CROSS-CULTURAL LEADERSHIP TRAINING

Managing the Cross-Cultural Challenges of the Nigerian Priests
on Mission in the United States with a Predeparture Training

*An international priest working in another culture needs to be aware that
doctrine is not enough to evangelize the host culture effectively. The gospel must
relate to the host culture to be transformative* (**Deck, 2012**).

LEONARD U. AHANOTU, PhD, EdD

CROSS-CULTURAL LEADERSHIP TRAINING

MANAGING THE CROSS-CULTURAL CHALLENGES OF THE NIGERIAN PRIESTS ON MISSION IN THE UNITED STATES WITH A PREDEPARTURE TRAINING

iUniverse books may be ordered through booksellers or by contacting:

iUniverse
1663 Liberty Drive
Bloomington, IN 47403
www.iuniverse.com
844-349-9409

Because of the dynamic nature of the Internet, any web addresses or links contained in this book may have changed since publication and may no longer be valid. The views expressed in this work are solely those of the author and do not necessarily reflect the views of the publisher, and the publisher hereby disclaims any responsibility for them.

Any people depicted in stock imagery provided by Getty Images are models, and such images are being used for illustrative purposes only.
Certain stock imagery © Getty Images.

ISBN: 978-1-6632-0785-2 (sc)
ISBN: 978-1-6632-0787-6 (hc)
ISBN: 978-1-6632-0786-9 (e)

Library of Congress Control Number: 2020917713

Print information available on the last page.

iUniverse rev. date: 10/27/2020

To my late father, Hon. (Sir) Thomas Ojukwu
Ahanotu, a customary court judge, the historian of
his community, and a teacher par excellence

He helped the Irish Catholic missionaries in Eastern Nigeria as the director and supervisor of many Catholic schools. He also served his Catholic diocese pastorally in different capacities, which earned him a couple of awards from his local diocese. His commitment to God to be a good husband and father helped me to know the importance of faith and the desire to serve God as a Catholic priest. I pray that the seed he has sown continues to blossom so many may see the liberating power of education and pastoral work in the social and spiritual development of human beings.

To my mother, Mrs. Veronica Ahanotu, whose support,
advice, and motherly care to me is second to none

CONTENTS

PREFACE

THE SOCIOCULTURAL DIFFERENCES BEAR ON THE ABILITY OF THE NEW arrivals in North America to settle and function at the best level of their potentials. Members of the clergy who come to serve as pastoral ministers are no exception to this reality but are even more so subjected to an unraveling cross-cultural coercion that has the potential to cripple their mission and jeopardize their pastoral work from the get-go. Certainly, when transitioning to the new culture is clogged due to an overwhelming cultural barrier, one's ability to integrate and carry out the pastoral ministry is stalled, along with one's pastoral proficiency. Predeparture training, as this book offers, will be a game changer for a smooth transition and integration to the North American culture, even though the data is collected only in the United States which does not have a significant cultural difference with Canada.

Looking through the North American sociocultural milieu with an open mind, one will understand the sensibility and sublimity upon which this culture is built, which will help to inform one's mindset before setting foot in the arena. The author of this book, thanks to his creative ingenuity, has developed a predeparture education and sociocultural orientation program to aid the new arrivals as they navigate through the culture of North America.

But what a strange feeling for a new arrival to North America, one who is tremendously equipped for the ministry and embodies great talents, erudition, and tested pastoral competences, to find himself in a new sociocultural setting, stripped of his ability to function let alone thrive. Integration into the new culture becomes an uphill task. The author employed an interpretative phenomenological approach and effectively divulged the experiences of these new arrival priests and how these encounters play out in their lives going forward. His interviews showed stunning experiences of culture shock, pain, regrets, and a sense of rejection. Many had to deal with a very detrimental social glitch for which excuses are non-admissible.

This book encapsulates the unraveling sociocultural hurdles that the new arrivals to North America encounter. A wide range of research and interviews—embellished with personal experiences—underscores the reality of this problem and makes the need to address it imperative. The author sets out to address and to pursue a remedial solution to the question, "What are the lived cross-cultural challenges and other experiences of Nigerian priests who have worked in North America for ten years or more?" The trajectory of his interview was on the common or shared experiences of the targeted group of the clergy.

Here is one who has ventured to address this issue with the motivation to make a difference in this process. This book provides an expansive exposé of the challenges as well as possible impacts on the life of the individuals affected, some of whom are left with injuries that may rise to the level of psychological, emotional, spiritual, and physical trauma that could potentially trickle down to frustration and despair.

This book demonstrates how culture shock affects the ill-equipped new arrivals. A well-directed orientation such as this text offers will both prepare and equip the intended missionary with the resources to navigate through the new culture.

The author, Rev. Dr. Ahanotu, makes a clarion call to clergy and all who intend to serve in North America to undertake the necessary preparations in advance of their arrival to North America. Understanding the culture and being able to play by the rules is key to successful missionary work. One can leverage the resources in this book to be better equipped for life and missionary work in North America.

Aside from walking you through the troubling reality of the problems, this book provides an effective and result-oriented training program model for the intended participants. I encourage for it to be offered to a much wider population than those captured by the title of the book, as I am positive it would benefit them as well. It is also tailored to accommodate all interested participants, even those who run a very busy schedule.

The training program focuses on specific elements of the North American sociocultural life that are known to be exceptionally challenging to the new arrivals. The goal is to provide them with the resources to deal with the initial culture shock and be able to navigate through the most unraveling period in the transitioning process.

The program offers a foundational education to the North American culture and life. Its methodology is comparative as it discusses in juxtaposition the known missionary's native culture and North American culture: the general perception of life, meaning and values, relationships, gestures, communications, and nuances. It also highlights on the no-go areas in North American culture as far as contacts and relationships. The program is intended to enhance the participants' skills as well as their flare for sociocultural adaptation in North America. It is my hope and expectation that this book and the training contained therein be made available to a wider population and demographics in Nigeria, America, and beyond.

Rev. Fr. Michael Chudi Mbonu, PhD

ACKNOWLEDGMENTS

CERTAIN PEOPLE INSPIRED AND HELPED ME TO ACHIEVE THIS RESEARCH work. I would like to thank Professor J. Morgan, Professor H. Hullinger, Professor A. Nwachukwu, Professor J. Faulds, and others who influenced my life through the grace of learning, research, and writing. Their humble way of guidance, encouragement, and insistence on producing good intellectual work whenever I write energizes me to leave no stone unturned to produce scholarly works that are educative for human development. I must always remain grateful to Professor Faulds, a decorated academician at Northeastern State University, Oklahoma, USA, and a Catholic Deacon, as well as Professor Hullinger for their interest in my scholarly and pastoral works. I thank Dr. C. J. Odunukwe, a great surgeon and friend, and his wife Professor S. Odunukwe, and Rev. J. Sommer for their continuous encouragement that keeps me aspiring high and working hard.

This book would not have been done without the cooperation of the Nigerian priests who gave their time to be interviewed and provided me the data for this research work. I cannot thank them enough.

I thank Ms. Theresa Fosburg, the secretary of my parish, who helped me to design the graphs in this work and assisted me in my pastoral duties so I may have time for this intensive research, and Ms. Earlyne Hutchens who offered me numerous supports and even took care of some of my duties to give me time to finish the work.

ABSTRACT

THE ISSUE OF CROSS-CULTURAL MOVEMENTS OF PROFESSIONALS WITHIN organizations in the twenty-first century's network style of the global organization has created the question of how to prepare professionals to meet the demands of satisfactory service in a culture different from their home environment. The absence of the cross-cultural preparation of the professionals is causing cross-cultural maladjustments among many professionals, and the Nigerian Catholic priests who move from Nigeria to the United States face this reality.

Given the shortage of priests in the United States, the US Roman Catholic Church recruits many priests from overseas, and a significant number of these men are being recruited from Nigeria, whose culture is very different from the United States. The work of these well-educated priests helps to solve the priest shortage problem but is creating new challenges in some Catholic parishes because of cultural differences. The priests continually face cross-cultural challenges to succeed in their pastoral work. There is little research on the cross-cultural challenges and other experiences of these priests in adjusting and carrying out their duties. This qualitative study investigated the cross-cultural experiences of Nigerian priests serving in the United States. Interviews with some Nigerian priests serving in the four different geographical regions of the United States yielded important discoveries: nineteen common challenges and twenty-five common strategies to facilitate adjustment. The findings indicated that some cross-cultural preparations before arrival to the United States could reduce the cross-cultural maladjustments and its effects on the pastoral works of these awesome priests. The discoveries influenced the recommendation of Kolb's learning theory to design a pre-departure cross-cultural training for Nigerian priests. The study offers an invaluable contribution to the tools that will help expatriates for cross-cultural adjustment and intercultural relations when they work in a foreign environment.

KEYWORDS

Priest shortage, foreign-born priests, expatriates, culture, cross-culture, cross-cultural challenges, strategies of adjustment, intercultural competence, acculturation, cross-cultural maladjustment, intercultural relation

CHAPTER 1

Introduction

As I indicated in the journal article published by SAGE (Ahanotu 2019), we live in an era of globalization where international mobility is increasingly common (Liu and Huang 2015) and professionals are increasingly moving from one culture to another (Ozar 2015). Many of these professionals struggle in unfamiliar cultures, and a body of research has examined the issues associated with the cross-cultural challenges faced by these expatriates (Ozar 2015; Smith and Khawaja 2011; Zhang and Goodson 2011; Hafitah, Tahir, and Ismail 2007). Antecedents have been identified for both psychological and sociocultural struggles among the expatriates, including personality traits, inability to handle life changes, disconnection with previous social support, lack of cross-cultural motivation, lack of prior experience of another culture, absence of well-defined goals, cultural distance, distance from home culture, language proficiency problems, discrimination, inability to develop social interrelation with the host nationals, and absence of cross-cultural training (Ozar 2015; Zhang and Goodson 2011; Hafitah, Tahir, and Ismail 2007).

Researchers have identified the cross-cultural struggles faced by the sojourners and expatriates, such as physicians, engineers, lawyers, accountants, teachers, historians, archeologists, professors, mediators, and managing directors of multinational companies (Albu 2015; Xin Morrison, Dharod, Young, and Nsonwu 2014; Roy 2013; Sandage and Jankowski 2013; Beck 1992). Only a limited number of studies have investigated the cross-cultural struggles and experiences of the Catholic priests who expatriated from other nations, especially Nigeria, to serve in the United States because of the US priest shortage.

The increasing cross-cultural movements of professionals within organizations in today's globalized world has made researchers face the challenge of how to best prepare all kinds of expatriates to meet the reality of competent cross-cultural service (Roberts 2007; Javidan 2008; Irving 2009). Globalization has led to the need for the skills to face the current global interconnectedness and ability for all kinds of expatriates to be effective both in their own culture and foreign culture (Klenke 2008; Eoyang 2005). All professionals, including Catholic priests, face this reality of the need for the knowledge of the cross-cultural perspective of service in the speedy, globalizing world (Javidan 2009).

From the 1960s, the US Roman Catholic Church started to witness a fast, continuous declining vocation to the Catholic priesthood among US men (Center for Applied Research in the Apostolate [CARA] 2014; Breitenstein 2014; Owan 2014; Gautier, Perl, and Fichter 2012). Lack of vocations to the priesthood by young men to replace the retiring population of elderly priests, as well as continued growth in the Catholic population, are the leading causes of the shortage of the number of priests (Schenk 2013; Welch 2009). The shortage of priests is such that many parishes are being closed or consolidated (Sheehy 2014).

In response to this problem, most of the US Catholic bishops began to recruit priests who were born and trained overseas (Gautier et al. 2012; Allen 2010). A significant number of these priests are being recruited from Nigeria and other countries whose culture is very different from the US culture. The presence and work of these priests help to solve the shortage problem, but the phenomenon is creating new challenges in some Catholic parishes because of cultural differences (Allen 2010).

International priests bring many gifts and talents to the church in the United States, but their presence is not without some challenges both for the priests and their parishioners because of cultural differences (Gautier et al. 2012; Allen 2010). While many of the foreign-born priests are finding it hard to adjust to the US social and ecclesial cultures, some of their host parishioners are not patient enough to allow them enough time to adjust to their new culture. In some cases, the cross-cultural problems are causing tensions and resentment of the foreign-born priests

(Gautier et al. 2012; Allen 2010; Goodstein 2008; Braxton 2008). Many US Catholic parishioners are asking that these foreign-born priests be given a better understanding of US culture before their assignment to the US parishes and other Catholic institutions (Allen 2010; Deck 2012; Goodstein 2008; Hoge and Okure 2006).

The US Catholic bishops have tried strategies such as postarrival training programs and the use of experienced priests as mentors to the foreign-born priests (Gautier et al. 2012; Schenk 2013). While these have helped to reduce the cross-cultural struggles among the international priests, the problem is still a major concern in the US church. Several studies have indicated the need to look into the cultural challenges of the Nigerian and other foreign-born priests working in the United States (Gray 2015; Gray, Gautier, and Cidade 2015; Owan 2014).

The phenomenon of the crisis of cross-cultural problems is not a new phenomenon because many expatriates in other professions have fully experienced it, especially in the multinational business corporations, which has led to research on cross-cultural training, predeparture training, and postarrival training (Shi and Wang 2014; Wurtz 2014; Joshua-Gojer 2012; Godiwalla 2012; Elmadssia and Hosni 2012; Shi and Lang 2009). The implementation of the cross-cultural trainings, especially a combination of predeparture and postarrival trainings in the international business corporations, has produced more success in adjustment and job performance by the expatriates in their host culture (Shi and Wang 2014; Wurtz 2014; Joshua-Gojer 2012; Godiwalla 2012; Elmadssia and Hosni 2012; Shi and Lang 2009).

The US church has spent a lot of money and time on postarrival cross-cultural training of the international priests but has not made a significant effort in the provision of predeparture training, and the problem is not yet as less as found among the expatriates in the international businesses since the international business corporations started to apply both predeparture and postarrival trainings (Gautier et al. 2012; Godiwalla 2012; Joshua-Gojer 2012). Perhaps the success of predeparture training in international business implies an analogous potential application to the predeparture training of Nigerian priests prior to their ministry in the United States. Hence the success of the addition of predeparture training in the international business precipitated the need for an in-depth study of cross-cultural predeparture training that will help Nigerian priests on mission in the United States so the priests would be ready for postarrival orientation, easier adjustment, and better performance (Owan 2014; Hoge and Okure 2006). If the addition of predeparture training to postarrival training could work among other multinational corporations, could it work in the Roman Catholic Church?

The study yielded a significant result that an addition of predeparture training to the postarrival training of the Nigerian priests can reduce the adjustment problems of the priests. The result showed that the success of the addition of predeparture training to postarrival training in other corporations could also happen among the international priests in Roman Catholicism. It confirmed the assertion of Hassan and Diallo (2013) that predeparture cross-cultural training could be applied to any intergroup context. Finally, the result of the study led to a design of a predeparture training for the Nigerian priests coming to serve in the United States.

STUDY BACKGROUND

Many authors such as Gautier et al. (2012) and Gray (2015) agreed that the United States is one of the countries where Catholicism is strongly established, but the problem of not having enough priests proportionate to the Catholic population has remained a critical one. Some of the US laity and clergy often discuss this problem. Given that lack of vocations to the priesthood and the continuous retirement of priests because of age have continued to exacerbate the problem, the US Catholic bishops have tried some strategies that have only led to a quasi-success that needs improvement (Schenk 2013).

When the issue of the priest shortage started, the first strategy by the US bishops was the recruitment of foreign priests from European countries such as Ireland and Italy, whose cultural heritage is more similar to that of the North Americans. Declining numbers of priests in Europe eventually led to another strategy. Young men were recruited from non-European countries such as Nigeria, Vietnam, Colombia, Mexico, India, and the Philippines and were trained in US Catholic seminaries in the hope that training them in these schools would help to bridge the cultural gaps (United States Conference of Catholic Bishops [USCCB] 2010).

The strategy worked for a while and stopped. According to the data of the USCCB in 1999, 11 percent of the US priests were foreign-born but trained in the United States. The number rose to 24 percent in 2002 and to 38 percent in 2003. Unfortunately, in 2009 the number decreased to 25 percent, and the decline has continued since then, thus the limited success of the strategy (USCCB 2010). This limited success of the strategy eventually led to a heavy reliance on priests who are born and trained overseas for the ministries in American dioceses/eparchies (Gray 2015; Gautier et al. 2012; Allen 2010). The support of this idea by the US Catholic bishops made the Bishops to reinforce their agreement on November 12, 2004, that stated, "with declining vocations among US Catholic men, more and more reliance will be placed on foreign countries, to carry out ministries in American dioceses/eparchies" (USCCB 2010b, see Report on Foreign Priests, 10). In other words, the decline of priests in Europe eventually led to the recruitment of priests from non-European countries like Nigeria, Vietnam, Colombia, Mexico, India, and the Philippines (USCCB 2010).

Currently Nigeria is one of the greatest suppliers of the foreign-born priests to the US church (Allen 2010; Gautier et al. 2012). The work of these priests contributes immensely to solve the problem of the priest shortage, but the cross-cultural challenges embedded in the strategy have remained a great problem. The cultural tensions between the foreign-born priests and many of their US parishioners have remained a significant problem and are not decreasing (Allen 2010; Gray, Gautier, and Cidade 2015).

Referring to the cultural tensions in the parishes of Nigerian and some other international priests, Henning and Mahfood (2009) said that unlike priests recruited from Europe, the culture gap between the foreign priests and US Catholic laity has widened. Owan (2014) agreed and indicated that usually the greater the cultural distance of the recruited priests, the greater the cultural complexities and tensions of interactions between the foreign priests and the US laity. Cerimagic and Smith (2011) concurred and said, "the more different an expatriate country of origin is to the host country the more difficult the adjustment" (393). The cross-cultural problems have led to some of the priests being sent back to their countries because of maladjustments (Goodstein 2008).

Many of the US Catholic bishops are addressing this problem of maladjustment among the foreign-born priests by providing different postarrival trainings to the priests (Henning and Mahfood 2009; Sperry 2012). Training programs for the priests are conducted at institutions such as Loyola Marymount University in California, Oblate School of Theology in Texas, and the Vincentian Center for Church and Society in New York (Henning and Mahfood 2009). Certain bishops prefer the strategy of allowing the newly arrived priests to remain in residence with more experienced priests to learn the US societal and ecclesiastical lifestyles from the experienced priests (USCCB 2010).

The programs are helpful to some extent but lack the authentic cross-cultural competency that will significantly reduce the cultural struggles of the foreign-born priests (Sperry 2012; Henning and Mahfood 2009). Sperry, Henning, and Mahfood described the postarrival programs as insufficient to achieve the cross-cultural competence and cultural sensitivity needed in the US church. Hoge and Okure (2006) described the programs as welcoming sessions so the priests can equitably adjust to the American style of ministry. Irrespective of what the authors said, the primary issue is that Nigerian priests on a mission in the United States still experience certain cross-cultural struggles, especially during their early years in the United States, and need the appropriate training and knowledge to handle their cross-cultural struggles and challenges (Owan 2014).

While the US Catholic bishops acknowledge the existence of the cross-cultural tensions in the parishes and other ministries of the foreign-born priests, they do not welcome the resentment of the international priests by their parishioners. The bishops reckon that the church is one and we live in a time of cross-cultural exchange of priests to meet the demands of the universal church (USCCB 2010; Braxton 2008; Gautier et al. 2012). Moreover, the potential resentment directed toward the international priests also challenges the rationale for using some US priests who do not adapt well or serve effectively in some parts of the United States due to some ethnic differences within the United

States (Braxton 2008). Borrowing the ideas of Popes Benedict XVI, John Paul II, and Paul VI on this issue, Braxton indicated that the US church should speak of the need to distribute the priests of the universal church in a more positive way so dioceses that do not have priests will benefit from those who have. Popes Paul VI, John Paul II, and Benedict XVI used some paragraphs in the documents of the church, *Optatam Totius* (Decree on the Training of Priests) and *Pastores Dabo Vobis* (Formation of the Priest in the Circumstances of the Present Day), to encourage the church to be sensitive to the realities of the changing world and the different cultural environments in the globe in order to meet the priestly demands of the church in our changing world.

The people of God should bear in mind that the church is intrinsically missional, genuinely diverse, and theologically open-minded while preserving her essential dogmas (Owan 2014). Adhering to the instructions from *Optam Totius* and *Pastores Dabo Vobis*, Braxton (2008) believed that differences in culture should not destroy the profound expression of the catholicity and universality of the church. The most appropriate thing, therefore, according to Braxton, is to understand that there are no perfect priests just as there are no perfect Christians and to develop a systematic way of helping the international priests to transition to the US culture and perform better.

In accord with Braxton's idea, Jenkins (2014) added that it is evidently true that the needed services of the international priests in the United States imply some cultural challenges, but the challenges could be reduced with a process of cross-cultural preparation while in their own country to expose them to the culture of the host country prior to their arrival. Gautier et al. (2012) also shared the same view. They advocated a systematic predeparture training of the international priests assigned to the United States to facilitate easier transition, adjustment, and job performance. Supporting Gautier et al., Hassan and Diallo (2013) persisted that, given the success of the combination of predeparture and postarrival trainings of expatriates in international business, it has become necessary to study how an addition of predeparture training to the present model of postarrival programs could be useful in the preparation of international priests intending to work in the United States.

In the international businesses, the addition of systematic predeparture trainings of expatriates to postarrival trainings have significantly reduced the maladjustments and cultural tensions in many multinational corporations, such that it is continuously being required for expatriates in the international businesses (Bank and Rothmann 2006). According to Cerimagic and Smith (2011), the combination of the two trainings has helped many expatriates in international businesses to adjust successfully in the host culture and perform better in their assignments. The success of predeparture training in the multinational corporations has been so great that many multinational corporations have decided to implement a mandatory predeparture cross-cultural training for their expatriates (Cerimagic and Smith 2011).

Agreeing with the mandatory predeparture cross-cultural trainings, Cerimagic and Smith expressed, "Companies should develop more tailored, relevant and realistic predeparture cross cultural training programs" (494). Chien and McLean (2011) have also encouraged multinational companies to establish training courses to help expatriates discover the cultural challenges they may encounter prior to their departure. In the world of multinational companies, the companies that engage their staff on psychological and intercultural preparation prior to departure to a foreign culture usually perform better (Osman-Gani and Rocksthl 2009). The predeparture training helps expatriates to learn some modes of human behavior and the framework of the interculture accepted by their host culture (Elmadassia and Hosni 2012).

Osman-Gani and Rocksthl believed that predeparture training has become a useful tool for both individual careers and companies' global success since the advent of globalization. In the fast-globalizing world and its need for intercultural efficacy of personnel, an expatriate can only be successful in a different culture if he is able to know and follow the rules of the host culture rather than the rules of the expatriate's culture (Hofstede 2009). Multinational corporations have proven beyond a doubt that the learning and knowledge of the host culture prior to arrival has the potential of being one of the instruments for quicker transition and less stressful adjustment.

Statements of the above-mentioned cross-cultural research experts are in agreement with many psychological hypotheses and theories about predeparture cross-cultural training. Psychological hypothesis— such as *Attitudinal Effects of Mere Exposure* by Zajonc (1968)—and psychological theories—such as *Met Expectations* by Vroom (1995) and *Solution-based Counseling*, also known as *Solution-Focused Based Therapy (SFBT)* by de Shazer (1988)—favor this strategy, as one would see in the literature of this work. A combination of the psychological theories and hypotheses and the assertions of the scholars of cross-cultural studies have played a significant role in seeking if predeparture training could reduce cross-cultural struggles and challenges.

From both the perspective of the well-acknowledged psychological theories and hypotheses and other studies of cross-cultural scholars, there seemed to be strong indications of a solid trust-based relationship between predeparture cross-cultural training and the competence to manage cross-cultural struggles and challenges. Both the psychological theories and hypotheses and cross-cultural research studies seem to indicate that the assignment of expatriates, which would include Nigerian Catholic priests on mission in the United States, require a very systematic predeparture cross-cultural training prior to departure to the host countries. The preparation could help them to adjust adequately and perform better. Therefore, an in-depth study that considers how the Nigerian priests could be socially, pastorally, and psychologically be prepared at home prior to departure on a US mission so they can adjust to US culture and perform better in their ministry has become a desideratum (Owan 2014).

PURPOSE AND SIGNIFICANCE OF THE STUDY

The purpose of this study is to understand the cross-cultural challenges and other relevant experiences of Nigerian Catholic priests who have worked in the United States for ten years or more and develop an improvement strategy. The continued need for international Catholic priests to serve in the United States as pastors and chaplains is increasing, and a significant number of Nigerian priests who have a cultural difference with the US culture are continuously recruited to minister in the United States (Breitenstein 2014; Sheehy 2014; Owen 2014; Owen 2014; Couturier et al. 2012; De Souza 2012).

While the problem of the priest shortage in the United States continues to revivify the recruitment of priests from Nigeria, the cross-cultural maladjustment of the Nigerian and other foreign-born priests has not declined (Owan 2014). The critical problems of cultural tensions in their places of work need to be addressed. A predeparture cross-cultural training of the Nigerian priests about US culture and context of pastoral work may help the priests to have some understanding of US culture and reduce both their cultural challenges and the cultural tensions at their places of assignment in the United States. The advanced preparation could help the incoming priests to adjust quickly and experience more success (Owen 2014). The genius of its importance also hinges on the expectation of the priests by the Americans to adhere to the traditions, customs, and manners of US culture (Panthaplamthottiyil 2006). Addressing a group of Indian priests working in the United States, Panthaplamthottiyil advised that international priests are expected to abide by the US cultural norms in order to be acceptable to the host nation and be successful in the ministry. He added that the faster the international priests get acculturated, the better their self-confidence and success will be.

Hassan and Diallo (2013) agreed with Panthaplamthottiyil (2006) by suggesting that predeparture training provides confidence and fastens transition and adjustment in the host nation. The studies, thoughts, and suggestions of the experts seem to favor the importance of an in-depth, systematic predeparture cross-cultural preparation of the expatriates prior to leaving for their assignment in a new culture (Osman and Rockstuhl 2009).

So, this study investigated the cross-cultural challenges and other relevant experiences of the Nigerian priests who are well educated and on a pastoral mission in the United States and suggested a predeparture training program for educating the Nigerian priests at home prior to departure so they can adjust to US culture and perform better in their ministry (Owan 2014).

Hopefully this research work would help the Nigerian priests to adjust and assimilate better into US culture. I do hope that it would normalize the ongoing cross-cultural misconceptions/pastoral threats that hamper the ministerial dispositions of Nigerian priests who come to the United States for missionary works, especially the misunderstanding of their cross-cultural struggles, which sometimes precipitate cross-cultural tensions in their missions. I believe that this work will assist the Nigerian priests to see the importance of cross-cultural improvement, with a great understanding that scripture becomes more transformative when it is acculturated. I also believe that this study is crucial at this time when cross-cultural maladjustments by the international priests are among the top discussions in the US Catholic church.

RESEARCH OBJECTIVES

The research objective of this study is to gather information about the cultural misunderstandings and conflicts as well as other challenges, which Nigerian priests in the United States encountered during their intercultural adjustments, and how the cultural problems affected their job performance. I believe that the systematic analyses of the gathered information will add to the enhancement of a good predeparture training and fast adjustment as well as easier cultural transition of the Nigerian priests going to mission in the United States.

It could reduce the insensitivity to cultural differences that can hinder the success of the Nigerian priests assigned to minister in the United States because the study will lead to some cultural information about the United States that the Nigerian priests need to know prior to coming to work in the United States. I agree with Braxton (2008) when he addressed the African priests working in the United States and indicated that even though the priests from both the United States and Africa are witnesses to the gospel of Christ, there are some cross-cultural problems that the African priests face in the United States because the respective continents are in some ways two distinct worlds.

The differences, according to Braxton, include complexity in ethnic, social, political, and linguistic issues as well as differences in ministry style, hence the necessity of this study to assist the Nigerian priests with getting acquainted with the US social and pastoral culture and being prepared to face the cultural challenges when ministering in the United States.

LIMITATIONS AND SCOPE OF THE STUDY

The United States is a vast and complex country made up of peoples from almost every country on earth, and so there are certain cultural and religious differences within the United States (Braxton 2008). Even though there might be a general US culture that unites all the geographical regions in the union, there are some regional differences concerning lifestyles in the four regions of the Northeast, South, Midwest, and Western states (Braxton 2008). Immigrants from different parts of the world who live in the same region have certain cultures they brought with them, and some aspects of those cultures are still part of their everyday lives. Thus, even though the dogma of the Catholic church is the same everywhere in the United States and is guided by the USCCB for the inculcation of the one dogma of the church, there is no doubt that the styles of application of the dogmas and the church within the regions might include their various cultural flavors without losing the universal teachings of the church (Braxton 2008).

OPERATIONAL DEFINITIONS

For the purpose of a clearer understanding of this research work, it will be appropriate to define certain terms used in this work:

1. Acculturation. Acculturation, according to Howell and Paris (2010), refers to the learning of appropriate behaviors of the host culture.
2. Cross-cultural training or cross-cultural preparation. Borrowing some ideas from Haslberger (2005) and Evans (2012), cross-cultural training refers to a complex psychological process of acquiring how to live comfortably outside one's own culture and function effectively in a foreign culture. It involves learning and understanding ways of diagnosing one's own culture, understanding a different culture, and being able to manage any differences and gaps. Without rejecting either a personal culture or the new culture, the person learns to adapt to the

new cultural situation by being open to learn and acquire the required behaviors of the new culture and refine and expand personal intercultural skills and flexibility in response to the new cultural situations (Dan 2014).

3. Culture. Aneas and Sandin (2009) said it is difficult to have a general definition of culture. In this work, we shall use the explanation of culture provided by Schwartz (2013), which refers to culture as the values and attitudes, beliefs, and norms that give meaning and significance to both an individual and their collective identity and justifies the social functioning of that institution.

4. Expatriates. Expatriates, according to Naithani and Jha (2010), are employees who transfer to a foreign country to work for a specified time.

5. Foreign-born priests. In this work, foreign-born priests, which is sometimes used in place of international priests, refers to the priests who were born and trained for the priesthood in another country and relocated to the United States to minister in US Catholic dioceses (USCCB 2010). Men who were born and reared in another country but had their seminary training and ordination to the priesthood in the United States are also included in this group by the USCCB.

6. Nigerian priests. Nigerian priests in this work refer to the men who were born and raised in Nigeria, had their seminary training in Nigeria, and were ordained Catholic priests in Nigeria.

CHAPTER 2

Review of Related Literature

APPROPRIATE CROSS-CULTURAL TRAINING PRIOR TO DEPARTURE TO work in a foreign culture has the potential of assisting workers to successfully adjust to the culture of the host country and perform better in their assignments (Cerimagic and Smith 2011). To scientifically justify and objectify these inquiries, we must consult other experts and professionals closely related to the subject of our research. It will help in the study to identify the appropriate areas of predeparture cross-cultural training that will aid the Nigerian priests on mission in the United States.

Many scholars have written about the importance of predeparture cross-cultural training of expatriates in multinational organizations for the purpose of cross-cultural adjustments and appropriate job performance (Shi and Wang 2014; Hassan and Diallo 2013; Meyer 2013; Godiwalla 2012; Joshua-Gojer 2012). Many scholars have also written about the need for predeparture cross-cultural preparation of the international priests intending to work in the United States (Holmes 2014; Gautier, Gray, Perl, and Cidade 2014; Schenk 2013; Gautier and Fichter 2012; Farh et al. 2010).

Owan (2014) even narrowed his own studies to the importance of having a program that considers cross-cultural training of Nigerian priests and seminarians in preparation for service abroad. He briefly mentioned service in Euro-America as an example. No thorough research has been discovered about the importance of having a predeparture cross-cultural program for Nigerian priests on mission in the United States or a particular predeparture program for the Nigerian priests.

Despite the comments of some authors about the cultural barriers between the international priests in the United States and their parishioners (Townsend 2013; Allen 2010), we are yet to see a major work on predeparture cross-cultural training of Nigerian priests prior to leaving for the United States.

The need for predeparture cross-cultural training of the Nigerian priests who fill in the gaps created by the scarcity of priests in the United States without having significant intercultural problems, the comments about the cultural barriers between international priests and their parishioners by some authors, and the success of predeparture cross-cultural training of expatriates in the multinational organizations are some of the reasons that spurred this research to seek the importance of preparing the Nigerian priests before they leave for United States for their missionary assignment.

The intention for this literature review, therefore, is to use other scholars' work to establish the following points, which will also inform the topics and topical organization in this chapter:

1. The priest shortage in the United States, which highlights the scarcity of Catholic priests in the United States and how the scarcity led to the recruitment of priests whose culture is totally different from US culture;
2. The clash of cultures between the international priests and their US parishioners, which tells us how the difference in cultures between the international priests and their parishioners made

the services of many of the priests and the recipients of their services a bumpy ride;

3. The examples of how the cultural beliefs of the international priests influence the cultural tensions;

4. The examples of how the cultural beliefs of the US laity influence the cultural tensions;

5. The antecedents of a better relationship between the Nigerian priests and US laity;

6. The signs of cross-cultural adjustments and better relationship between expatriates and host nationals;

7. The acquisition of intercultural competence by both the Nigerian priests and US laity as a necessity for the reduction of cultural clash;

8. The present cross-cultural training of the Nigerian and other international priests serving in the United States;

9. Cultural competence for both the foreign-born priests and the US church as an antecedent for successful pastoral ministry;

10. The success of predeparture cross-cultural training in multinational corporations;

11. The effectiveness of cross-cultural training in multinational corporations, which exposes the importance of cross-cultural preparation for expatriates;

12. A study of the positive effects of predeparture pastoral and psychological training of the Nigerian priests from the perspective of psychology;

13. The present cross-cultural training of the international priests working in the United States, which expresses the acknowledgment (by many authors) of both the success and need for a more appropriate cross-cultural program for priests from other cultures; and

14. The success of predeparture cross-cultural training in other organizations, which indicates that predeparture cross-cultural training already successfully exists in many multinational corporations for the preparation of their expatriates and therefore can be analogously a successful venture in Roman Catholicism.

Basically, there are two different inquiries in this chapter:

1. An inquiry pertaining to scarcity of priests, recruitment of priests, and cross-cultural training of the recruited priests; and
2. An inquiry about the success of predeparture cross-cultural training of expatriates in multinational corporations.

Both are relevant for this chapter because the success of this model in multinational corporations implies an analogous potential application to the preparation of the recruited Nigerian priests assigned to mission in the United States. The searches for the review included: chapters of certain books, research articles, digital dissertations, and scholarly journals using electronic databases. The key search items used were "priest shortage in the United States," "international priests working in the United States," "Nigerian priests working in the United States," "cross-cultural training," "success of cross-cultural training," "failure of cross-cultural training," "pre-departure cross-cultural training," "models for cross-cultural training," "cross-cultural psychology," and "psychological theories that support job performance in an unfamiliar environment."

2.1. PRIEST SHORTAGE IN THE US PARISHES

The issue of priest shortage has been scientifically covered by the Center for Applied Research in the Apostolate (CARA), "a national, non-profit, Georgetown University affiliated research center that conducts social scientific studies about the Catholic Church" (Gray 2015, 2). CARA serves to increase the church's self-understanding, research the needs of church decision-makers, and advance scholarly research on religion, particularly Catholicism.

According to Gray, Gautier, and Cidade (2015), CARA has continuously advanced social science research for the Roman Catholic Church in the United States since 1964 at the request of the USCCB and frequently provides the USCCB with the statistical information about the shortage of priests in the United States and its impact on the US church. In 2012, CARA conducted a survey of young men's interest to the Catholic priesthood and did not have an encouraging result for more vocations to the priesthood (Gautier and Gray 2012). Referring to the survey, Gautier and Gray said,

> In winter 2012, the Secretariat of Clergy, Consecrated Life, and Vocations of the United States Conference of Catholic Bishops (USCCB) commissioned the Center of Applied Research in the Apostolate to conduct a national poll of never-married Catholics regarding their consideration of a vocation. CARA partnered with Knowledge Networks to conduct the survey in May and June 2012. The survey was completed by 1,609 respondents ... in a margin of sampling error of plus or minus 2.6 percentage points ... The report included where possible, comparisons by CARA in previous years which questioned about vocations to national samples of U.S. adult Catholics. (9)

The data, which was collected in 2012, were compared with the 2003 and 2008 data and then analyzed. The analysis, which was reported in the 140-page work of Gautier and Gray, indicated a continuous drop of interest in becoming priests among the male respondents. A follow-up study by CARA in 2015 clearly indicated that while the Catholic population in the United States is steadily increasing annually from the late 1960s, the number of young men being ordained to the Catholic priesthood is steadily declining from the late 1960s (CARA 2015).

The same study indicated that in 1965 58,632 priests were serving the Catholics in the United States, but the number declined to 37,192 in 2016. Within the same period, the number of Catholics increased from 48.3 million to 67.7 million (the number in the Official Catholic Directory) or 74.2 million (the number of self-identified Catholics).

CARA's analysis mirrored the finding of Breinstein (2014) that nationally, the ratio of priests to parishioners in 1950 was one priest to 652 parishioners, but the number changed in 2010 to one priest to 1,653 parishioners, excluding those who are not registered with a parish. After a careful study of the gradual decline of the Catholic priests and the gradual increase of the Catholic population, Sheehy (2014) said it has become evidently clear that while the number of Catholic population in the United States continues to grow, the number of priests who are supposed to serve them keeps declining.

Bogan (2011) studied the cause of priest shortage in the region of Southern Illinois and concluded that a third of the priests were either retired or inactive in the ministry, with another fourth expected to retire within five to ten years. Bogan believed that the situation in Southern Illinois represented a national trend of the shortage of priests since the phenomenon started in the last half of the 1960s. Welch (2009) described the phenomenon as a situation where a few priests are scrambling to meet the needs of a growing Catholic population that the continuous immigrant population in the country generated.

Mann (2012) interviewed Bishop LaValley, the bishop of Ogdensburg, New York, and reported that according to the bishop, the issue of priest shortage in his diocese and the United States is a difficult one because many priests are retiring and dying, and young men are no longer interested in becoming priests. The bishop said that the shortage is very daunting and there are no signs of hope in having many US priests.

Writing further about the continuous decline of the number of priests in the diocese of LaValley, Mann (2012) reported that in the diocese of LaValley, 92 priests were covering a 12,000-square-mile area in 2002, but the number of priests per 12,000 square miles dropped to 62 in 2012 and might plummet to 40 over the next decade.

Agreeing that the phenomenon of Catholic priest shortage in the United States is not a made-up story, Sheehy (2014) asserted that the inadequate supply of priests is true and caused by a decline in ordination and the aging of the present priests with the average age of sixty-three, and the situation has led to the closure or consolidation of parishes. In his own report about the issue, Breistein (2014) concluded that nationally it is estimated that one out of five parishes still do not have a resident priest. Hoge and Okure (2006), who were sponsored by the US National Federation of Priestly Council to do a study about the priest shortage in the United States, reached a conclusion that

> America needs immigrant priests to fill in the gaps in
> its priest shortage. While the number of Catholics in
> the United States has been growing … the number of
> priests has been declining … American seminaries are
> not producing ordinations rapidly enough to meet the
> need. (15)

Hoge's and Okure's study became prophetic when the result of the survey carried out by CARA in 2015 on behalf of the USCCB indicated a continuous decline of the number of priests and a continuous growth of the Catholic population (CARA 2015).

Recently Hopfenspenrger (2019) reported that the priest shortage in the United States is such that about one in six Catholic priests in the United States now are foreign-born. So, when Schenk (2013) noted that the situation of priest shortage has led to the closing down of some parishes and others being merged, he was not unerring because the shortage has become so insolvent that continuous reliance on foreign-born priests is inevitable. It is worth knowing that the priest shortage is also affecting both parishes and other institutions, such as the military and Catholic schools.

2.2. Priest Shortage in the US Military

Catholic priests do not only serve as pastors of regular parishes. They also serve in the US military and are referred to in the military as chaplains. Some authors (Walker 2014; Shrinkman 2013; Sugg 2013; Jones 2009; Hershkowitz and Tenenbaum, 2008) have also indicated that the shortage of Catholic priests in the United States has extended to the US military chaplaincy.

Writing about the gradual shortage of priests in the army, Hershkowitz and Tenenbaum (2008) lamented, "the military is currently experiencing a critical shortage of Chaplains both in deployed units and in the Reserve Forces at home" (24). To explain the cause of the critical shortage of the chaplains, Sugg (2013), a Catholic priest and a major in the U.S Army, said, "one third of Catholic priests in uniform were aging and ailing. The chaplain service was forced to medically retire them …

Today, we continue to struggle with a shortage of priests" (16) to provide religious services to military personnel, their family members, and civilians who assist the military.

Jones (2009) reported how a soldier, Captain Matt Foley, became a military Catholic priest because of the shortage of Catholic priests in the army and the great need for their services. Walker (2014) commented how many military priests in active duty, especially overseas, have been asked to pull double or triple duties because of the scarcity of chaplains. According to Walker, it is not uncommon to see one priest at a post that has 25,000 to 35,000 troops running all the Catholic programs alone.

Writing about the scarcity of the Catholic military chaplains and the need for them, Shrinkman (2013) reported that some Catholic military men and women who came back from Iraq and Afghanistan had no chaplains to offer them religious and social compassion after many years of bloody and brutal warfare. According to Shrinkman, as these military men and women transition from the years of bloody and brutal warfare to appointments to the military bases in the United States, the troubling trends of priest shortage have left Catholic military priests (or chaplains) shorthanded with regard to ministering to the officers.

Timothy Broglio, the Catholic archbishop of the US military personnel and head of the Catholic Church Military Services in the United States, was asked about the greatest challenges in his job, and he immediately responded that one of his greatest challenges is a severe shortage of military chaplains, both at home and abroad (Walker 2014). Brogolio's response, according to Walker, indicates that the priest shortage in the military is presently more acute than before.

2.3. Priest shortage in US Catholic Higher Education

Although a small number of colleges and universities represent the Catholic higher education in the United States, by and large, these institutions have produced a huge number of outstanding graduates and "leaders in business, education … law, religion and the highest offices of government" (Petriccione 2009, 1).

The Catholic colleges and universities amazingly have hundreds of thousands of students and graduates who are proud of their institutions and are a blessing to United States (Petriccionne 2009). Catholic clergy and nuns once ran most of these Catholic institutions, but this number has plummeted from 23,000 in 1965 to 13,000 in 2009, a decline of over 43 percent, as reported by Georgetown University's Center for Applied Research in the Apostolate (Matheson 2009). It is even worse today, given the continuous shortage of priests.

More than thirty years ago, these colleges and universities had priests and nuns as presidents, and they also comprised the largest percentage of the faculty members. Yet a priest shortage and lack of vocations to the priesthood and religious life have made the presence of priests and nuns in the colleges and universities very scarce (Reedu 2007; Cernera 2005).

Watching the number of the priests and nuns decline in the Catholic colleges and universities, Matheson (2008) thought it was about time to acknowledge the reality that the shortage of Roman Catholic clergy is not only being felt in regular parishes but also in Catholic higher education. Matheson was concerned that the institutions founded and run by the Catholic clergy across the United States for many years were struggling to retain the distinct religious identities of these institutions as they face the continuous decline of the number of priests and nuns.

Petticciones (2009) concurred and added, "Today as in the foreseeable future, most Catholic colleges will have dominant numbers of lay faculty, coaches, staff, consultants, administrations and trustees" (26). Referring to the publications of CARA, which had continuously informed the Catholic community about the decline of priests since the 1960s, Peticionne expressed that the days of having Catholic priests as presidents in most of the Catholic colleges and universities were over and a rise of the number of lay presidents and lay faculty members are just inevitable. Citing an undocumented statement of Richard Yanikoski, the former president of the Association of Catholic Colleges and Universities (ACCU), Peticcionnes reported that "about one-half of American Catholic colleges and universities are led by lay women and men and the numbers are rising every year" (7). The former president of ACCU was particularly worried about the decline of the number of the Catholic clergy in the colleges and universities because of the traditional commitment of the institutions to the pursuit of actual truth and great leadership skills, which must be systematically inculcated into the students of the Catholic colleges and universities by the faculty (Matheson 2008).

The shortage of priests and lack of their presence in the Catholic colleges and universities has become so noticeable that Matheson (2008) wondered if the leadership of the institutions, which was moving into the hands of the laity, would aspire to preserve the religious aspect of the mission statements of the institutions. Cunningham (2005) also wondered if the lay leaders would "aspire to articulate and model the Catholic idea of education as an education is wisdom where faith and reason breathe as two lungs of a single body" (84).

Thinking that the shortage of priests and lack of their presence in the Catholic colleges and universities could affect the overall quality of the institutions, Pope Benedict and some US clergy met with the presidents of the colleges and universities when the pope came to the United States, and the pope reminded them to always remember the mission statements of the institutions in their day-to-day business of the colleges and universities (Matheson 2008). Providing examples of La Salle University in Philadelphia, St. Joseph University in Philadelphia, and Xavier University in Chicago, Matheson indicated that the day-to-day running of most of the Catholic colleges and universities have been affected by the change of times and there will continue to be a difference between the way they would be run by the original stewards who know and clearly understand the origin of the mission statements and the way they are run by the laity.

2.4. Clash of Culture between the International Priests and the US Laity

I already indicated that the work of the international priests in the United States helps to fill in the gap created by the shortage of priests in the United States (CARA 2014), but the dedication of these international priests in their ministry is not without challenges, among which are cultural misunderstandings between the international priests and the US laity (Owen 2014; Gautier, Gray, Perl, Cidade, 2014; Allen 2010). Unlike before, when priests were recruited from Europe, these days "the culture gap between international priests and US Catholic laity has widened" (Henning and Mahfood 2009, 63) because of the complexity of cultures and cultural differences existing between the US parishioners "and the priests arriving from non-European cultures in Africa, Asia, the Pacific Islands, and South and Central America" (Henning and Mahfood 2009, 63). The wider the cultural distance, the greater the cultural complexities and tensions of the interactions between the international priests and the US laity (Owen 2014; Lefevere 2006). Using the words of Cremagic and Smith (2011), "the more different an expatriate country of origin is to the host country the more difficult the adjustment" (393). Some authors (Owen 2014; Estes 2012; Henning and Mahfood 2009; Cave 2009; McMohon 2008; Levefere 2006; Hoge and Okure 2006; Braxton 2008) have given examples of the causes of the cultural misunderstandings and clashes between the foreign priests and the US laity. The causes of the tensions are not one-sided. Rather, both the international priests and the US laity contribute to the tensions (Owen 2014; Hoge and Okure 2006; Henning and Mahfood 2012; Lefevere 2006).

The intention of reporting the causes of the cultural tensions is not to personally critique the authors but to report their ideas. We shall look at the examples of how the cultural beliefs of both the international priests and the US laity contribute to the tensions. The causes of the tensions are written in paragraphs, followed by some of the suggestions given by certain authors to ameliorate the cultural clash.

2.5. EXAMPLES OF HOW THE CULTURAL BELIEFS OF THE INTERNATIONAL PRIESTS INFLUENCE THE CULTURAL TENSIONS

First, there is a cultural mentality of superiority of men over women. Some of the foreign-born priests have problems with accommodating the role of women in the US church and found it hard to work with women who have leadership positions in the administration of the pastoral works (Lefevere 2006). "Women's opinions are not elicited or needed" by some of the foreign-born priests (Hoge and Okure 2006, 17).

Many of the foreign-born priests, according to Hoge and Okure, "are not used to working with women who speak up, especially if they are on their parish staff" (18) because the priests come from a culture where the staff take instructions from the priest and are not expected to object or offer personal opinions. This leadership method, according to Hoge and Okure, has no place in the United States and so has a great tendency to create tension between some foreign priests and their parishioners.

In addition, Braxton (2008), who has visited the birthplaces of some of the international priests, brought a great enlightenment to this discussion about working with women. He observed that some of the priests come from cultures where women are not highly educated, unlike here in the United States where some women have degrees, even in theology and leadership studies, and are willing to use their knowledge to serve the church in one way or another. A purposeful neglect of the usefulness of these educated and useful women simply because they are women tends to create tension (Braxton 2008).

Second, some of the priests come from countries where priests are put on a very high pedestal (Hoge and Okure 2006) and are used to the autocratic style of leadership influenced by the tribal-chief-autocracy in their own culture (Braxton 2008). Unaware of the US style of leadership where culturally "everybody is thought of as equal since everybody is human" (Estes 2012, 12), they exhibit a leadership that demonstrates power instead of service (Hoge and Okure 2006). Reporting on an observation made by an instructor at the Cultural Orientation Program for International Ministers at Loyola Marymount University in California, Cave (2009) indicated that some of the international priests serving in the United States expect special regards and are surprised or even offended when some parishioners call them by their first name, which is usually not offensive among American priests. They need to "abandon that overweening clericalism that would set them apart from lay people and their daily interests and concerns" (McMohon 2008, 2). Authors like Cave (2009) believed that undoubtedly the foreign priests genuinely come to serve in the United States, but what they know in their original culture shaped their expectations.

Third, there is what Hoge and Okure (2006) referred to as "English competency and accent reduction" (16). Henning and Mahfood (2009) described it as "lack of language instruction or accent reduction" (63) for a better English. In some of the US Catholic dioceses, there are no established programs or efforts to address linguistic boundaries, even though many US parishioners "have a strong interest in the question of accent reduction and English language skill development" (Henning and Mahfood, 67). Nevertheless, in the dioceses where accent reduction is offered, some of the priests from the English-speaking countries like Nigeria and India resist the lesson, claiming they already know the language, which actually happens to be the King's English that is spoken with their tribal accent (Hoge and Okure 2006). The study of Hoge and Okure revealed that "there is no doubt … that language problems with international priests need more attention than they have gotten" (15–16) so Americans will understand them better and work better with them.

Fourth, there is cultural bias (Goodstein, 2009). Prior to arrival to the American shores, some of the international priests had already developed some personal perception of Americans, which does not represent the present US cultural and social lifestyles anymore, or at least in entirety. Goodstein believed that the international priests' knowledge of the US history, which includes US racism, the struggles of the civil rights movement, and the Ku Klux Klan, makes some of the international priests develop a stereotype that causes them to be afraid of parishioners, defensive, and sometimes antagonistic instead of acknowledging that they genuinely need some cultural adjustments that will help them in their pastoral ministry in the United States. Adequate preparation prior to their ministry in the United States, according to Hoge and Okure (2006), could reduce this issue.

Fifth, there is the lack of the ecclesiological context of preaching in the United States (Lefevere 2006). The unacceptance of the foreign priests' style of homily, according to Lefevere, is unspoken to the priests but manifests itself by people dozing during the homily or leaving the church when they see who is officiating the liturgy. The parishioners, according to Goodstein (2009), believe that the priests are good priests but do not know how to be clergy in the United States.

Besides the difficulties in language and accent, the international priests need to know that there is a difference in the styles of delivering homilies in various cultures and should learn to preach and organize liturgy in the US cultural context (Lefevere 2006). The international priests, according to Hoge and Okure (2006), must know the US context of officiating the liturgy and delivering the homily.

Cave (2009) reported how the attitude of dancing in the church by some African priests during their homilies could be disconcerting in some Euro-American parishes where parishioners are more individualistic and do not want to stay in the church beyond a certain period of time. Even though the international priests minister under the Roman Catholic principle of *ex opera operantis,* a meaning that incorporates the sacramental efficacy of an ordained Catholic priest independent of his communication skills or abilities or spiritual state (Lefevere 2006), he needs to understand the church's recommendation of being sensitive to acculturation (Hoge and Okure 2006) in order to have a better rapport with his parishioners and revitalize US Catholicism (Lefevere 2006).

Sixth, some of the international priests come from a culture that is structured in a way in which the oldest in the group assumes the leadership role (McMohon 2008). The problem with such priests when they come to the United States is the inability to exercise appropriate leadership in the parish, especially if the priest is young and never led before. Using McMohon's words,

> Some international priests come from highly structured cultures, in which a young man is not allowed to take action or join a group unless given permission either by the oldest person involved or by the person with the senior role. Such a cultural background might keep a young priest, for example from joining other clergy or staff ... if the oldest ... in the group doesn't make him feel welcome. (2008, 3)

In other words, part of the cultural problems in the parishes of some international priests is the inability of the priests to take initiatives in their leadership role because of their cultural background where the oldest in the social or church community is the one who initiates activities.

Finally, knowing that there are some other cultural problems of some international priests that might cause tensions in the parish, like lack of the knowledge of the US context of time and money management (McMohon 2008) as well as lack of the US church business administration and other social and ecclesial matters (Lefevere, 2006), one cannot claim that they have exhausted all the cultural baggage of the international priests that trigger tension in parishes.

However, Schroeder's (2009) general advice for international priests seems to be an essential tool for working in a different culture for the avoidance of cultural clash. Schroeder (2009), a US Catholic priest who worked as a missionary priest in Papua New Guinea for several years, used his own personal experiences in another culture to advise that a culture clash between foreign-born priests and the laity of the host culture can be reduced if the foreign-born priests receive an adequate knowledge of the host culture and become sensitive about the ways of doing things in the new culture. Schroeder understood that "the underlying dynamics and levels of cultural adjustment are complex" (82) but insisted that the foreign priests in the United States must value cultural competence and need "to be open to understanding the situation in the United States" (82). They are expected to adjust to the US lifestyle and be quick about it (Lefevere 2006). "In order to sell your product, you need to understand your audience. You have to understand their culture" (Deck 2012, 6).

2.6. Examples of How the Cultural Beliefs of the US Laity Influence Cultural Tensions

First, there is cultural bias by some US laity (Lefevere 2009). Borrowing an expression from Professor Yang of St. Paul Seminary School of Divinity at the University of St. Thomas in St. Paul, Minneapolis, Lefevere said that some Americans tend to consider anything that is un-American as inferior. Likewise, they look at the international priests as second-rate priests who did not have the adequate preparation and qualifications for the priestly ministry. Thus, some of the US parishes do not accept international priests simply because they are not Americans (Hoge and Okure 2006).

Expressing this issue in a different work, McMohon (2008) referred to the work of Hoge and Okure (2006) and indicated that many Americans "prefer not to have these priests in their churches, saying that … the screening of such priests isn't adequate before they arrive for service in the United States" (2). Addressing this idea of some of the US parishioners, the US Catholic bishops expressed their dissatisfaction of this misconception by some of the US parishioners in the document of the United States Conference of Catholic Bishops about International Priests (USCCB 2010).

The bishops presented several systematic methods that the different bishops of the various dioceses in the United States use for assessing the adequate screening of the international priests before they are invited to work in the United States (USCCB 2010). The bishops indicated that the situations where some international priests were advised to go back to their home countries or leave the United States are not based on inadequate priestly life but rather inadequacy to work in the American cultural context after arrival or other reasons unrelated to their adequate priestly formation (Goodstein 2008).

Allen (2010) said the same thing when he indicated that some of the international priests had been sent back to their home countries, but it is due to the problem of maladjustments and other personal issues unconnected with their general seminary formation. This is why (Goodstein 2008) highlighted that other than a few of the international priests, the idea of having them has yielded good results.

Allen (2010), who concurred with Goodstein (2008), also added that most of the international priests have many gifts and talents, which they bring to the pastoral ministry in the United States. What they need is to understand how to adjust to the clerical ethos of the American parishes. Goodstein (2008) hopes the US laity recognizes their cultural biases and works with the missionaries from other cultures.

Second, there is lack of a collaborative approach that hinders the consideration of the culture of the international priests (Henning and Mahfood 2009). According to Deck, "What is good for the goose is also good for the gander" (2012, 8). The US laity should "develop intercultural competence" (8) and hospitality and "foster ecclesial integration, rather than assimilation" (12). They should also assist the foreign priests in their journey of adjustment.

Deck would like the American Catholics to understand today's reality in which Roman Catholicism involves a great diversity in the priesthood and embraces intercultural awareness and sensitivity. After all, "the Gospel aims at transforming each person and identifying him or her, first and foremost with Jesus Christ, and not with American culture, or any other for that matter" (Deck 2012, 9).

For Deck, Americans need to acknowledge the present-day cultural reality and ask, "What do we do?" (5) to work together with the foreign priests and laity as a people united by the one teachings of Jesus Christ. "To do that successfully, one must get to the level of culture, be consciously aware of it and discern the shared meanings and values that constitute one's lived reality" (5). Making further emphases on the importance of cultural sensitivity toward the foreign clergy and foreign laity, Deck expressed,

> At least ten percent of today's U.S. Catholics no longer identify with the church of their baptism, and the number of fallen-away Catholics would constitute the second largest religious denomination in the country! This is occurring because we do not appreciate culture, how it works and how it truly defines who we are and what we are about. Culture does this not consciously, but unconsciously or subconsciously ... We are not here just because, "Oh my goodness gracious! All of these diverse, exotic seminarians are showing up," or "My goodness, one-third of our seminarians are international," or "Oh, a growing number of presbyterates are more international than local in origin. (5)

Deck believed that one of the reasons the cultural clash between the international priests and some Americans is happening because "the Americans need to understand what is really at play in the experience we are having right now. It is about accomplishing the church's overarching purpose which is, unity and communion in difference; community and diversity" (Deck 2012, 5).

Sympathizing with the international priests, McMohon (2008) expressed a personal belief that American missionaries would expect patience and support from the host nation if they also went to work in a different culture and therefore needed to understand that the foreign priests suffer disconnection from their families and home culture and expect patience and support in their transition to US culture.

Third, there is the understanding of the international priests as opportunists rather than missionaries (Hoge and Okure, 2006). Hoge's and Okure's study indicated that even though the foreign priests "see themselves as missionaries to America; the Americans do not recognize them as missionaries" (21), rather "there is a suspicion among some Americans that priests from developing nations are here partly to enjoy the higher standard of living and the more numerous educational opportunities here" (21).

As much as there is no doubt that most of these priests are happy to minister in the United States, they "are having a revitalizing effect in some parishes, where they bring their own spirituality, their music, and their devotions as a breath of fresh air" (17). Hoge and Okure questioned "if the level of wealth determines who is a missionary" (17).

Referring to the Second Vatican Council decree, *Ad gentes*, a Catholic Decree on the Missionary Activity of the Church, Owen (2014) cited a sentence that reminds Catholics everywhere that the international priests and lay missionaries are disciples "divinely sent to the nations of the world to be to them 'a universal sacrament of salvation', the church driven by the inner necessity of her own Catholicity and obeying the founder" (2–3).

The decree Owen cited, using Mark 16:16, reminded men and women of all cultures in the church that we as a church are called "to proclaim the gospel to all men" and women irrespective of cultural and economic differences (Owen 2014, 3).

Fourth, some Americans see their country as one that sends missionaries, not receives them (Ortiz 2012; Deck 2012). Some of the international priests, according to Ortiz (2012), might see this kind of mentality as a subtle snub that has its roots in environmental microaggression that asserts that only people of certain ethnicity are able to lead, and non-Western priests cannot be trusted. The essential theology of the church lacks in such a conversation about the countries that are perfect enough to be teachers of others and those who are not good enough to play the same role (Deck, 2012). Acknowledging the natural tendency of a negative reaction when some people in the Western world get a priest from a Third World, Deck insisted that such a mentality is not the Church's mentality.

Theologically, the church is essentially missionary, and so everywhere in the world, the church remains both a sending and receiving church, and the church in the United States needs to face this reality (Goodstein 2008). Thus, "We are talking about something rooted in the essence of the Christian faith and identity in the very mission entrusted to the Apostles by the Lord" (Deck 2012, 6). "This is the foundation of the Catholic Church's mission, ad gentes, to all people without exception" (6) and cannot be replaced by an ideology of some people (Deck 2012).

According to Deck, the cultural clash is partly due to a misunderstanding of intercultural unity that requires hospitality and openness to missionaries and all children of God. The American laity needs to accept the present reality of working with all good priests "whatever their differences may be—cultural, ethnic, race, or social class—because that is how the church maintains her remarkable worldwide unity and communion" (7) and "the reality of diversity in the church and the world" (Deck 2012, 7).

2.7. Potential Antecedents of a Better Relationship between the Nigerian Priests and US Laity

The movement of different professionals, including priests, from one culture to another made Ozar (2015) and Liu and Huang (2015) express that, given the continuous globalization of the world, it is becoming increasingly common for all kinds of sojourners and expatriates to move from one culture to another. The expatriates from the different professions relocate from their culture to another either as organizational expatriates (OEs), i.e., expatriates sent by an organization, or as self-initiated expatriates (SIEs), i.e., those who took the decision to relocate and were not sent by any organization (Peltokorpi 2008).

Most of the Nigerian priests who relocate to the United States are OEs, and they struggle in the unfamiliar culture of the United States. Some researchers have examined the issues associated with cross-cultural struggles as well as the antecedents of a better relationship when the home and heritage cultures meet (Ozar 2015; Zhang and Goodson 2011; Smith and Khawaja 2011; Hafitah, Tahir, and Ismail 2007; Hullinger and Nolan, 1997).

Little or nothing has been done about the cultures of the Nigerian priests and US laity. The antecedents of a better relationship when two cultures meet do not exclude the relationship of the Nigerian priests and US laity when two cultures meet. Unfortunately, cross-cultural researchers have given little consideration to international Catholic priests in the US culture when they study the cross-cultural struggles and challenges faced by professionals and expatriates in multinational assignments. Thus, a limited amount of studies has been done about the antecedents of a better relationship between the Nigerian priests and the US laity. The truth remains that the shortage of priests in the United States led to the recruitment of priests from Nigeria. As long as the world continues to be a global market, Catholic priests will continue to move from Nigeria to the United States. The service of the Nigerian priests and other foreign-born priests will still be needed in the United States due to globalization and priest shortage in the United States.

Researchers (Ozar 2015; Ortiz and McGlone 2012; Deck 2012; Zhang and Goodson 2011; Henning and Mahfood 2009; Peltokorpi 2008; Hafitah, Tahir, and Ismail 2007) identified certain antecedents of both psychological and sociocultural rapport when different cultures meet. These antecedents will be helpful to both the Nigerian priests and the US laity. The antecedents include:

1. Language proficiency by the expatriates. When the expatriates interact better with the host nationals, it increases better interrelationship. Furthermore, an understanding by the host nationals that the expatriates were not born and raised in the

host nation and therefore need time to be improve in their language proficiency reduces unnecessary clash.

2. Tolerance and optimism. A situation where people from different cultures are tolerant and optimistic to work together reduces cultural clash.

3. Social support. The expatriates need a support system that will help them to adjust better in the host culture; the host nationals should be sensitive of the loss of the social support that the expatriates had at home and then help them to get adjusted to the new culture.

4. Intercultural personality. Those who develop attitudes such as being flexible, tolerant, open-minded, patient, sensitive, stable, and respectful to other cultures and individuals who are different from them tend to have the ability to work together with people of other cultures. Both the expatriates and nationals need intercultural personality.

5. Ability to handle life changes. Both the expatriates and nationals need to understand that we live in an era of globalization, a period of mobility from one culture to another, and appreciate intercultural relationship.

6. Replacement of discrimination with acceptance. Morgan (2005) used the moral teachings of Abraham Joshua Heschel to express that human beings need to be human to one another irrespective of backgrounds and different cultures.

7. Well-defined goals. A better cultural relationship is enhanced when the expatriates and nationals have well-defined personal and professional goals and responsibilities to one another.

8. Acknowledgement of cultural distance. The need appreciate a knowledge of different cultures in an era of a globalized world

where people are expected to celebrate diversity enhances unity and good rapport.

9. Cultural competence. The capacity to respect and appreciate other cultures by both the expatriates and nationals is a *sine qua non* for living and working together.

10. Social interrelation. The ability to develop social interrelation by both the expatriates and the host nationals could decrease cultural clash.

In addition to the above-mentioned antecedents, the expatriates need to develop the necessary attitudes of the people of the host culture. If the expatriates could learn and master the ability to integrate both their heritage and domestic cultures during cross-cultural trainings, their cultural struggle and clashes with the host culture will be lessened.

2.8. Signs of Cross-Cultural Adjustment and Better Relationships between Expatriates and the Host Nationals

"Cross-cultural adjustment refers to the degree to which expatriates are psychologically comfortable and familiar with different aspects of a foreign culture" (Peltokorpi and Froese 2012, 735). It is the perceived degree of psychological comfort and familiarity an individual has when working within the new culture (Okpara and Kabong 2011, 24). It involves a feeling of less uncertainty, and comfort in the new culture (Ozar 1015). It is a period when expatriates are comfortable to imitate the appropriate behaviors of the host culture because of a genuine willingness to be a member of the culture (Nolan and Morley, 2014). It is a process in which expatriates begin to be comfortable and add new behaviors, norms, and rules of the host culture to the knowledge of the norms of their home culture (Peltokorpi and Froese, 2012).

Given the increased momentum of cross-cultural struggles and challenges in the recent years, studies on cross-cultural adjustment to assist both OEs and SIEs have also gained momentum in the recent years (Nolan and Morley 2014; Peltokorpi and Froese 2012; Hafitah et al. 2007). Both the OEs and SIEs struggle with certain cross-cultural problems before some of them eventually adjusted to the host culture. Some scholars have used three factors to measure the existence of cross-cultural adjustment in an expatriate: general adjustment, interaction adjustment, and work adjustment (Nolan and Morley 2014; Okpara and Kabongo 2011; Peltokorpi 2008).

According to Nolan and Morley (2014), general adjustment refers to the comfort and familiarity that the expatriate has with the general living conditions of the host country. Peltokorpi (2008) said it is synonymous with the sociocultural adjustment within the environment of the host culture. Interaction adjustment refers to the comfort of interaction with the host nationals (Nolan and Morley 2014), which Peltokorpi emphasized as the joy in interacting with the host nationals in their different interpersonal communication styles. Work adjustment refers to the happiness of the expatriate concerning their performance of work responsibilities and conditions (Nolan and Morley 2014). Peltokorpi described it as the comfort an expatriate gets from their work performance and values.

2.9. Acquiring Intercultural Competence by Both the Nigerian Priests and US Laity: A Necessity for the Reduction of Cultural Clash

The term "cultural competence" emanated from the term "multicultural competence," which appeared first in a mental health publication by a psychologist, Paul Pederson, and gradually became popular in culture-related and other academic conversations (Martin and Vaughn 2010). Today, different authors have given different definitions, descriptions, interpretations, and analyses to cultural and intercultural competence, and in some cases, one sees some disagreements in some of the authors' definitions and descriptions (Owan 2014).

More interesting is that the definitions of some of the authors are influenced by their fields of study. Owan captured the varied definitions influenced by the authors' academic backgrounds: health care, liberal arts, social work, English as a Second Language, military, missionary or ecclesiastical, and so forth. Even though there are variations in the definitions and explanations of cultural competence, there are also some commonalities, especially the recognition of cultural diversity and development of the skills to embrace the idea of unity in diversity.

For the purpose of the pastoral response to the cultural clash between the international Catholic priests and American Catholic laity, the definition given by Sperry (2012) shall be our guide. According to Sperry, "cultural competence is the capacity to recognize, respect and respond with appropriate words and actions to the needs and concerns of individuals from different ethnicities, social classes, genders, ages or religions" (43). This definition is not different from the understanding of intercultural competence given by Ortiz and McGlone (2012), "the capacity to notice, respect, appreciate and celebrate individual difference" (24). This description discourages the idea of focusing on differences and encourages focus on a person as a child of God (Ortiz and McGlone 2012). Sperry (2012, 42) acknowledged the description as a high level of cultural competence and indicated that it is essential for effective ministry in the church. Both the international priests and American laity need to know and acknowledge the importance of this cultural competence in order to develop an actual sense of one community of Christ and work together as a united people even though they have cultural differences (Cave 2009).

The fundamental nature of the Catholic Church is a community of one people united by oneness of faith (Gaillardetz 2010). The people who make up the church may have cultural differences, but these cannot be a threat because "the church's catholicity is a differentiated unity—a unity in diversity" (Ortiz and McGlone 2012, 37). Reflecting on the importance of understanding the church as a unity in diversity, the US Catholic bishops produced a document titled "Unity in Diversity" and said,

> The presence of so many different cultures and religions in so many different parts of the United States has challenged us as a Church to a profound conversion so that we can become truly a sacrament of unity. We reject ... the nativism, ethnocentricity, and racism that

continue to re-assert themselves in our community.
(USCCB 2000, 2)

The bishops believed that the call to one communion challenges every Catholic parish and diocese in the United States to celebrate the presence of people from different cultures and social backgrounds as a gift to the church (USCCB 2000).

Writing further about the church as a unity in diversity (or as one people, though, from other cultures and social backgrounds), Deck (2012) related the unity in diversity to the doctrine of the Blessed Trinity in order to theologize the idea of the church as a people of different cultures and backgrounds who are united in one faith. For instance, "in the Christian theology, particularly in the central teaching of the early Christian Church, we begin with the doctrine of the Blessed Trinity which is, about otherness" (Deck 2012, 6).

In this theology of the Three Persons in one God, which is a great mystery, "one finds a fundamental regard for difference, reaching out to what is other, ... It is a great mystery, but it is profoundly about otherness" (Deck 2012, 6), an acceptance of the other and not a denial or rejection of the other. So, it is not surprising that Otirz and McGlone (2012) called for an understanding of the importance of intercultural competencies in the present Roman Catholicism because the unity in Christ is a unity where cultural differences do not separate people. Rather it is a unity that accommodates all people, no matter their cultural and social backgrounds (Ukwuegbu 2008).

Cultural competency may not be the easiest aspect of life because it is a process that requires the ability to move beyond one's own worldviews and nationalistic admirations and accept people of all cultures for who they are in God's creation (Sperry 2012; Ortiz and McGlone 2012). However, in our increasingly globalizing world where cultural competency and working with people of different cultures are inevitable (Friedman 2005), the essence of cultural competence surpasses the difficulty of adapting to it, and it should really be accepted as a good thing for the increasing globalizing world (Sperry 2010).

When positively received, such competence generates a cultural awareness that engenders an attitude of welcome, respect, and openness in our association with people of other cultures, thereby engineering a cultural sensitivity that results in an effective and productive community irrespective of the cultural differences (Sperry 2010).

Contrary to seeing cultural competence as merely learning how to get along, which is only a part of it, cultural competence essentially proposes "an attribution of goodness and dignity to other individuals, especially to those who may be ethnically, racially, linguistically and culturally different" (Ortiz and McGlone 2012, 29). With that in mind, Ortiz and McGlone believed that both the international priests and receivers of international priests could find God in their various cultures and work together if they could develop "(a) awareness of the other, (b) knowledge about the uniqueness of the other, (c) sensitivity to the dignity of the other, and ultimately, (d) a set of skills to enter into dialogue and listening with otherness" (26).

Along the same line of thought, Lefevere (2008) wrote to the US laity about the international priests.

> We need to help these priests feel that they are indeed part of a family and to do that, we may need to learn about the culture in which the newly … arrived priest grew up … Our invitation and willingness to be brothers to the priests who are now serving in the United States and to help them experience aspects of life that we take for granted can open opportunities to build the kinds of relationships that invite dialogue and awareness in less threatening ways. (3)

Deck (2012), a US Catholic priest and author, added to the above statement by saying that the Catholic Church teaches the universality of the church and both the US Catholics and the foreign-born priests need cultural competence to have a fairly good integration. "We are challenged to get beyond ethnic communities living side by side 'for in one spirit we were all baptized into one body, whether Jews or Greeks, slaves or free persons and we are given to drink of one spirit (1 Cor. 12:13)" (USCCB 2000, 2).

2.10. The Present Cross-Cultural Training of the Nigerian and Other International Priests Working in the United States

The style of acculturation of the Nigerian and other international priests in today's US church and how it lacks authentic cultural competence for the ministry cannot be overlooked if one genuinely wants to confront the cultural clash between the international priests and US laity (Sperry 2012).

Believing that cultural competence is a process and not an event, Sperry has critiqued the present postarrival cross-cultural acculturation method being used in the US church to ameliorate the cross-cultural struggles and challenges facing international priests and their effect on the US parishes and institutions. Sperry does not deny the goodness of the method. However, he described it as a method that is "hardly sufficient to achieve the high level of cultural competence, particularly cultural sensitivity, needed in today's church" (42).

The different bishops of the various dioceses in the United States have adopted different forms of this postarrival acculturation method (USCCB 2010), but none is sufficient (Sperry 2012; Henning and Mahfood 2009; Hoge and Okure 2006).

The different statements of the US Catholic bishops about their various acculturation plans for the international priests arriving in their dioceses are clearly postarrival and can be partitioned into four different styles. Each bishop applies a style that suits him most (USCCB 2010b). A review of the bishops' plans indicates that

1. In some dioceses, the newly arrived priests remain in residence with some seasoned priests and learn the US societal and ecclesiastical lifestyles.
2. Some bishops send the new priests to institutions with established acculturation programs.
3. Some bishops have their own diocesan formal transition programs to meet their identified needs.
4. Some bishops have no specific protocol for the cross-cultural adjustment of the foreign priests.

Rather they have more of policies of welcome, even though it addresses some sort of acculturation (Hoge and Okure 2006). According to Hoge and Okure (2006), the acculturation styles or policies of welcome contain very little postarrival cross-cultural training of the priests so they can fairly adjust to the American culture and style of ministry. They are not strong enough to help an international priest to handle his cross-cultural struggles and conflicts. This is why Henning and Mahfood (2009), referencing the work of Hoge and Okure (2006), said that there is nothing in the protocol of the bishops that suggested any kind of strong cross-cultural training of the international priests or acknowledges the importance of predeparture cross-cultural training prior to coming to the United States.

In light of the different methods used by the US bishops, Hoge and Okure recommended a combination of predeparture and postarrival trainings of the international priests before their assignment to particular US parishes or institutions.

Given that cross-cultural programs are not conducted in the homes of most of the cultures of the international priests prior to their arrival to the United States, Henning and Mahfood suggested six recommendations, which Sperry (2012) thought are good but not good enough for a high cultural competence. The first recommendation is that the bishops need a fair implementation of the guidelines for receiving pastoral ministers in the United States (Henning and Mahfood), which was issued in 1999 by the Bishop's Committee on Migration. In the guidelines:

> The Committee called for orientation programs that would take place before the priest arrived in the US (pre-departure orientation), time to adjust upon arrival in the US and pre-placement orientation, and ongoing orientation and spiritual direction for the first three years. (Henning and Mahfood 2009, 63)

The second recommendation by Henning and Mahfood is that the US Catholic bishops should take the advice of Popes John Paul II and Benedict XVI about making use of the world's present technology of cyberspace and "insert media instruction into pastoral formation programs" (Henning and Mahfood 2009, 65). The authors and the popes were referring to the kind of current distance learning and online programs that are popular in many institutions of higher education since the advent of digital technology.

Henning and Mahfood suggested that on a simple scale, a tool such as Skype could be used to orient a priest about five months before he leaves his country for United States.

> On the more complex level, culture specific lessons could be developed and delivered online ... to priests who are or might be coming to the US. Such lessons need not be formal lectures but be a mixture of video and text with interactive components such as an attendant discussion board or online seminars with live interaction. (2009, 65–66)

Henning and Mahfood (2009) admitted that this idea would need the use of the internet, which is not available in every place in Third World countries, but it is still possible because "internet cafes have become common throughout the developing world" (65). With the use of the distance learning technology, an international priest could be learning about the social and ecclesial cultures of the United States while still in his home country, and the priests and parishioners in the United States would be learning something about the foreign priest and his home culture.

This, according to Henning and Mahfood, has the potential of starting a rapport and establishment of bonds between the foreign priest and his future US parishioners prior to his arrival. The distance learning technology like video conferencing, blogs, web pages, and so forth have the advantage of helping both an international priest and his future US parishioners to introduce themselves, share cultural differences, and know some aspects of their backgrounds, interests, and needs, as well as allowing room for advice and establishment of a support system from future parishioners.

The other four recommendations by Henning and Mahfood

(2009) are preparation of the host community for the arrival of the international priest, expansion of the acculturation programs, provision of mentors to the international priests upon arrival, and consultation of the international priests for the development of the acculturation programs.

Sperry (2012) believed that the six ideas of Henning and Mahfood (2009) and other ways of gaining knowledge of other cultures like having "a set of intercultural guidelines, an intercultural workshop or series of workshops or a brief immersion experience in another culture" (Sperry 2012, 42) are fine but can only be a good starting point for learning another culture because they are never sufficient to obtain a real cultural competence.

The acculturation programs for international priests presently taking place at "Loyola Marymount University in Los Angeles, California, Oblate School of Theology in San Antonio, Texas, and the Vincentian Center for Church and Society in Queens, New York" (Henning and Mahfood 2009, 63) and many other places are described by Sperry (2012) as an event for "cultural knowledge and awareness" (46). They can be a very good starting point, but "they are hardly sufficient to achieve the level of cultural competence, particularly cultural sensitivity, needed in today's church" (42).

Sperry (2012) believed that being culturally competent is a process that consists of "growth and transformation of the cognitive and emotional domains" (45). At the early stage of the growth of the two domains, each develops separately and independent of the other, but if they continue to develop unimpeded, "a transformation occurs in which both domains interact and eventually become integrated" (45).

At this early stage of development, the behaviors of individuals are often egocentric and lack empathy, and culturally, individuals tend to be insensitive (Sperry 2012) because at this stage that Sigelman and Rider (2012) call the preoperational stage (a term they borrowed from Piaget 1977), individuals tend to lean toward emotional pleasures and avoid pains, which include tolerance of a foreign culture (Sperry 2012).

Individuals, according to Sperry, lack the understanding that things might appear different to people of other cultures at this early stage, but as the cognitive domain begins to extend in the same direction with the emotional domains, then the individuals will begin to develop "the capacity to think and make more rational decisions" (Sperry 2012, 45). They will gradually begin to exhibit some intercultural tolerance, a sign of the capacity for cultural competence. Borrowing a term from Piaget (1977), Sigelman and Rider (2012) called this stage the stage of formal operations.

According to Sperry (2012), actual cultural competence occurs when there is a cognitive-emotional development, which means that individuals would have developed a capacity of the integration of cognitions and emotions and tend to act realistically and logically (Sperry 2012). As rightly put by Sperry, "Despite influences that may be operative in cultural situations, such individuals have the capacity for a high level of cultural sensitivity" (45).

When an individual reaches this stage of cultural competence, which is popularly known as postformal stage, they undergo a transformation that makes the person able to internalize and integrate the cultures of other people into their worldviews (Sperry 2012). From then on, the transformation genuinely influences the way the person thinks and acts with people of other cultures. The individual will begin to exhibit "the capacity to recognize, respect and respond with appropriate words and actions to the needs and concerns of individuals from different ethnicities, social classes, genders, ages or religions" (Sperry 2012, 43).

According to Sperry, there are four components of this actual cultural competence. The four levels and how they work together are worth citing in their entirety.

> There are four components to cultural competence: cultural knowledge, cultural awareness, cultural sensitivity and cultural action. Cultural awareness builds on cultural knowledge with the added capacity to recognize a cultural problem or issue in a specific individual and a particular situation. Cultural sensitivity is an extension of cultural awareness and involves the capacity to anticipate likely consequences of a particular cultural problem or issue and to respond empathically. Cultural action follows from cultural sensitivity. It is

the capacity to translate cultural sensitivity into action
that results in an effective outcome. Cultural action is
the capacity to make appropriate decisions and respond
skillfully with effective actions in a given situation. (43)

The above description by Sperry indicates that there is an
interconnection among the four components. The development of
each component flows from the previous component, which means
that there is a developmental process. Similarly, the development from
the preoperational stage to the postformal stage explained earlier is a
transformational process that occurs gradually and is not a discrete
event.

Therefore, participating in a course or workshop, or acquiring
cultural knowledge through reading, observation, language acquisition
or conversation is useful and necessary, but it is not sufficient to increase
cultural competence. Similarly, increasing cultural awareness by direct
involvement in the lives of others from a different culture through
immersion experiences is useful and necessary, but it is not sufficient to
increase cultural competence. (Sperry 2012, 45)

Unless individuals had a capacity of the integration of cognitions
and emotions, which only occurs in the sequential four components of
cultural knowledge, awareness, sensitivity, and action, individuals may
not be very culturally competent.

2.11. CULTURAL COMPETENCE FOR BOTH THE FOREIGN-BORN PRIESTS AND THE US CHURCH: ITS IMPORTANCE FOR SUCCESSFUL PASTORAL MINISTRY

Recent studies of both some international and US priests have
demonstrated the need for cultural competence as a key for success in
ministering in a foreign culture (Owan 2014; Ortiz and McGlone 2012;
Deck 2012; Schroeder 2007; Lefevere 2006). In his dissertation for a
doctoral degree from Kent University, Owan (2014), a Nigerian priest
who has worked in the United States, asserted,

> To enhance the chance of success through effective
> ministry, the church must institutionalize the
> importance of cultural competence in priestly training
> and service, especially service abroad where there are
> different cultures. This means adopting a comprehensive
> training program that would ensure that priests sent
> abroad for services possess the appropriate level of
> cultural competency to be successful in the field. (368)

The new training mirrors the purpose of the new evangelization advocated by Popes John Paul II and Benedict XVI, which calls for a new kind of ministry in the church that requires recognition of the cultural diversity and ignores superiority either by the priest or laypeople (Owan 2014). The purpose of the new evangelization and its intended success, according to Owan, have triggered the Committee of Cultural Diversity of the United States Conference of Catholic Bishops to promote "the importance of engaging cultures as the key to fruitful evangelization so that all ecclesial ministers will have 'a basic level of familiarity with cultural and intercultural relations and communications'" (190).

Moreover, since cultural competence has become the challenge of the church in our present time (Ortiz and McGlone 2012; Sperry 2012), acquiring the skills for it will strengthen the effectiveness of the priestly ministry, especially in the present reality of globalization and multiculturalism (Owan 2014). This is why Kilbourn (2006) expressed that ministry in both global and domestic context requires cultural competence. Lefevere (2006) believes it will help to reduce the cultural clash between the international priests and US parishioners because the international priests will move to the United States with both "the cultural ambience of their native setting … and a knowledge of "the ecclesial culture of the US Catholic church" (2). Lefevere's comments were motivated by some words of frustration of a foreign priest in his forties.

> Nobody briefed us about the situation here, or how to
> function. It was like, "Ok, we'll send you and try to do
> the best you can. We'll drop you in the water. Try to

swim. If you swim, fine. If you don't you die." That's their approach and I think it is wrong. (2a)

A training and acquisition of cultural competence prevents this kind of uncertainty in a job situation because it helps one with anticipation and cultural sensitivity (Sperry 2012). It helps priests to undergo a transformation experience in which they have an internalization and integration of the worldviews of people of another culture (Sperry 2012). A foreign priest working in another culture needs to be aware that "doctrine is not enough in order to effectively evangelize" (Deck 2012, 11) in the host culture.

Instead a combination of the knowledge of the doctrine and cultural competence for appropriate deliverance of the doctrine in the host culture would produce a more effective outcome. For Deck:

> The gospel must be translated in a way that it can be received by others. Doctrine becomes life through culture. When what the Gospel proclaims is somehow received into the heart and identity of a person, when it is inculturated, then it is transformative. Conversion is taking place. Short of that, one is merely hearing without really listening. (2012, 11–12)

The skill of cultural competence is not only useful for the training of priests for intercultural ministry (Sperry 2012). An extension of the skill of cultural competence to the laity of our universal church will help the receiving parishioners of an international priest to develop the habit of charity and tolerance of their foreign pastor (Owen 2014). Parishioners would develop a "post-formal thinking and processing of specific situations and circumstances" (Sperry 2012, 46) about an incoming foreign priest who can help to deescalate the tensions between international priests and the host parishes.

Cultural sensitivity, which is part of cultural competence, "involves both a welcoming attitude and the capacity to anticipate the consequences" (Sperry 2012, 47). Host parishioners need the knowledge that the church has always been a community where people cannot be divided by their cultural differences but a community of the Pentecost where people of different cultures are united by one Holy Spirit and one faith in Christ (Gaillardetz 2010).

Agreeing with Gaillardetz, Ortiz (2012) reminded everyone that at the Pentecost, the Holy Spirit came down upon the believers despite their differences in language and culture, which indicates that "the Holy Spirit does not erase difference but renders difference non-divisive. The account suggests that the church born of the Spirit, is from its beginning open to diverse languages and cultures" (Ortiz 2012, 38).

Cultural competence will help the American parishes with a foreign pastor to understand that "the Pentecost narrative essentially underscores how the first-century church moved from an ethnocentric congregation in Jerusalem to a multiethnic congregation . . . This is the vision of the intercultural, spirit-filled church we should strive as a community to recapture" (Ortiz 2012, 38).

The Pentecost narrative, which presents the church as a multiethnic church, motivated Ortiz to use the recommendations of the vicar for clergy at the Archdiocese of New York, Rev. William Belford, to suggest that the US parishes need to embrace cultural competence for a better relationship with foreign priests. Borrowing a portion of Belford's speech, Ortiz wrote that every "international priest deserves assistance and repeated answers from the time of arrival until he is confident and competent" (30) because in our multiethnic church we are one people in the Spirit of God and are our brothers' and sisters' keepers. Hence, "we should write things down for the newcomers, and urge them to ask how things are to be done in this place" (38).

The host parishioners need to "articulate a vision of church and society that invites the spiritual inheritance of diverse cultural groups to complement and enrich each other" (Ortiz 2012, 37–38) and have the capacity to recognize a cultural issue in a foreign priest positively and translate cultural sensitivity into an effective outcome (Sperry 2012). This can only be possible if people are able to "anticipate the need to work through the stressful feelings of … fear or anger that are inevitably evoked by the challenges of meaningfully engaging with persons unlike ourselves" (Ortiz 2012, 39).

2.12. The Importance of Predeparture Cross-Cultural Training in Multinational Corporations

Even though the focus of this particular topic is predeparture cross-cultural training in multinational corporations, the researcher would like his readers to understand that predeparture cross-cultural training is only an aspect of cross-cultural training. Cross-cultural training has more than one component, among which are predeparture and postarrival trainings (Shen and Lang 2009).

Some authors like Varner and Palmer (2005) have even written about a third aspect of cross-cultural training known as repatriation training, which is training for easier readjustment in one's own home culture when one goes back after a mastery and full immersion in a host culture. Varner and Palmer believed that despite the initial culture shock in the host culture, some expatriates eventually get adjusted very well, master the culture and then love and immerse themselves in the host culture so much that they hate to go back home. If they are repatriated home because of the need of their services at home, they find it difficult to readjust in their home country, thus the need for repatriation training.

However, our focus on this particular topic is on the importance of predeparture cross-cultural training in multinational businesses in order to learn the importance of predeparture cross-cultural training among expatriates in general, which does not exclude church expatriates. Given that the predeparture aspect of cross-cultural training in multinational businesses could be understood better when one fully understands what cross-cultural training is, this topic is divided into two subtopics: the importance of cross-cultural training in multinational corporations and the effectiveness of an addition of predeparture cross-cultural training within the big family of cross-cultural training.

Shen and Lang (2009) had a better explanation of the two subtopics when they said that a general knowledge of cross-cultural training helps one to understand not only its importance in multinational corporations but also the distinctiveness and importance of predeparture cross-cultural training with regard to fast adjustment and better job performance in a host country.

2.13. Cross-Cultural Training in Multinational Corporations

Shen and Lang (2009), who preferred to use "CCT" for cross-cultural training, used the work of Littrell, Salas, Hess, Paley, and Riedel (2006) to describe cross-cultural training as follows;

an educative processes that improve intercultural learning via the development of cognitive, affective and behavioral competencies needed for successful interactions in diverse cultures. Although CCT can be used for domestic employees, CCT in its traditional form is focused on preparing international assignees and is more specifically designed for targeting cultural issues ... CCT for expatriates aims to develop the awareness, knowledge and skills needed to interact appropriately and effectively with host-country nationals. (Littrell et al., 2006, 371)

In today's world of increasing globalization, the relocation of staff from one culture to another in multinational corporations is common, and so is the cross-cultural training of the expatriates for better adjustment and job performance in a different culture (Shi and Lang 2014; Neill 2008). In their study, Shi and Wang (2014) described why the expatriates of multinational corporations needed a cross-cultural training in this new age of globalization:

> In the current age of economic globalization, more and more business expatriates have been sent for cross-national investment and overseas operation. However, the expatriates' adaption is not always successful in a culturally different environment, since they are supposed to adjust to both the local working environment and the life environment, which are usually very different and challenging. (23)

Cross-cultural training, according to Neil (2008), serves the great purpose of preparing expatriates to adjust and perform well in the host cultures. Research has continuously shown that cross-cultural training enhances expatriates' intercultural adjustment and job performance

(Shi and Wang 2014; Wurtz 2014; Joshua-Gojer 2012; Godiwalla 2012; Shi and Lang 2009; Neill 2008).

According to Wurtz, (2014), there is a continuous assembly of educative resources to improve cross-cultural training in multinational companies so expatriates can bridge cultural distances and perform better in the host nations. Wurtz expressed that technical competencies for bridging cultural distances have become very popular among multinational corporations since many international companies continuously see the effectiveness of CCT toward the success of multinational corporations. Acknowledging the importance of CCT for easier adjustment and better performance in an unfamiliar culture, Joshua-Gojer (2012) said,

> The basic premise for CCT stems from the belief that it will help acclimatize the individual to the new culture and be effective in the new role. CCT can facilitate adjustment by involving the gradual development of familiarity, comfort, and proficiency regarding expected behavior and the values and assumptions inherent in the new culture. (52)

After assessing the success and failure of cross-cultural training in multinational business companies, Joshua-Gojer asserted that lack of cross-cultural training has led to more failures than success in many multinational companies. It has led to more loss of money, a premature end to international assignment, noncompletion of work, damaged relations with a host country, low performance, loss of business confidence, expatriate failure to frame arguments, repatriation, departure from a company shortly after assignment, and other adjustment problems.

The failures of known successful staff when assigned to a foreign culture made Liu and Lee (2008) insist that expatriates who are good in domestic positions need some cross-cultural skills and abilities to accomplish the same job they performed successfully at home for the assignment in a foreign environment.

We need to acknowledge that Joshua-Gojer's (2012) study also indicated that all repatriations or premature termination of assignment are not caused by lack of CCT. Some are caused by other reasons like organizational flexibility that leads to transfers to other positions within the same organization, better job offers in other companies, or expulsion for breaking the general rule of the organization. Nonetheless, Joshua-Gojer strongly believed that a good number of the repatriations and premature ends of international assignments are caused by inability to adjust to the host country by the expatriates or lack of the needed cross-cultural skills and support. He indicated, "Studies have found that between 16 and 40 percent of all expatriate managers end their foreign assignments early because of their poor performance or their inability to adjust to the foreign environment" (57).

The percentage of those who leave because of maladjustment is often higher than other reasons for repatriation. After a separate study about CCT for expatriates, Godiwalla (2012) expressed a view that is similar to Joshua-Gojer's (2012) findings and noted that poor performance and inability to adjust in a foreign culture are often caused by lack of training for cultural differences. According to Godiwalla (2012),

> The expatriate's strange and difficult-to-fathom foreign environment causes him to be anxious as he works hard to adjust and be effective. The obstacles of dealing with the different business customs, social etiquette, and language differences make it difficult for communication, operating environments, and building professional relationships in an appropriate manner. He has to deal with the strangeness and unfamiliarity during the initial period after his arrival in the foreign country. This is further compounded by the pressing need for him to show good performance and produce results in his foreign assignment. (Godiwalla 2012, 32)

Shin, Morgeson, and Campion (2007) did their own study to find out if there is a truth in the thoughts of some people that the expatriates' inabilities to cope with the anomalies and incongruities really hinder the expatriates to concentrate and fulfill their goal in a foreign culture and discovered;

A positive relationship between cognitive failures (failures of memory, reasoning and perception in everyday life) and stress susceptibility ... Problem-solving ability is negatively related to stress level. In a similar vein, uncertainty can be caused by an individual's inability to adequately structure or categorize information. In turn, such perceived uncertainty may lead to intolerance of anomalies and incongruities and a strong need for explanation of cause-and-effect relationships. This suggests that the expatriate's work will have higher reasoning ability requirements than domestic work because of stress, uncertainty, and the anxiety associated with unfamiliar situations. (35)

Cross-cultural training is meant to inculcate the reasoning ability, capability, and tenacity to handle the anomalies and incongruities in a foreign land and prepare the expatriates for the uncertainties and stressful situations in the different culture (Elmadssia and Hosni 2012). This, according to Joshua-Gojer (2012), is why the "the past few decades have seen an explosion in research on expatriates and cross-cultural training" (47) in order to appropriately address the problems of maladjustments, premature end to foreign assignments, and other cross-cultural problems among expatriates.

2.14. THE EFFECTIVENESS OF PREDEPARTURE CROSS-CULTURAL TRAINING IN MULTINATIONAL CORPORATIONS

According to Bakel et al. (2011), who wrote about the success of multinational companies in our present time, cross-cultural training before departure to the foreign country hastens adjustments on arrival. It leads to lesser waste of time before production and increases better performance. Better performance is enhanced by the reduction of cross-cultural stress inculcated in the expatriates with the predeparture training. It gives a prior knowledge of the possible difficulties the expatriates may encounter and how to manage them (Elmadssia and Hosni 2012; Farh et al. 2010).

The addition of systematic predeparture training to postarrival training among expatriates has improved the success of many multinational corporations such that it is continuously increasing in importance (Bank and Rothmann 2006). In the training, the expatriates are taught new rules and modes of behavior and given a framework of the intercultural norms accepted by their host culture (Elmadassia and Hosni 2012).

Arguing on whether predeparture or postarrival training is better for expatriates, Elmadssia and Hosni (2012), who favor both trainings for expatriates, indicated that a comparison of expatriates who received only training upon arrival and those who had a predeparture training indicated a greater importance of predeparture training. However, a combination of the two connoted that predeparture training is a powerful tool that supports postarrival training for easier adjustment and better performance in a foreign culture. So, a combination of both is very essential.

According to Godiawalla (2012), the effectiveness of predeparture cross-cultural training is clear and simple: it helps the expatriate to "be an effective expatriate right from the start, upon arrival in his foreign assignment" (33). Making the same point in another way, Joshua-Gojer (2012), who expressed that the effectiveness of predeparture cross-cultural training is a reason "there have been many more studies done on pre-departure training than post-arrival" (56), asserted that "the time taken to adjust to the new culture will be shorter if the expatriate is aware of what to expect in the host culture" (54) prior to arrival. Explaining his assertion more, Joshua-Gojer said,

Pre-departure training would lead to improving the learning curve upon arrival in the foreign assignment, resulting in fewer costly mistakes; successful adaptation to local organization, culture, logistics, industry and society. The training would lead to improved capabilities in dealing with the host country people and ... the training should enable him [expatriate] to build effective relationships and influence network in work and non-work environments. The training would enable him to be more confident in managing stress, ... unfamiliarity and ambiguity. (2012, 36)

On the same par, Godiwalla (2012) compared predeparture and

postarrival training. Acknowledging the importance of both, he still stated that if he must choose between the two, he would choose predeparture training. Elaborating his reason for the choice, he said,

When an expatriate gets a pre-departure training, his knowledge of the local environment and his developing of his own ways of dealing with the local situation would be helpful in the transition to the host country environment. His enhanced problem-solving skills and cognitive reasoning (i.e., ability to recall, perceive, and reason in everyday situations) would improve his ability to correctly understand and analyze the situation. His confidence will be better, and his stress level will be lower. (2012, 37)

It is the observations of people like Joshua-Gojer (2012) and Godiwalla (2012) that made Shi and Wang (2014) conclude that the majority of researchers and managers of multinational business companies believe that predeparture training works better for adjustment and greater performance.

Littrell et al. (2006) used the theory of met expectations to further explain why predeparture cross-cultural training could be very effective. According to them, the theory of met expectations proposes that if an individual has expectations about a situation and the initial expectations are consistent with the reality, the individual gets adjusted, satisfied, and committed. Accordingly, if predeparture training is done very well, the theory of met expectations gets fulfilled in the work of the expatriates because their predeparture training will match the realities they would face on an arrival to the foreign culture. This would help them to adjust faster and start work without a big setback by culture shock.

The general effectiveness of the theory of met expectations in job performance made Bank (2007) borrow some of the explanations and analyses about the theory given by Vroom (1995) and Ormond (1999) and summarized the theory of met expectations as a decision theory of motivation that directs individuals toward goals, increases energy and activity level, and promotes initiation and persistence. Bank suggested the use of the theory for the predeparture training of expatriates to help them with the knowledge of the reality they will face so as to increase their ability level when they face the reality.

Neil (2008) also believed that predeparture cross-cultural training does help expatriates to adapt and work in a new environment because of its power of equipping an individual with the preknowledge of the host culture and expectations prior to departure. However, he questioned if cross-cultural trainings (predeparture or postarrival) are the only contributing factors for easier adjustment in a foreign culture.

The work of Petison and Johri (2008) had a response to Neil's (2008) question. They expressed that even though cross-cultural training, especially predeparture training, is a great factor for adaptation in a foreign culture, the ability of having a good relationship or the inability to have a good relationship with nationals could enhance faster adaptation or vice versa. They asserted that sometimes the success or failure of expatriates is caused by a smooth or rough relationship with the host country nationals. It is therefore necessary to provide the expatriates with a training that should lead to a solid trust-based relationship with the host nationals (Petison and Johri 2008; Sanders-Smith 2007).

This idea of Petison and Johri had surfaced before in the work of Shin, Morgeson, and Campion (2007), who reported that cross-cultural adjustment and performance in a foreign culture are sometimes affected by the relationship that exists between the local host-country workers and the expatriates. Hence, there should be a relationship dimension of predeparture training because it would help the expatriates to interact comfortably with the host nationals and relate appropriately with them (Shin et al. 2007). Given that the expatriates are meant to function in the host country context, Joshua-Gojer (2012) also proposed that building good relationships and networking in work and nonwork environments are important and require knowledge of the local language, good communication, and good manner of communication. Wurtz (2014), who also concurred with Petison and Johri (2008), Morgeson and Campion (2007), Godiwalla (2012), and Shin et al. (2007), said that a good relationship in and out of the work area leads to appropriate association and teamwork between the expatriate and nationals. When an expatriate develops an interpersonal skill that leads to a good relationship with the host nationals, it helps to improve communication competence, cultural adjustment, and job performance (Shin et al. 2007).

Fan and Lai (2014) and Osman-Gani and Rockstuhl (2009) have also brought up the importance of including an intense self-efficacy development in predeparture cross-cultural training. Fan's and Lai's (2014) study of "169 managers from four different national backgrounds ... on overseas assignments in Asia" (277) indicated that an inclusion of intense self-efficacy in their predeparture cross-cultural training increased their adjustment ability and effectiveness in job performance. The two authors believed that when self-efficacy is very strong, the individual becomes self-confident, adjusts better, and performs appropriately. Even though the focus of predeparture cross-cultural training is to have a solid basis for adjustment and job performance, the expatriate needs a strong self-efficacy in order to be effective upon arrival in the unfamiliar culture and work setting (Godiwalla 2012).

Without denying the importance of self-efficacy, Shen and Lang (2009) shared the opinion that self-efficacy and appropriate job performance are hard to achieve when there is no preparation to handle culture shock. Culture shock, according to Joshua-Gojer (2012), is "a normal process of transition, adaptation and adjustment in which an individual who enters a foreign environment for an extended time period experiences cultural stress involving some degree of anxiety, confusion, disruption, helplessness, and irritability" (54). After studying the different theories and definitions of culture shock, including the explanations of culture shock given by Kalervo Oberg, the anthropologists who introduced the term "culture shock," Shi and Wang (2013) made the following clarification of culture shock,

On the whole, culture shock can be described as the anxiety or stress an expatriate feels immediately due to the unfamiliarity of social practice in the host country. A big challenge faced by expatriates is that those who are inadequately informed of the host country's culture or unaware of cultural difference are most likely to fail. (24)

According to Joshua-Gojer (2012), in cross-cultural training, culture shock is also addressed as the effect of cultural problems, and it has a significant negative effect on adjustability. If cross-cultural training is taken before departure, it helps to lessen the stress from culture shock and other cultural problems (Shi and Wang 2013). The study of Shen and Lang (2009) suggested that the combination of predeparture training and intermittent continuation after arrival in the host culture are more effective to subdue culture shock easily and develop a faster cross-cultural adjustment. Both factors, predeparture and postarrival training, according to Shen and Lang, support behavioral management and lessen the stress that emanates from culture shock. Explaining how the two factors work together, Godiwalla (2012) said that the predeparture training tends to be more motivational, which tends to support expatriates with the behavioral management of their postarrival culture shock. The postarrival training strengthens the behavioral management and reduces the stress that comes from the culture shock.

Joshua-Gojer (2012) believed that both the predeparture and postarrival trainings are important, but also very important are the personal attitudes of the expatriates to both the CCT trainings and their willingness to be genuinely involved in the host culture. No matter the number of the different types of adjustability given, "personal attitudes of the expatriates play a role in the end result of the CCT" (Joshua-Gojer 2012, 55). He asserted that it is the degree of the expatriate's mental involvement and the effort they put into the training and learning, in association with personal determination to succeed, that lead to success.

2.15. Analyzing Positive Effects of Predeparture Pastoral and Psychological

Preparation of the Nigerian Priests from the Perspective of Psychology

According to some cross-cultural psychologists like Triandis, Malpas, and Davidson (1971) and a social psychologist, Morgan (2012), psychologists are primarily interested in understanding the determinants of both human behavior and experiences to build wellness and resilience. Psychologists also see "their main purpose as the development of general laws and of human behavior and application of these laws to different situations" (Triandis, Malpas, and Davidson 1971, 1).

Just as physicians of today practice more expertly to meet present health needs (Johnson 1953, 24), psychologists, especially pastoral psychologists, have the duty to consider the present needs of pastors and most functional way to address the needs in our present time. It is necessary for pastoral psychologists to constantly review their arts or science and religion for a proper application of human behavior in various situations since different situations require the appropriate behavior for each circumstance. The pastoral psychologists and cross-cultural psychologists who prepare the Nigerian priests on mission in the United States are expected to be familiar with the fact that new situations require fresh skills and knowledge. Hence, they must help the Nigerian priests to systematically acquire the style of pastoral ministry that presently works in the United States. The priests should know the importance of scientific accuracy and practical effectiveness for great ministry in the present United States prior to departure. They must learn how to be students of personality prior to departure in order to have a quick understanding of their parishioners in the United States and how to be proactive in defusing emotional conflicts and anxieties, which cultural conflicts and maladjustments may cause. Joshua-Gojer (2012) was probably thinking of these factors when he advocated that the predeparture preparation of any expatriate must include how to understand a new people in a new culture in order to manage the unfamiliarity and ambiguity in the new culture and build effective relationships with the host country people and associate with them in both work and nonwork environments.

A social psychologist, Zajonc (1968), has studied and noted the positive effect and importance of prior knowledge before actual contact and advocated the hypothesis of attitudinal effects of mere exposure, which is also called the familiarity principle in social psychology. In the hypothesis, Zajonc was not only referring to the actual physical exposure to a real situation but also an exposure to something familiar to what a person or animal will eventually encounter in order to reduce fear and increase social attachment to the situation upon encounter. Zajonc started his hypothesis with the effect of a prior knowledge of the meaning of unfamiliar words to a quick familiarization with the words when faced with the things and events that the words represent. The hypothesis clearly demonstrated the power of a prior knowledge of anything in cultivating an effective attitude to the actual thing when an individual encounter it. According to Zajonc, "with an exposure-enhancement mechanism, a strange reaction to something new could be reduced and even appreciated" (1968, 19).

His argument was based on several experiments, and all indicated that the first encounter with the novel stimulus evokes fear, uncertainty, and conflict, but prior knowledge before the encounter enhances familiarity and better interaction. This is why most animals and humans prefer a familiar image or device to a new one most of the time. In the conclusion of his work, Zajonc asserted, "novelty is thus commonly associated with uncertainty and with conflict ... it will produce more negative than positive effect" (21). This highlights the importance of prior knowledge with regard to reducing fear and increasing readiness to interact with new situations.

The "attitudinal effects of mere exposure" is a good argument for advocating that if the Nigerian priests assigned to the United States are exposed to or familiarized with US culture through different sorts of learning about US culture, the priests could adjust and perform better upon arrival to the United States.

Zajonc's hypothesis has a little similarity with the theory of met expectations discovered by Victor Vroom and the Yale School of Management. This theory, which has been briefly explained above, needs to be explained further from a pure psychological standpoint. According to Lunenburg (2011), Vroom's theory of met expectations, which Porter and Lawler (1968) further later clarified, differs from the content theories of Maslow, Alderfer, Herzberg, and McClelland, in that Vroom's expectancy theory do not provide specific suggestions on what motivates organization members. Instead, Vroom's theory provides a process of cognitive variables that reflects individual differences in work motivation ... The expectancy theory has some important implications for motivating employees. It identifies several important things that can be done to motivate employees by altering the person's effort-to-performance expectancy, performance-to-reward expectancy, and reward valences. (1)

In other words, the intention of the theory is "to explain what motivates people in the workplace" (Lunenburg 2011, 1). The theory highlights that "employees do not act simply because of strong internal drives, unmet needs, or the application of rewards. That is to say, they are rational people whose beliefs, perceptions, probabilities and estimates influence their behaviors" (5). The expectations of people influence their reactions and outputs in a workplace.

In other words, the expectancy calculation affects their behaviors and production in a workplace. Expectancy theory is based on three assumptions: Individuals are motivated by the belief that (a) their efforts will lead to expectancy, (b) performance will be rewarded, and (c) the value of the rewards will be highly positive (Lunenburg 2011). Vroom (1964) also described the theory in a mathematical way: Motivation = Expectancy (anticipation) x Instrumentality (selected behavior and performance) x Valence (attractiveness).

This is why Lunenburg (2011) agreed with Littrell, Salas, Hess, Paley, and Riedel (2006) that in expectancy theory, motivation increases when the initial expectations (or prior knowledge) are consistent with the reality because the individual easily gets adjusted, satisfied, and committed. Thus, expectancy theory has some important implications for motivating employees if the employees get into the job with the expectation that their past experiences will help them to perform the job successfully (Lunenburg 2011).

The application of this theory to the Nigerian priests intending to work in the United States implies that if the priests are given the knowledge of the challenges and other cultural experiences they will encounter and how they could tackle the issues and the knowledge accords with actuality upon arrival, the priests could face the difficulties without a great setback. The prior knowledge would help the Nigerian priests to adjust faster and start work without a huge culture shock.

This is why Bank (2007) described the theory of met expectations as a motivation theory. Bank was thinking of its ability to make an individual forge ahead because of their prior expectation of the difficulty and a possible positive achievement at the end. The theory of met expectations could definitely be a great theory for the preparation of the Nigerian priests assigned to United States because it will help them understand that if they know and prepare for the reality they will face, their ability level to adjust and transition to US culture will be more positive than negative when they face the real situation.

The theory of solution-based counseling would be another thing to be considered for the cross-cultural predeparture training of the Nigerian priests intending to work in the United States. A husband and wife, Steve de Shazer and Insoo Kim Berg, and their team of workers originally developed this theory in the 1980s (Berg 2016). Their aim was to focus on a therapy that is based on a time-limited solution building rather than problem-solving. According to Berg, "It is about being brief and focusing on solutions, rather than on problems" (1). Berg believed that the therapy is needed because "so much time and energy, as well as many resources are spent on talking about problems, rather than thinking about what might help us to get to solutions that would bring realistic and reasonable relief as quickly as possible" (1). Thus, both Shazer and Berg thought of three ways of building the solution: (1) acknowledgment of the present problems, (2) looking at the past situation of the client to identify the cause of the problem, and (3) exploration of current resources and future hopes of the clients so that with the application of the resources and the hopes for success the clients will use their own strengths to solve their problems (2016). This therapy is also known as solution-focused brief therapy (SFBT).

Using the words of Iveson (2002), "Solution-focused brief therapy is an approach to psychotherapy based on solution-building rather than problem-solving … It has great value as a preliminary and often sufficient intervention and can be used safely as an adjunct to other treatments" (149). Even though the therapy is time-limited, many psychotherapists incorporate the therapy to other long-term therapies in order to achieve long-lasting effects on the clients (Oliver, Hasz, and Richburg 1997).

The Counseling Directory by Memiah (2016) has a good summary of what this theory is all about. According to the directory, the concept of the theory is built on the belief that (1) change is certain and also constant, (2) clients have the potential to change, (3) clients have the ability to outline their own goals toward change, (4) clients have the strength to overcome their problems, (5) the focus of the therapy should be the use of the past history of clients to achieve a better future for the clients, and (6) there must be emphasis on what is changeable and its possibility during the application of the therapy.

Believing that human beings often do many more positive things than they are fully aware of, Berg (2016) believed that bringing the positive aspects of clients to their awareness could make the clients to be more confident to improve their lives. She holds the opinion that the knowledge of the clients' potential successful behaviors, no matter how small, could help them be hopeful of more and bigger successes, which could lead them to creating a better life for themselves or surmounting the difficulties that psychologically frightens them. Berg believed that

Repeating these successful behaviors is easier than learning a whole new set of solutions that may have worked for someone else … Thus, the brief part was born. Since it takes less effort, people can readily become more eager to repeat the successful behaviors and make further changes … The model continues to evolve and change. It is increasingly taken out of the therapy or counseling room and applied in a wide variety of settings where people want to get along or work together. (2016, 1)

According to Iveson (2002), the clearer a client is about their successful behaviors and future goals, the more likely they will strive to achieve the goals. That is why Berg and Miller (1992) expressed the view that both the therapist and client should be interested in finding out the goal of the client, hence the description of the therapy by Oliver et al. (1997) as a "mind-set that sees possibilities rather than impossibilities" (263). It encourages the importance of building on existing strengths and setting small and attainable goals while watching expectantly for a gradual change to occur. Iveson (2002) called it "the seed of client's own solution" (149).

Applying the theory to missionaries, Oliver et al. expressed the importance of patience in a new culture in order to allow the existing strengths to be helpful in mastering the principles of the new church setting, such as style of worship and evangelism and the way the host culture conducts ceremonies and meetings. The Nigerian priest preparing to mission in the United States should learn how to be patient, remain hopeful in mastering the pastoral style of ministry in the host culture, and avoid the imposition of his own cultural style. He needs the patience that involves listening, a belief in the successes he has made in his life, and a hope for bigger success, while bearing in mind that unless he changes from his home cultural style of ministry to the host country's unsatisfactory relationships or other depressing and self-defeating situations may occur (Oliver et al. 1997).

Emphasizing more on the critical importance of personal change in transition into a new culture, Oliver et al. advised that those preparing cross-cultural missionaries should master and teach the general principles of change, patterns and stages of change, process of change, and the difficult aspects of cultural change. These would also apply to the trainers of the Nigerian priests departing to the United States for missionary work so the priests will be aware of their strengths and be open to personal change prior to arrival to the host country.

Concurring with Oliver et al., Wong and Wong (2006) expressed that personal transformation is a very important strategy to be successful in a foreign culture and suggested that the trainers of the departing missionaries should clarify the critical concepts in stress and coping in a foreign culture for the departing missionaries. The trainers should teach the priests all the personal and collectivist values in coping in a foreign culture as they seek to give the missionaries the psychological skills that enhance intercultural adjustment for pastoral work in a foreign land. All the positive aspects of this theory can be helpful for a missionary to an unfamiliar place.

Given that some of the Nigerian priests assigned to work in the United States may encounter some cross-cultural problems, the predeparture training might include the use of cognitive behavioral therapy (CBT), which Morgan (2015) recognized as the "most advanced form of cognitive behavioral therapy" (417). CBT, which emanated from Albert Ellis' theory of rational emotive behavior therapy (REBT), is one of those developments from Freud's psychoanalytic theories until it was modified and refined in the 1960s by A.T. Beck (Morgan 2015). Acknowledging the great contribution of Beck on this psychotherapy, Morgan explained Beck's cognitive behavioral therapy as essentially based upon the cognitive model … Thoughts, feelings, and behaviors are interconnected and that any improvement in the emotional life of a troubled individual can only occur when the client is able to overcome his difficulties by acknowledging, identifying, and addressing dysfunctional ideas and thoughts as well as counter-productive behaviors and distressing emotional responses to life's situation. (417)

Like the SFBT that originated from Shazer and Berg, one of the greatest things about the cognitive behavioral therapy is the emphasis that the client "is empowered to collaborate with the therapist in developing strategies for altering, changing, or modifying ... counterproductive ideas, emotions, and behaviors to foster, nurture, and solicit self-affirmation and self-fulfilling ideas, emotions, and behaviors" (Morgan 2015, 417). This therapy could work for the preparation of the Nigerian priests who are assigned to the United States and are struggling with the trouble of certain personal assumptions.

With the use of this therapy, the basic assumptions that are troubling to the Nigerian priests could be altered with positive redefined information and insights that are helpful in restructuring one's view about the troubling issues. Morgan might be thinking of the usefulness of this therapy on the cure of certain personal assumptions when he said, "In cognitive therapy, the client is called upon to be proactive in working with the therapists in exploring alternative ways of thinking about situations and imagining alternative ways of responding to those situations" (419).

With the use of this therapy, a Nigerian priest assigned to the United States but troubled about his new mission will be helped by the predeparture trainers with the process of questioning the priest's stress-causing situations as well as knowing his strengths in order to obtain a positive assessment of the priest's personality in handling problems and use it to replace his negative views. Morgan explained the process as building analytical skills in assessing one's situation or perception and then reconstructing and innovating a process where the client becomes his own therapist to take care of his own situations in a constructive, positive way.

The application of Morgan's explanation of the therapy to predeparture training for an unfamiliar culture has the potential to help the Nigerian priests on mission in the United States. Morgan's ideas have affinity with Oliver et al.'s (1997) description of the therapy as a mindset that sees possibilities rather than impossibilities. Their analysis of this therapy has an indication of a good therapy for predeparture preparation. Iveson's (2002) and Berg's (2016) contribution to the knowledge of the therapy as a solution-building therapy that has great value in preliminary and often sufficient intervention also makes the therapy a great tool for preparing a Nigerian priest for the intervention and solution of the cross-cultural problems he might encounter. The therapy could help him to focus more on realistic solutions rather than being pessimistic.

CBT and SFBT share the commonality of approaching the problem of an individual by avoiding a lengthy psychoanalytic approach in treatment. They approach a problem through an in-depth probing of the past for a short behavioral solution by empowering the client to be their own therapist. A preknowledge of the two psychological theories have the capability of helping a Nigerian priest on mission in the United States to probe his past and find out the things that may not work in his present situation and then make the necessary changes that will help him to adjust better in the host country. The Nigerian priest must not forget Morgan's idea that CBT and behavior-modification technique have a collaborative relationship.

SUMMARY

This literature began with the problem of priest shortage in the United States and the manifestation of the shortage in the US Catholic parishes and colleges as well as military institutions. The shortage led to the recruitment of priests from Europe, and the priest shortage in Europe led to the recruitment of priests from non-European countries, whose culture is very different from the US culture. Presently there are many priests from the non-European countries working in the United States, and the cultural differences between the foreign-born priests and the Americans they serve sometimes generate conflicts in the ministry.

Certain cross-cultural programs are being implemented to alleviate the problem. Research revealed that the programs are helpful but are mainly postarrival in nature and there is need to improve the cross-cultural programs with the inclusion of a predeparture program. The need for improvement has attracted some suggestions, such as cultural competency and distance learning by the incoming foreign priests about the culture of their future US parishioners.

Some of the authors also suggested a learning of the culture of the incoming priests by the US laity in order to increase cultural competency in both the US laity and foreign priests so that both could appreciate one another's cultures and happily work together as one people in faith amid the differences in culture.

Given the continuous problems of cultural clash between the foreign-born priests and the US laity, the church can also learn intercultural teamwork from the multinational corporations, which have already included intercultural programs in the training of their expatriates who work in other cultures since the increasing globalization of our world. Research indicates that the success of expatriates in the multinational businesses became better since the business corporations included predeparture training. Studies of some psychological theories also favor the importance of predeparture cross-cultural training of priests prior to taking up their assignments in a different culture.

If predeparture training works for the expatriates in multinational corporations and is also favored by some psychological theories, it might work for the priests in Roman Catholicism and therefore could be used to prepare the Nigerian priests intending to work in the United States for adequate adjustment and better job performance upon arrival.

From both the perspective of well-acknowledged psychological theories and the studies of cross-cultural scholars, there are strong indications of a solid trust-based relationship between predeparture cross-cultural training and the competence to manage cross-cultural struggles and challenges. So prior training could be very instrumental in lessening the cross-cultural struggles and challenges of the Nigerian priests serving in the United States, especially if it is combined with the postarrival training that is being used currently. According to some researchers, the combination lessens cross-cultural struggles and challenges (Elmadssia and Hosni 2012; Godiwalla 2012; Joshua-Gojer 2012).

Thus, adequate research needed to be done to psychologically and pastorally prepare the Nigerian priests on mission to the United States given the continuous influx of Nigerian priests to the United States and the cross-cultural maladjustments among some of them.

CHAPTER 3

Methodology of the Study

3.1. STYLE OF STUDY

THE METHODOLOGY OF THIS STUDY TOOK A QUALITATIVE STYLE, utilizing the phenomenological approach of qualitative research. "Qualitative research involves an interpretive, naturalistic approach to the world. This means that qualitative researchers study things in their natural settings, attempting to make sense of, or interpret phenomena in terms of the meanings people bring to them" (Creswell 2007, 36). "Qualitative researchers are interested in understanding the meaning people constructed, that is how people make sense of their world and the experiences they have in the world" (Marriam 2009, 13).

While there are different designs in qualitative research, for instance, phenomenology, ground theory, or ethnography, the essence of every qualitative research is to be attentive and understand the participants' perceptions about how they lived and experienced the phenomena (Creswell 2007). Using the popular "analogy of 'believing is seeing' versus its antithesis, 'seeing is believing,'" O'Dwyer and Bernauer (2013, 32) expressed that a qualitative researcher leans toward the former because of their interest in constructing a meaning that is based on lived phenomena and experiences. Qualitative method was very appropriate for this study because of its ability to facilitate an understanding of the actual lived cultural struggles and conflicts and other cultural experiences of the Nigerian Catholic priests who have lived and served in the US pastoral missions for ten years or more. The knowledge of their actual lived phenomena and experiences were very essential for the cross-cultural predeparture training of the Nigerian priests assigned to the United States for pastoral duties.

Given that qualitative method of research seeks the meaning and reason attributed by participants to events and circumstances, the method was a good research method for providing rich and deep understanding of the lived complex cross-cultural phenomena needed to gather information for this study. As indicated by Joshua-Gojer (2012), predeparture cross-cultural training must consider the appropriate behaviors to be engaged in or avoided when in a host country in order to gain the confidence of the host-country. So, the lived phenomena and experiences of the Nigerian priests who have lived and worked in the United States were necessary for the predeparture cross-cultural training of the Nigerian priests assigned to mission in the United States.

This qualitative study took the phenomenological approach because phenomenological researchers have the general concern of returning "to embodied experiential meanings aiming for a fresh, complex, rich description of a phenomenon as it is concretely lived" (Finlay 2009, 1). According to Wertz (2005), the phenomenological design "glories in the concreteness of person-world relations and accords lived experience, with all its indeterminacy and ambiguity, primacy over the known" (175). This particular method, which included the cognitive, affective, and experiential approach (Ko and Yang 2011), was effective for the study. It allowed an in-depth phenomenological interview approach, the most appropriate approach to study the participants' lived phenomena and experiences for this study. The approach enhanced the recommended techniques for collecting information from the participants usually involved in the qualitative approach of study, such as this.

Some scholars have used phenomenological design to study predeparture cross-cultural training. Ko and Yang (2011) used it in their study. They used it to study the insights of some Taiwanese expatriates to find out if predeparture cross-cultural training has some effects on cross-cultural adjustment and job performance. Ko and Yang applied an interview protocol for their data collection while using the qualitative methodology with a phenomenological approach for the study. "Eight former expatriate managers were recruited ... ranging in age from 33 to 65, with 3 to 27 years of work in overseas assignments" (163). The result of the study indicated a positive impact of the "ability to build up a good relationship with the local staff, to reach the goals of their overseas assignments and ... enhance job-related performance" (169).

O'Donnell, McAuliffe, and O'Donovan (2014) also used the phenomenological approach of qualitative method to study the experiences of Irish medical students who take international health electives (IHEs) and travel to developing countries to further their knowledge of health care. "One-on-one, semi-structured interviews were conducted in person to record the experiences of the participating students" (3).

Purposive sampling was used for the selection of the students (participants) who had travelled to developing countries. Fourteen students were chosen as participants and "Fourteen interviews were conducted from April to June 2013. The Interviews lasted for an average of 55 minutes in each case" (3). Data were then analyzed thematically. After the study, O'Donnell et al. "recognized the need for formal pre-departure training and debriefing on return" (7) from the mission trip.

They concluded that there is much to be gained from exercising this type of study. They also observed that the method helped them to observe that there has been "a situation of unexamined good intentions" (7) and recommended a scrutiny of the program, among which is the preparation of students prior to traveling overseas. Here is a part of the conclusion:

The fact that inadequate preparation prior to IHE can lead students to placing themselves in distressing situations is obvious and should be addressed. Irish medical schools need to recognize the need for formal pre-departure training and debriefing on return and their role in the governance of funds raised by their students. The possibility of formal agreements with institutions in several countries, with a view to developing long-term sustainable partnerships should be explored where regular short-term rotations for students and staff, and possible reciprocal arrangements could be arranged. (O'Donnell et al. 2014, 7)

Interpretative phenomenological approach (IPA) was the best

phenomenological qualitative approach for this study because "IPA is concerned with the detailed examination of personal lived experience, the meaning of experience to participants and how participants make sense of that experience" (Smith 2011, 1). The aim, according to Smith, is a detailed exploration of the participants' sense of their personal and social world. Biggerstaff and Thompson (2008) explained the essence of IPA more by saying,

Its theoretical underpinnings stem from the phenomenology which, ... attempts to construct a philosophical science of consciousness, with hermeneutics (the theory of interpretation), and with symbolic interactionism, which posits that the meanings an individual ascribes to events are of central concern but are only accessible through an interpretative process. (4)

Therefore, IPA suited the assessment of the cognitive inner world of the Nigerian priests who have ministered in the United States and provided a method to explore how the priests ascribed meaning to their experiences. Since this research made use of a small number of twelve participants with semi-structured interviews, an IPA was more suited for the study. IPA encourages a small number of participants "to illustrate, inform, and master themes by firmly anchoring findings in direct quotes from participant accounts" (Finlay and Ballinger 2006, 21). Its method of data collection, according to Smith (2011), "is in-depth semi-structured interviewing ... conducted on relatively small sample sizes" (10).

3.2. RESEARCH QUESTION

The overarching question for the research is: what are the lived cross-cultural challenges and other experiences of Nigerian priests who have worked in the United States for ten years or more?

3.3. PARTICIPANTS

One of the most important steps in phenomenological study and other qualitative studies is to carefully choose the appropriate participants who have a good experience of the phenomenon and to whom the researcher could gain access and establish a rapport with, in order to collect the essential data for the study (Creswell 2007). Research explains it as sampling.

According to Onwuegbuzie who wrote about qualitative sampling, "Sampling is an essential step in the qualitative research process. As such, the choice of sampling scheme is an important consideration that all qualitative researchers should make" (Onwuegbuzie 2007, 241). Bearing in mind that the form of sampling in phenomenological qualitative study considers the sites and size of participants with the intent of not generalizing suggestions "but to elucidate the particular, the specific" (Creswell 2007, 126), twelve Nigeria Catholic priests were selected from the four geographical regions of the United States.

The twelve Nigerian Catholic priests were selected, three each from the South, West, Midwest, and Northeast regions of the United States, to capture the cross-cultural struggles and the pastoral effects on the Nigerian priests in the four regions of the United States. Each region included priests from a rural parish and a city church. I used purposeful sampling because it helps researchers to choose the participants who can provide the best information about the research phenomenon under examination (Creswell 2007). I believe that the twelve participants provided the best information about the phenomenon under examination because they had both the willingness to participate and the ability to communicate experiences articulately and reflectively as recommended by Palinkas, Horwitz, Green, Wisdom, Duan, and Hoagwood (2013).

There were five criteria for participation:

1. They must be Nigerian-born priests who had their priestly training and ordination in Nigeria before coming to work in the United States as full-time priests.
2. They must not have lived in the United States before experiencing the culture as priests in the United States.
3. The priests must have lived and worked in the United States for ten years or more and therefore have a fresh memory of their experiences.
4. The priests must not be students who are pastoral helpers.
5. Priests who had participated in a formal cross-cultural training program prior to coming to the United States were excluded.

I thought that foreign-born priests who spend more time for their personal studies and less time with parishioners may not provide complete experiences about adjustability and pastoral performance in a foreign culture.

Diocesan directories of the Catholic Church in the United States were used to select the priests in situations where the researcher does not know the priest or priests who have worked in the geographical regions for ten or more years. During the study, I intended to add more participants if saturation were not reached. Creswell (2007) advised that "sampling can change during a study" (126). Fortunately, I reached saturation and did not add more participants.

3.4. DATA COLLECTION

The data for this study were collected through semi-structured interviews that consisted of audio-recorded interviews from twelve Nigerian Catholic priests conducted over a four-week period and transcribed verbatim by me. Drummond, McLafferty, and Handdry (2011) encouraged a lower number of participants for the interpretative phenomenological approach because it "allows for a richer depth of analysis that might be inhibited with a larger sample" (21). Nine of the twelve interviews were a face-to-face interview, and three were done with the use of telephone.

The interviews were conducted in accordance with Creswell's (2007) recommendations for phenomenological interview technique. So, before the interviews, personal experiences of the researcher, a Nigerian Catholic priest, was written down as reported at the beginning of the methodology discussion to make sure that my personal story did not interfere with the participants' stories (Creswell 2007). The research question guided the collection and analysis of the data and facilitated the identification of the struggles and challenges that affect the cultural adjustment and job performance of the Nigerian priests within the pastoral sector. The twelve priests were known to me personally.

Following the recommendation of Gill, Stewart, Treasure, and Chadick (2008), interviews varied from thirty-five to sixty-five minutes in length. Gill, et al., believed that a long time of interviewing could lead to a distraction from the central purpose of the interview unless essential experiences were not retrieved from the interviewee. Two major factors guided the collection and analysis of the data.

1. Identification of the struggles and challenges that affect the adjustment of Nigerian priests into the US cultural environment within the pastoral sector.
2. A discovery of the impact of cross-cultural adjustments on the priests' job performance in the United States.

As already indicated twelve Nigerian Catholic priests were selected, three each from the four geographical regions of the United States, to capture the cross-cultural struggles and other experiences of the priests in all the areas of the country. Selections from each region included priests from both rural and city parishes. I applied interpretative coding and thematic analysis. The emerged information was used to recommend a better improvement strategy to reduce the cross-cultural struggles and improve cross-cultural assimilation and better performance in the host country.

Following the recommendations of Chan, Fung, and Chie (2013) about the avoidance of bias in the difference phases of research, bracketing was not restricted to the collection of data and data analysis but started before reviewing the literature and continued until the end of data analysis and evaluation. The participants' experiences were approached with an open mind, seeking the essence or the commonalities of the shared experiences that are inherent and unchanging (Langdridge 2007). The participants' understanding of their experiences was not influenced to let unexpected meanings emerge (Giorgi 2011; Langdridge 2007). Heeding to the recommendation of Chan, Fung, and Chie (2013), reflexivity was also applied during the interviews to strengthen honest inquiry. The instrument for this study is a one-on-one in-person semi-structured interview of the selected participants.

3.5. PROCEDURES

The primary research question was not asked directly. Rather following the methodology of data collection in IPA, the primary question was presented as a general issue and not as a direct question to avoid a limitation of the inquiry (Creswell 2007). As advised by Creswell, subquestions based on the primary question were also investigated during the interview, and the responses were thoroughly analyzed for the emergence of informative themes that revealed the essence of the participants' experiences. The primary questions were influenced by the suggestions of Jia and Van de Vijver (2012), who explained three options of instruments: adoption, adaptation, and assembly for cross-cultural research and recommended "assembly" as a better option because of its high ecological validity in studying people of the same culture.

Malda, Van de Vijver, and Temane (2011) and Davis and Silver (2003) have the same opinion. The use of assembly involves a compilation of new interview questions for the target culture. Therefore, the suggestions of

Jia and Van de Vijver (2012) served as a guide to formulate the following questions for the study.

1. What is your general pastoral background, and what was your knowledge of US culture before missioning in the United States?
2. What are the cross-cultural struggles and challenges you have experienced in the United States, especially pastoral struggles and challenges?
3. What strategies are helpful to you to effectively adjust from Nigerian culture to US culture?
4. Could you please briefly describe the important knowledge of the US culture that a Nigerian priest coming to mission in the United States should have prior to departure to the United States?

While the listed interview questions served as a guide for the semi-structured interview, the following factors were also considered for the interview procedure.

1. The participants were screened and contacted early before the interview and assured of necessary ethical principles, like confidentiality and anonymity.
2. For the purpose of a productive interview, the interviews were done in non-distractive locations that were suitable for the interviewees and at the time most suitable for them.
3. There was an establishment of rapport before the interview and an application of attentive listening to the interviewee during the one-on-one in-person interview.
4. The interviews were audio-recorded.
5. During the process, an emotionally neutral body language was adopted along with encouraging responses to facilitate more information and clarifications.
6. There were probing remarks when necessary for the sake of more information and clarification.
7. Leading questions that may influence the participant's emphases in his perspective of his personal experiences were avoided so the participants could express their opinions and convictions.
8. At the end of responses to the questions, each participant was asked if he has something else to add in relation to our discussion to facilitate a freely open-ended expression of some tangible information that might not have been captured during the interview.
9. After the interview, the recorded discussions were transcribed verbatim.

After the transcription, the interviewees reviewed their various information for the purpose of accuracy, and inductive method of analysis was applied to sort out the texts of the interviews into themes. So, the themes were dependent on the content of the interviews. With conceptual or relational analysis in mind, the frequency and intensity of some contents in the interview were used to reorganize the keywords or phrases in the interview text for the purpose of coding. In the coding, the ideas of the interviewees or participants were made short and clearer. In other words, the participants' important expressions because of their frequency of appearances or power in their effectiveness were short listed as phrases, sentences, or inferences. With this technique, the researcher was able to explore the participants' lived experiences and narrate them for informative knowledge.

Addleman, Nava, Cevallos, Brazo, and Dixon (2014) used this analytical method in their study, "Preparing Teacher Candidates to Serve Students from Diverse Backgrounds: Triggering Transformative Learning through Short-term Cultural Immersion." They used Creswell's (2007) recommendation of identifying and coding significant statements to analyze the immersion field experiences of twenty-four teacher candidates for their better knowledge of the culturally, ethically, and linguistically diverse students they teach. In the analysis of their studies they wrote,

We compiled candidates' reflections and analyzed them for significant themes related to their cultural immersion experiences; then we analyzed these patterns … and described the ways in which participants' practicum experiences provoked disequilibrium, reflection, and transformative learning. In the coding and analysis process, we followed Creswell's (2007) definition for identifying significant statements. (Addlemana et al. 2014)

Gao, Tilse, Wilson, Tuckett, and Newcobe (2015) use the same method in their study, "Perceptions and Employment Intentions among Aged Care Nurses and Nursing Assistants from Diverse Cultural Backgrounds: A Qualitative Interview Study." The aim of their research was to understand individuals direct care workers' (nurses and nursing assistants) perception of rewards and difficulties and how these are related to their employment intentions, along with the variation of perceptions between nurses and nursing assistants and among the cultural diversity of the nurses and nursing assistants. The study was done in Australia, and sixteen nurses and nursing assistants were interviewed. The authors coded the data to capture the major themes in the interview for the opportunity to analyze exactly what the participants experienced, said, and thought.

3.6. Interpretative Coding and Thematic Analysis

The interviews were audio-recorded and transcribed verbatim by me, as mentioned earlier. After multiple readings of the transcriptions, general ideas discovered in the words of the interviewees were identified, labeled, and assigned codes. Codes related to similar ideas were clustered into categories. From the categories, overarching themes emerged. The themes were given meaningful names.

3.7. Potential Sources of Bias

The fact that the author of this work is a Nigerian priest who has spent nearly twenty years of his priesthood in the United States as a pastor might be an element that objectifies this monograph, but the possibility of personal bias was not taken for granted. I have my own personal experiences with regard to cross-cultural struggles, challenges, and adjustments, and I am aware that those could engender personal bias.

Nonetheless, bearing in mind that a phenomenological study describes the meaning of the lived experiences of a concept or phenomenon for the individuals being studied, I was mindful that my personal experiences have the potential of undermining the basic purpose of phenomenology (Creswell 2007). Hence, I had a strong desire to focus on reducing my individual experiences by using the methodology of presenting my personal experiences separately, as Creswell (2007) advised. I was always reminding myself that discovering the meanings that are universal among the participants required an open attitude and suspension of my own presuppositions in order to allow the meanings to emerge from the participants.

3.8. Assumptions

The assumptions for this phenomenological inquiry included the following:

1. Extreme rigor in bracketing was applied throughout the study since a Catholic priest from Nigeria did the study. The researcher's personal cross-cultural struggles were separated from the participants' experiences. Phenomenological inquiry suggests this separation to avoid the infiltration of the researcher's idea to the essence of the inquiry (Creswell 2007).
2. It was also assumed that the researcher could accurately uncover the phenomenological essence embedded in the individual narratives.
3. It was assumed that the Nigerian priests interviewed were glad to be involved and open for the required rapport and transparency needed for a phenomenological study like this.
4. It was also assumed that even though the United States is made up of a diversity of cultures and values, there is still some major US cultural values that the participants could have encountered, irrespective of their work.

3.9. Transferability

This study may not be transferable to certain cultures within the United States that are not considered or represented in the information given by the participants. The study was limited to twelve participants and therefore poses a problem of generalization because the twelve participants may not accurately represent the cross-cultural struggles and challenges of all the Nigerian priests in the United States. However, the findings would not underscore the fact that some of the detailed and validated nature of the result of the study will be valuable to the Nigerian priests on mission in the United States.

SUMMARY

Many researchers, including those who studied cross-cultural training, have used qualitative phenomenological method to inquire the essence of the lived experiences of the targeted population. Given that the methodology has been successfully used in the past, this study was done with a similar approach to inquire the essence of the lived experiences of twelve Nigerian Catholic priests who have worked in the United States for ten or more years.

Purposive sampling, a semi-structured one-on-one in-person interview, and data analysis were used in this phenomenological study to make the inquiry and identify the significant themes in the inquiry in order to accomplish the purpose of the study. The methodology aimed at establishing the required facts that can guide Nigerian missionaries on mission in the United States to a huge success.

CHAPTER 4

Data Presentation, Analysis, and Interpretation of Results

As already indicated in the introduction and chapter 3 of this work, the qualitative phenomenological method of inquiry is used in this study because of its psychological, interpretative, and idiographic importance of capturing and examining the lived experiences of the individuals who encountered the actual phenomenon. It gave the researcher the opportunity to analyze exactly what the participants experienced, said, and thought. Then the narrator narrated and described what the participants lived and examined it for the informative knowledge that came from the participants' experiences. With the research question in mind—that is, "What are the lived cross-cultural challenges and other experiences of Nigerian priests who have worked in the United States for ten years or more?"—the researcher asked the primary questions and some pertinent subquestions to the participants to ascertain the cross-cultural problems that are essential for the predeparture cross-cultural training of the incoming priests from Nigeria.

The primary questions never changed, but the subquestions differed according to the responses of each participant to the primary questions. Before using the primary questions, the questions were piloted among a group of seven Nigerian Catholic priests in the Diocese of Tulsa, Oklahoma, and there was no need to refine the questions.

With the use of the phenomenological methodology, I explored the experiences of the twelve different priests from the four regions of the United States. The experiences were gathered through a one-on-one in-person interview. Twenty-nine priests from the various four regions of the country were first contacted by telephone to ascertain their willingness to participate in the research. All of them agreed to be interviewed.

Two separate priestly ordination ceremonies of Nigerian-born young men who might attract a physical appearance of many of the priests who were reached via the telephone for participation were targeted. The telephone discussions happened from November 16, 2015, to December 13, 2016. The two young men were ordained for different dioceses in two separate regions within a time frame of two months in 2016. Seventeen of the twenty-nine priests who expressed their intention to be at either of the ordination ceremonies, as well as their willingness to be interviewed, showed up for either of the two ordinations. My intention was to interview three priests from each region, that is, interviewing a total of twelve priests. The choice of the total number of twelve priests, three from each of the four regions of the United States, was based on their regions of pastoral work and qualification for this study.

Prior to interviewing each priest, the priest or interviewee signed a letter of consent to indicate his willingness to participate in the study and also to assure him of the confidentiality discussed during the prior telephone conversation. The interview protocol was once again described to him as already described during the telephone conversation. Each of the interviews lasted between thirty minutes to sixty-five minutes and was recorded. Each interviewee received the same designed questions but different subquestions as a follow-up to the participant's answer to the primary questions, for the purpose of clarity and gaining further insights from his answers to the primary questions.

The subquestions were based on the facilitation to obtain the actual experienced phenomenon and not on challenging the shared experience. During the interviews, repetitions by the different participants were noted for the sake of knowing when the data had reached saturation

(Creswell 2007). On the same token, the consistency of the data indicated that sufficient information for analyses had been obtained.

All the interviewees were supportive of the study and gave informative answers to the questions they were asked. All the questions and answers were done in English, except very few sentences or phrases that were made in Ibo language by three priests, but they were transcribed in English. The process of coding was used to categorize the ideas of the various participants into meaningful themes for comparison and analysis. So, with the process of coding, related pertinent ideas, concepts, terms, and phrases discovered in the words of the interviewees were labeled together as related thoughts for one theme or category. I strictly coded the themes from the direct answers given by the participants on the interview questions.

There was other significant information that developed during the coding but did not perfectly fit into the already existing codes. Those are the important themes that came out by themselves and are usually referred to as "dimensionalising" by Strauss and Cobin (1990) because the additional codes help to make sure that all the important dimensions of the data are explored. However, the experiences under these themes were so small and not stringently different. I added them to the various existing themes that contain the experiences that share relations with them.

To meaningfully and methodologically organize the various ideas, concepts, terms, or phrases to the various themes or codes they belong, the significance of using memos during the coding process was highly valued and used to keep notes of related thoughts during the reading of the interviews of the various participants. The memos were used to track phrase repetitions and significant words in the interview text, metaphors, and analogies that are informative and relate to particular themes, poetic narratives that belong to certain themes, and logical implications that lean toward certain themes.

With the traditional technique of sorting and cutting related information and putting them into piles, separate envelopes were used to pile up related ideas in the memo, and the related ideas were then coded after carefully rereading them to make sure that each pile could make up a code or theme. After the coding, the coded themes were then used to analyze the entire data to obtain the common shared cross-cultural problems of the priests and other informative ideas that are essential for the predeparture cross-cultural training of Nigerian priests for pastoral mission in the United States.

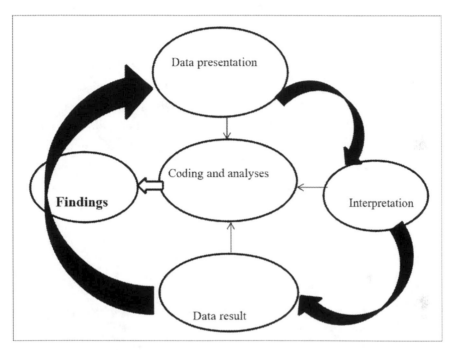

Figure 1: Model for the entire research and evaluation.

4.1. THE COLLECTED DATA

As narrated in the design of this study, the data were collected via one-on-one in-person interviews that were recorded, reviewed, and systematically analyzed to enhance validity and reliability of results. Here are the collected data. In keeping with the confidentiality agreement with the interviewees, the actual names of the interviewees are not used to report their recorded experiences. So instead of using their actual names to report their experiences, I decided to use alphabets to represent the participants' names in the interview.

As already indicated in chapter 1 of this study, before collecting the data, being a Nigerian priest, I wrote my own experiences to avoid research bias by a researcher. Since a phenomenological study describes the meaning of the lived experiences of individuals being studied, I am aware that my personal experiences have the potential of undermining the basic purpose of the study, if I am not careful. This is why Creswell (2007) recommended that a researcher of this kind of study could avoid this aspect of bias by writing his or her experiences prior to seeking the participants' experiences. I have my own personal experiences with regard to cross-cultural struggles, challenges, and adjustments. Given my strong desire of suspending my own presuppositions and avoiding research bias in order to allow only the participants' experiences to emerge, I used the methodology of presenting my personal experiences separately, as Creswell advised. Here are my own personal experiences.

Interviewer's Personal Experience to Avoid Researcher's Bias

4.1.1. Researcher's General Pastoral Background and Knowledge of the US Culture before Missioning in the United States

I was ordained a Catholic priest in 1994. I had my seminary training in Nigeria after college graduation at Duquesne University in the state of Pennsylvania, United States. As a seminarian and a young priest, I lived and worked in Nigeria. I also worked with some Americans in Papua New Guinea (PNG) and Australia before coming to mission in the United States as a priest. So, I first experienced the US culture prior to my pastoral assignment to the United States, which might make my own pastoral experiences in the United States a bit different from those of the participants of this study. In other words, I had a small in-living experience in the United States and a small exposure to the US culture prior to my pastoral work in the United States. Nonetheless, I still had some cross-cultural struggles in the United States when I came back for pastoral work.

The Cross-Cultural Struggles or Challenges I Experienced in the United States, Especially Pastoral Struggles or Challenges

My priestly work exposed me to certain aspects of US culture that I did not experience the first time I came to the United States as a student. Born and raised in a country where leadership was mainly the work of men and collaborative leadership was not significant as one might see in the United States, I struggled with the US promotion of collaborative leadership that embraces people with various types of ideology. Thus, working with some women with strong feminist ideology was a big struggle for me. For instance, praying in a place where I was not allowed to use "He" for God was a struggle for me.

I know we have closet gays and lesbians in Nigeria, even though it is culturally a taboo. I have no problem working with them in the United States, but I struggled with the US legal approach to same-sex marriage before I got used to it. I understand that the US church does not permit same sex marriage but having open gays in the pastoral team of my church was a challenge.

Americans have the culture of great patriotism, but the patriotic spirit leads some of them to put down other people. For some of the Americans, everything American is the best, including human beings, even if the foreign one is better. I was never happy to see some Americans put down my home culture or me. Some parishioners would always prefer a national priest to a foreign-born priest, no matter the greatness of the foreign-born priest or the lousy performance of the national priest. I never agreed with this kind of cultural patriotism. It could be annoying sometimes and made me think that some of the citizens sometimes exaggerate American patriotism.

Given that in Nigeria children are expected to always respect their elders, which I did when I came to the States as a younger person, I struggled with the present-day US culture where freedom has made some children talk to their elders as if they are age-mates or even call people who would be about the same age of their father or mother by their first names without any respectful prefix. I hated situations where some of the US children would talk to their elders disrespectfully in some social and church gatherings, just as I hated situations where children in some places in Nigeria were expected to behave like servants to their elders. I admire the rule of law in the United States, which gives every man, woman, and child an equal freedom, but I hate the situation where some children think or behave as if the freedom makes them age-mates with their elders.

Even though I had lived in the United States before, I struggled with the US culture of starting occasions at the exact agreed time. It is good, but I struggled with it because in Nigeria, people do not take timing very seriously. It has a nickname, "African time." Changing from African time to being time conscious (which is good) was a struggle.

Again, despite my living in the United States before, I had communication problems, just as I had when I came to the US as a young student. I could understand the American accent, but some could not understand me. I also could not understand all the American symbolic expressions.

I struggled with the issue of discrimination because of my accent, ethnicity, or skin color. It was annoying and irritating. Why should my accent, ethnicity, or skin color automatically make me a second-class person? Even though legally the United States is a nation where everyone is equal, practically there is an unspoken culture of treating people of certain ethnicities, especially blacks and browns, differently. The US church preaches against it, but it happens in some parishes, just as it does in the society. I struggled with it and still do.

I value interrelationship and community spirit. I think interrelationship is part of the Nigerian culture, which is why the extended family system is still strong in Nigeria. The American formal lifestyle and individualism remain a problem for me. Unlike in Nigeria, I rarely had an informal relationship with my neighbors when I came to work as a priest in the United States. I also experienced lack of informal interrelationships in my parish except with the individuals or families who were good friends. There was a good relationship with the parishioners, but it was a careful and formal relationship most of the time.

The Strategies that Are Helpful to Me to Effectively Adjust from Nigerian Culture to US Culture

Whenever I feel confused, I pull back and become a participant observer until I discover a strategy to take care of my problem. I already know that certain people in the United States detest any form of discrimination, even though some of them like it. So, I try to relate more with those people who do not discriminate and avoid those who might look down on me because of my accent, ethnicity, or skin color. I minister to them with more caution and make sure that I only visit their homes when I am pastorally needed. I was less cautious and more open in the homes of those who do not detest having a colored man in their place of residence.

I am also aware that Americans respect professionalism in whatever a person does. With the use of an alarm clock and smart phones, I try to avoid lateness and make sure I prepare very well for any activity. I was also aware that, the more a foreigner values American culture, the more he or she is welcomed and accepted. The awareness made me try my best to learn the American culture and accent every day. The need for knowing their culture and accent better helped me to socialize more with them than previously.

Given that communication was one of my problems, I tried to improve my accent by listening carefully to how certain words were pronounced on the television. I also read many books about the US church and the US ecclesial lifestyle in order to assimilate myself into the society.

Even though it is not easy to put one's culture aside and embrace another's, my ambition to be productive in the society and my love of the pastoral ministry I do motivated me to try my best to embrace the culture. I often asked questions in order to learn. I was never shy to ask questions if I must ask to learn. My conscientious questioning of myself about how to be productive in the United States motivates me every day to learn my host culture and their ecclesial lifestyle.

Knowledge of US Culture that a Nigerian Priest Coming to Mission in the United States Should Have Prior to Departure to the United States

Given that my prior knowledge of the United States helped me to adjust without much difficulty, an incoming priest must have a good knowledge of the country before he comes. If possible, the priest who will be assigned to work in the United States should be given the opportunity of a minimum of three months of vacation in the United States before his assignment. The incoming priest must know that the US culture is totally different from the Nigerian culture, as well as the things that make the cultures different. Nigerians speak English, but it is the British English with the Nigerian accent. The incoming priest needs to get acquainted with the American accent by listening to Voice of America on the radio and watching some American television channels while at home. If those are not available, some CDs and DVDs should be made available to him. He must know that his English, as good as it may be, will need some adjustments with regard to writing and speaking. He should therefore be helped to develop a mindset that the English accent and spellings of certain words he knows before may not work for him in the United States because the Nigerian English, which is British-oriented, has words that are written differently (e.g., *labour* and *labor*) and spoken differently. Apart from accent and spelling of some words, he should also know that a good grasp of the US communication skill includes knowledge of the US symbolic expressions and the meanings of the symbols. Certain symbols in the United States might be familiar to a Nigerian, but the meaning could be different. I would also advise the incoming priest to read as many books and magazines as possible about US culture, cities, and rural and urban lifestyles as a proactive preparation for wherever he might be sent to mission upon arrival. I would also suggest a prior knowledge of the US Constitution because Americans admire their Constitution and expect every resident to know and comply with the Constitution.

Apart from the above-mentioned suggestions, the incoming priest could attend seminars organized by some people who have lived and worked in the United States for many years. Through the seminars, he could learn the way Americans think and appreciate their culture. Prior to leaving Nigeria, he should start working hard toward putting his home culture aside without losing it and embracing the US culture upon arrival. Americans are so patriotic that they have no sympathy for those who live in their country but do not embrace the US culture and lifestyle, even in pastoral work. The priest must be taught the importance of professionalism, work ethics, collaborative leadership, equal treatment for all, being at every activity on time, and finishing on time. There is nothing like "African time," that is, being late for social and pastoral activities.

The incoming priest needs to know that it is the cultural beliefs of the host people that their lifestyle as well as their cultural expression of their belief that would guide the priest to enrich the faith of the host people and not the cultural beliefs of the missionary priest. Unless the priest immerses himself into the hosts' culture, he will find it hard to have interpersonal relations with the host people and might be lonely and perhaps suffer rejection.

I would also suggest that the priest be participant observer at the early stage of his residence in the United States in order to master the American culture better before exercising his duties fully. The participant observation requires patience, humility, and an open heart in order to absolve the new way of life in the host culture. He should not be shy or afraid to ask for explanations in order to know the social and pastoral culture. Without mastering the culture, his priestly ministry in the host culture may not yield any fruit. It might even be problematic to the people he has come to serve. Finally, the Catholic culture might be the same all over the world, but the way of expressing the Catholic dogmatic teachings can only resonate when they are expressed within the cultural context of the people.

PARTICIPANTS' EXPERIENCES

PARTICIPANT A

4.1.2. WHAT IS YOUR GENERAL PASTORAL BACKGROUND, AND WHAT WAS YOUR KNOWLEDGE OF US CULTURE BEFORE MISSIONING IN THE UNITED STATES?

I was ordained in July 1990 in Nigeria. I worked in Nigeria for some years before I came to the United States sixteen years ago. My work routine here in the United States includes administering all the church sacraments to parishioners as an associate pastor and a full-time hospital chaplain. I never worked in the United States prior to coming. My only experience of working in another culture was an intramission apostolate in two other tribes within Nigeria. I worked in both the Yoruba and Hausa tribes for a couple of years apiece. The tribes are different from mine but not in comparison with the US culture. They are just microcultures that are different from mine.

WHAT ARE THE CROSS-CULTURAL STRUGGLES OR CHALLENGES YOU HAVE EXPERIENCED IN THE UNITED STATES, ESPECIALLY PASTORAL STRUGGLES OR CHALLENGES?

Upon arrival, one of my greatest problems was the use of time. Here, Americans are very time conscious. For instance, I got into trouble a couple of times with parishioners for celebrating Mass for more than one hour. Everybody wants to be out of the church for other businesses after a maximum of one hour. In Nigeria, when people come to Mass on Sunday, their definition of Mass time is "the time for God." They surely would not like to be at Mass more than necessary, but they rarely complain because the Mass lasted for more than one hour.

Americans are also very sensitive, and there are expected cultural norms for every situation and occasion. I had zero knowledge of the cultural norms, and so I was often stressed out by thinking of what to say and what not to say without getting into trouble or what to do and what not to do without getting into trouble. The fear of the unknown irritated me very much. The lack of knowledge of the norms, especially the ones that were complex to me, gave me some kind of mental torture. There was nobody to ask or seek advice from. So, I felt helpless because I needed the knowledge to operate better in my ministry.

The cold weather has always been one of my problems, especially driving on the icy road. I am still struggling with it up until today, but I am getting better at it. It has become my habit to check the temperature every day in order to know how to dress, which could be stressful sometimes. Moreover, the predicted temperature of the day changes certain times, even though it does not happen very often.

Another cultural challenge is how to address the people. In my parish, about 90 percent are more than seventy years old. Back home, one does not look at an elder in the eye when talking to them. It is a sign of disrespect. It took me time to realize that here in the States, it is the other way around. When I first arrived, I never liked it when kids looked at me in the eyes and asked my name. I thought they were being disrespectful. It is never done in my home culture. After living in the States for several years, I understood that it was just their culture. It is no longer a problem to me. However, I am still struggling with calling people older than me by their first names or calling their names without using a prefix like Mr., Mrs., or Ms. It would be considered highly disrespectful in Nigeria, and that is how I felt when some people, especially children, called my name directly without a prefix that signified that I am older than they are. I am not referring to the church norm of calling a priest "Rev." I am referring to an acknowledgement that one is an elderly person through the way they are addressed. I call my parishioners the names with the use of prefix. Some of my parishioners understand my reason for doing it, and they appreciate it. Some, I guess, misunderstand it as being unnecessarily formal, or probably see me as a timid African who respects the white man.

Life here is also more formal than I experienced at home. There are no casual visits unless by a very dear friend. Back home I was having constant visits by parishioners. For the parishioners at home, these visits are a sign of showing that they care and love their pastor. Here in the

States, a casual visit without prior information is often regarded as an intrusion into somebody's space. In most cases, a priest is not expected to visit a sick person at home without prior notice. Back home, such a visit will be appreciated.

Among the list of my problems are differences in food. I never loved eating cheese, or anything made with cheese and many other American foods. When I first arrived, I did not know how to handle the situation. The chickens here do not even taste as good as those at home. Certain kinds of food, such as rice, might look similar, but the way they are prepared, and the ingredients used to prepare them make them different.

The high level of feminism and dealing with the power of women in this country were challenging to me initially. I have great respect for women, and I learned about feminism at school in Nigeria, but I did not know that feminism is this strong in the United States. Unlike home, here in the United States, attention is given more to women than to men, and one has to be more careful when dealing with women than with men, or he may be accused of being discriminatory and probably end up in jail. The women here are very powerful, and it took me time to know that men must acknowledge and respect the feministic power of women in this culture, or they may get into trouble. Having such feministic women in the parish leadership was a problem.

Easy communication with the Americans was and is still a problem. Many still complain about my accent, and sometimes it is hard to know whether the problem is honestly an accent problem or a kind of microaggression. Whatever the case, I am aware that I have an accent, just as I am aware that my English pronunciations may not be very difficult for anybody who is aware of globalization and its manifestation in our present global intercultural relations, especially when communicating with people from other nations. I often feel irritated whenever my accent is misinterpreted by some, including those who cannot read or write, as lack of the ability to speak English. I am irritated when some Americans use their cultural values and standards to mark me as unfit to be a priest in the United States instead of grasping a natural understanding that a person from a totally different culture could be suffering from a discontinuity of a known cultural lifestyle and values to an unprepared exposure to a different lifestyle and values.

Nonetheless, even though I had a negative feeling about some Americans labeling me as unfit, what annoyed me most was the failure of preparing me at home for the complex experiences I encountered. I am referring to things like knowing the importance of feminism in the United States when working together with women, the US symbols and their meanings, effective ways of interaction in America for better intercultural relations with parishioners, the dissimilarities between Nigerian and American cultures, ways to assimilate myself to the US culture, different ways of intercommunication in the United States, or all the cultural values of Americans if I may use one sentence to summarize the complexities I encountered, which stressed me out on a daily basis. The preparation would have saved me from a feeling of loss of self-esteem, unnecessary fears of meeting the pastoral expectations from people, and my own misinterpretation of the Americans' cultural values and their honest opinions about me, which made me angry in my early years in the country and my parish.

Finally, another cultural challenge (a good one) I observed is the morality or goodness of some people in this country, even though they do not go to any church or believe in God. Some of the Americans have great moral values even though they do not believe in God or any supernatural being. I am still trying to comprehend that because, from my own perspective, it is not common. I have encountered some people who are morally wonderful but not interested in any religion. I am also struggling to comprehend how some groups that are popularly known as racist groups, like the Ku Klux Klan, have legal permission to exist.

WHAT STRATEGIES ARE BEING HELPFUL TO YOU TO EFFECTIVELY ADJUST FROM NIGERIAN CULTURE TO US CULTURE?

Humility, courage, and emotional support were the keys to my success. After knowing some people, especially those who were sensitive enough to know that I was suffering from stress, I started asking them questions about US cultural values and expectations from priests. They never resisted offering their help. I made every occasion and situation a learning moment and never failed to ask questions, even to younger people, in order to get the knowledge that would help me assimilate into the country, have a feeling of acceptance, and be pastorally productive. Patient and desperate to learn, I never let the negative labeling of me by some people stop me from being mentally and socially engaged in my learning process. I had no option but to have faith in myself and become humble and fearless to ask questions and learn. It is quite unfortunate to go through some mental torture before figuring out what to do in order to learn and be a part of the society I came to serve. The stress could have been lesser if I had had some kind of preparation about US values and expectations from a priest before I left Nigeria.

Another thing that helped me to adjust was the cultural orientation program I had at a time, which was helpful to some extent but did not fill in all the gaps that would help me as an individual and a priest on mission in the States. The program was set up for all the international priests from different countries. It was helpful but not very much because each international priest came from a culture different from those of others, and each priest wanted to know the differences between certain things in his own culture and those of the US.

Moreover, the instructors were more interested in accent reduction and child abuse, and we did not do much about other things about the pastoral work in the country. I must remain grateful for the easy availability of internet, books, and magazines around me. I read a lot in order to understand the US culture better.

I must acknowledge that my motivation to learn the complexities in the American culture was constantly increased by some Americans' appreciation of the hard work and good efforts by some foreigners to learn the US culture and be a part of it. I often get compliments from people for making improvements on different areas of the US culture and ecclesial lifestyle. Often there are phrases like "great improvements," "good job," and "nice to have you." Comments like those helped me to work harder to improve more.

The food problem became better when I knew about food buffets and ethnic restaurants. The buffet gives me the opportunity for choices, which is good. Eating at the Asian restaurants helped to alleviate my food problem because some of the restaurant food is not very different from my home cuisine.

The cold weather was a big problem for me, but with the help of friends, I knew about certain kinds of clothes to wear in winter, such as long johns, which I put on first before my usual dress, and then a winter coat. The friends also introduced me to the use of electric blankets, which keeps my bed warm. They also introduced me to the best tires for icy roads and how to maneuver the car when the roads are icy.

COULD YOU PLEASE BRIEFLY DESCRIBE THE IMPORTANT KNOWLEDGE OF US CULTURE THAT A NIGERIAN PRIEST COMING TO MISSION IN THE UNITED STATES SHOULD HAVE PRIOR TO DEPARTURE TO THE UNITED STATES?

I will strongly suggest that there should be some kind of preparation back home to give the missionary a kind of mindset about where he is going. Do not throw a person inside an ocean expecting him to swim well without teaching him how to swim and about the ocean. Help him to know about the ocean and how to swim in that particular ocean. Secondly, I will advise that a new person in this culture needs to begin his life like a chicken sent into an unfamiliar place. Usually when a chicken arrives at an unfamiliar place, it stands with one foot until it understands its surroundings.

A new foreign-born priest in the United States must understand that he is in a different culture and be humble enough to be a participant observer in order to master the host culture. Without that, he might see himself imposing his own culture on the host people. I believe that we are all members of one church, but we are not members of one culture.

Unless you minister to the people in their cultural way, you might make them lose interest in the church. So, people at home should be mentally prepared at home before they come. In fact, I encourage a curriculum or a seminar that prepares priests assigned to mission in the United States. The curriculum or seminar should include the US cultural values and lifestyles, what to expect upon arrival, how to take care of the unfamiliar situation, how to assimilate oneself and be a part of a society, how to mission in the United States, and the difference between the US English and Nigerian accents. Such a program will help the missionaries have appropriate tools that will reduce their stress and culture shock upon arrival.

Before leaving Nigeria for the United States, a person needs to know what to do and avoid and many other things that will help him pastorally and socially because US culture is totally different and sometimes complex to people like me who are not from the Western world.

Participant B

4.1.3. What is your general pastoral background, and what was your knowledge of US culture before missioning in the United States?

I am a Nigerian priest. I was ordained in Nigeria and worked in Nigeria for fourteen years before I came to the United States. I have worked in the United States for ten years. I am an associate pastor. My ministry in the States includes administering the sacraments, meeting with different volunteer groups, teaching religious education in a primary school, and hospital chaplaincy. I had no knowledge of US culture prior to coming to work here. I lived in another tribe in Nigeria as a kid, which gave me a little knowledge of working with Nigerians who are not from my tribe, but I had never been in the United States or had knowledge of US culture prior to coming. So, the change to a totally different culture was a big challenge.

What are the cross-cultural struggles or challenges you have experienced in the United States, especially pastoral struggles or challenges?

My primary challenge when I arrived was the absence of major similarities between my culture and US culture, especially the ways of speaking English and relating with people. There was a total lack of the knowledge of the US lifestyle as well as the expected verbal and nonverbal behaviors. Before I left Nigeria to the US soil, nobody told me about US culture, their way of speaking English, the history, the diversity within the country, what they do and do not appreciate, and what to expect, wear, and say (and not). So, upon arrival, I felt like a kid learning how to walk again. I was hunted by a feeling of helplessness that was always irritating. I was just raw.

I was making mistakes and learning from them. The mistakes constantly generated a fear of doing something that might cause me legal, moral, or physical injuries. I was living in a complex situation that is hard to explain. I would do things with a good heart, but my parishioners often misinterpreted them, and I could not understand the reason for the misinterpretation. Thus, I was constantly irritated to the extent of having a mental breakdown. I felt a loss of self-esteem and unacceptance in the society.

I wish I had known about the US weather, food, language, ethnic and regional differences, the role of slavery and civil right acts in the US history, the gap between the rich and the poor, and how today's United States came into existence. I believe that the lack of this kind of background knowledge enabled my misunderstanding of the American social and pastoral culture and caused me mental stress.

The lack of the necessary knowledge I needed affected the skills I needed in order to assimilate myself into the society and do the work that brought me here. Remember that the knowledge of why and how the rules and regulations exist contributes to having a quick understanding of the rules and regulations in a culture and how to avoid getting into trouble naïvely. Without the knowledge, I felt like one who just woken up and see himself in the middle of an ocean but does not know how to swim. There was a lack of continuity between what I know and what Americans expected from me, and it affected my pastoral work heavily. The lack of the knowledge of the US way of seeing and doing things gave me a culture shock. I became a loner who was struggling every day to adapt to the new way of life I found myself.

Before I left Nigeria, I thought I would not have a problem with speaking English because I have always been confident with my English grammar. I was speaking English every day in Nigeria, and I also taught English grammar and literature in a minor seminary in Nigeria. Upon arrival at the New York airport, I was shocked when I heard people telling me, "say it again," "excuse me," "speak slowly," "I cannot understand you, sir," and other things that made me gradually realize my deficiency with regard to the US English grammar and accent. I felt belittled and was angry with the Americans each time they made me feel like one who does not know English. I believed that "English [grammar] is English [grammar]," and if it were spoken very well, it would be understood, irrespective of the accent. I understood the British Broadcasting Corporation (BBC) news in Nigeria even though the accent I heard on the BBC news is different from the Nigerian accent. Being mocked because of my English accent or told that I lack the communication ability was annoying. A man once told me that he left the church because he could not understand me. I found the statement insulting.

I had a great problem with the climate when I came to the United States because I arrived during the winter season. Honestly, I nearly went back because I could not handle the cold weather. For two years, I was constantly sick because of the weather changes, especially the change to winter season. I know that some Americans enjoy the winter season, but I do not. Sometimes I felt like I was wearing my whole wardrobe just to be warm. Driving to the hospital or nursing home on the icy road was giving me a nervous wreck. I hated it.

Even though I now enjoy some of the American food, particularly salad, I never thought of eating an uncooked vegetable. I never ate uncooked tomatoes, carrots, cucumbers, and others. Do not misunderstand me. There are one or two vegetable leaves one can eat raw in Nigeria, but those are not here. The ones I see here are usually cooked before they are eaten if it were in Nigeria. Apart from salad, I see different kinds of meat that I honestly have seen in Nigeria, but they are prepared in a totally different way with various spices. Moreover, they are cooked very well in Nigeria, but here in the States, they are sometimes served with blood inside them. I am still struggling with the habit of eating meat that is not well cooked, and I doubt if I will overcome it. It took time for me to understand that one could request a well-cooked meat or egg, and I wish I had known that prior to my arrival. As a matter of fact, I lost many pounds because of a food problem until I discovered African stores or shops where I could buy the food, even though they are unbelievably expensive. Nonetheless, I still buy them because nobody works with an empty stomach, pastoral or nonpastoral work.

Throughout the time I was in Nigeria, I worked with women, but my work relation with them is totally different from what it is in the United States. In Nigeria, everybody, including women, could give a suggestion or advice to a priest, but without a strong feminist ideology. In the United States, the ideology of feminism is so strong that a woman cannot understand why her idea cannot be considered. Some of the women who work with me in the parish administration often misunderstand the non-implementation of their ideas as a purposeful negligence because they are women. They expect their advice or suggestion to be implemented, without considering if the pastor has a better suggestion from either the bishop, former pastors of the parish, or somewhere else.

I admire how patriotic Americans are about their entire ways of doing things, but I detest their superiority complex. I detest the demeaning of my own culture. For them, "made in America" is the best, and that includes culture, way of dressing, behavior, food, language, sports, socializations, and even human beings. If one is not born in America, the person automatically becomes an inferior individual. I may be wrong, but that is my experience, and I see it even in the church. One woman told me that she prefers their own priest because she thinks that foreign priests are not trained very well. I do not think there is any research that supports her belief. Both the liturgy and theology of the church are the same everywhere, and they are primarily endorsed at the Vatican for the church everywhere in the world. Yes! The church allows enculturation, but that does not destroy the same dogma and liturgy of the church, which is monitored by one magisterium and taught in every seminary in the world. As much as I wish I had known about this superiority complex prior to my coming to the United States and how to handle it for the sake of peace and pastoral ministry, it is still unfair to think that a person is better than the other simply because they are born in a particular country. Such belief undermines the indiscriminate gift of God, which does not know boundaries and cultures. After all, different colleges, universities, hospitals, and scientific laboratories in the United States have people who are not born in the United States.

Nevertheless, much of the US lifestyle is admirable, like freedom of speech, noninterference to what a person does as long as the individual is not a nuisance in the society, great work ethics, more respect of the law compared with home [Nigeria], and good patriotism. As much as I admire these, especially the freedom in this country, the legal existence of some racist supremacist groups like the White League, or the White Knights of the Ku Klux Klan remains a shock to me.

WHAT STRATEGIES ARE HELPFUL TO YOU TO EFFECTIVELY ADJUST FROM NIGERIAN CULTURE TO US CULTURE?

Confronting bigger cultures is not easy, but a couple of things helped me, and some still are. When I arrived, I took a lesson on enculturation or acclimatization for six months, and the lesson helped me to understand US culture and social life better, but not fully. The lesson that was organized by the diocese I work for was very short and did not take care of all my cross-cultural problems. The diocese could not financially afford my being in the program for more than I did, and moreover I needed to start work as soon as possible. Nevertheless, the program opened the door for me to see the differences between US and Nigerian culture and the importance of knowing the antecedents for better adjustments in a new culture. I started doing whatever I could to fill in the gap of discontinuity between the culture I knew and the new host culture.

Moreover, through patience and reflection, I came to an understanding that my appreciation of my culture also implies that my host nation appreciates her culture and I must respect the host culture and make myself a part of it in order to fit in. This thought made me to look inward to find out where I have been imposing my culture and where I have not been doing well with regard to respecting the host culture. So, I was humble and embraced what I may call "personal cultural exorcism" in order to align myself to the culture of the people who welcomed and embraced me and hoped I would deliver the pastoral work that brought me to this country. Hence, I started to figure out ways to be part of US culture. I took classes on US history, cultural competence, and intercultural studies in the university near my church. I also read books and magazines that exposed me to US culture and never fail to ask questions in order to know. Both on- and off-campus and at church gatherings, I started to teach myself accent reduction by paying attention to the Americans when they speak. With more reflections, it became obvious to me that the Americans sometimes misunderstand the Nigerian accent, just like it was sometimes difficult for me to understand the American accent. A grasp of this very reality energized me to make strong efforts about my accent reduction.

At every party I attended, I observed the common behaviors and accepted norms. Through those efforts, I started to be more knowledgeable of the various US cultural values and how to communicate better and assimilate myself into the culture. I also embraced collaborative leadership, which is not very common in the Nigerian parishes, and started to find ways to work with the women, especially the feminists, as well as children, gays, and lesbians. A threat for lawsuit must make you find a way to accommodate their suggestions.

My parish secretary was also very helpful. She was always helping me with some ideas that Americans and my parishioners appreciated. The secretary also introduced me to checking the weather every morning in order to figure out how to dress for the day.

By appreciating both my culture and US culture, I came to an understanding that knowledge and embracement of another culture increases both personal cultural enrichment and the ministry. When you genuinely know what to learn and what to bring to the ministry and put them together in the ministerial work, it makes the pastoral ministry richer.

Finally, I must acknowledge that the missiology class I took while in the seminary in Nigeria was very instrumental in my adaptation to US culture. The class is helpful, even though the class was not mainly on US mission, but on missioning in a different culture other than mine. The class reminded me the importance of being mentally, physically, and socially resilient when challenged by cultural difference.

COULD YOU PLEASE BRIEFLY DESCRIBE THE IMPORTANT KNOWLEDGE OF US CULTURE THAT A NIGERIAN PRIEST COMING TO MISSION IN THE UNITED STATES SHOULD HAVE PRIOR TO DEPARTURE TO THE UNITED STATES?

He should know that he is coming to live in a place where people prefer to do what they would like to do and not what somebody else would like them to do. The leadership here therefore involves more of a consultation of the people than a top-down leadership. He should know the importance of symbols in a culture, the US symbols, and the symbolic meanings and avoid presuming that his own tribal or national meanings of certain symbols have the same meanings for the symbols in the United States. A particular symbol could mean different things in various cultures. The person should be exposed to both the negative and positive aspects of the United States. He should know that upon arrival, he should talk less about his own culture or himself because the more he talks about the goodness of his culture or his own personal success, the more he will definitely lose his audience. He must be humble and come in with an open heart and then start learning the new culture and the people like a person in a preschool. He should use the examples of the host people, their culture, and their situation in life to facilitate his ministry. He should work with the people and not be a boss of the people. He should solicit their cultural gifts, vocabularies, and food and know that he is in the world of the host people and their culture. He should know of what will help enrich the faith of the host culture and not the culture of the missionary. Without joining them, he will not be important to them because they do not want anybody to come and colonize them ideologically. Unless a foreign-born priest embraces the culture wholeheartedly, he will remain stressed and useless to the people he came to serve. Without embracing the culture, the priest cannot work with the host people to transform an inherited situation to something better or greater, which he is expected to do no matter how good the circumstance was before he arrived.

Finally, based on my experiences, it is absolutely necessary that a prior knowledge of a foreign culture before arrival is very important because a person cannot work well in a different culture without knowledge of the host culture, especially if the work involves relationships with human beings. More importantly, the prior knowledge of US culture by an incoming Nigerian priest and the requirements to adapt to the culture would help the priest to know if he could really adjust to the culture upon arrival and decide whether to come or not. If he decides to come, the prior knowledge and preparation would help him to remain patient and tough to face the mental, psychological, pastoral, and social struggles he might encounter until he assimilates himself to the host culture. The prior knowledge and preparation would also help him to know what to collect at home and what not to take and research more on certain issues that frighten him the most. He should have a mindset that could lessen helplessness, a feeling of complexities, and misinterpretation of the behaviors and values of the host culture, which often arises from using personal cultural values as a standard for right and wrong in a foreign culture that has different ways of seeing what is good or bad.

PARTICIPANT C

4.1.4. WHAT IS YOUR GENERAL PASTORAL BACKGROUND, AND WHAT WAS YOUR KNOWLEDGE OF US CULTURE BEFORE MISSIONING IN THE UNITED STATES?

I was ordained nineteen years ago and worked in Nigeria for five years before I came to the United States. My work here includes administering all the sacraments of the church and working as the chaplain of the primary school in the parish. (The parish has a school.) I celebrate Mass for the students and counsel them on a regular basis, either individually or as a group. I do more office work in the parish than I expected. Parents of the students and staff are always calling my office, and I have to take the calls and attend to them. The calls are often about students' issues.

I had zero knowledge of US culture before coming to work in the States. I was so lost with the differences between the two cultures that I could not do anything for two years, not even to celebrate Mass. I usually stood there at the altar with the pastor and did or said nothing. Outside the church, I did nothing but listening and learning. Neither the pastor nor I opposed the idea of engaging myself in learning and understanding the society first before active duty in order to avoid any kind of the damage control that maladjustment could cause. I somewhat stepped back and learned, and it helps me now to work better with the people.

WHAT ARE THE CROSS-CULTURAL STRUGGLES OR CHALLENGES YOU HAVE EXPERIENCED IN THE UNITED STATES, ESPECIALLY PASTORAL STRUGGLES OR CHALLENGES?

During the two years I was asked not to be involved in any pastoral work, I was not happy with the decision of not being involved in any pastoral duty, and it made me disengage myself in almost everything, including the learning of US culture. Looking back now, I would have used the opportunity to learn. Priestly work here in the United States is different than in Nigeria or Africa in general. I was surprised with the involvement of women in the ministry here. The priests here in the States do more office work than we would do in Nigeria. There is more office work than pastoral visits. Life is more formal than informal. In Africa, people just walk in and visit with the priest or vice versa. Here, apart from those who are very close to you, you cannot visit anybody without a formal appointment. Things are very structured.

The leadership style of the priest in the United States was complex to me when I arrived here. Unlike home [Nigeria] where people listen to you, here, one has to put his feet down to facilitate issues but in a highly diplomatic, political, gentle, and respectful way with the members of the group that make the primary decisions. In Nigeria, the popular leadership style of the priest is also diplomatic, but the priest is more of an unchallenged figure who makes almost all the decisions, unless he chooses to contact others. Even though he sometimes seeks suggestions from some of the parishioners, his administration is often more of a one-man leadership than a collaborative leadership. In some places, not everywhere, women are sidetracked during suggestions without much opposition, especially in the northern part of the country. In the United States, if you do not work with women as you would with men, you will be inviting trouble because the women here want to be heard and treated equally as men. Feminism is popular in US culture, and so, if one does not collaboratively work with both men and women on equal status, he will immediately get the heat of feminism. In fact, a person once told me that I should remember that I am no longer in Africa but in the United States. I was offended then, but knowing what I know now, I had no reason to be offended. Looking back at the issue that led to the person's statement from a cross-cultural point of view, she was right. Nonetheless, I may not consider myself wrong either because I was doing what I thought was appropriate, given what I knew then.

I would like to use the case of the woman as an example of what I might describe as doing wrong as a result of not knowing the cultural values of my host country or doing wrong as a result of using my own cultural way of doing things as a yardstick for assessing wrong and right. When I realized that my knowledge of wrong and right is mainly based on my cultural heritage and not meant for US culture, I became confused and afraid to make mistakes. I found myself in a situation of discontinuity without some materials to start anew. I discontinued making plans and judgments for my pastoral work, but unable to replace it with what works in the United States. I wish I had put more effort into mastering the culture during the two years I was supposed to be. I saw myself in a complex situation because of not knowing what is culturally or socially right in the States. It was depressing, and I have never seen a thing so irritable like that kind of situation. I was always thinking of how to behave or do things without being in trouble. I saw myself in a situation of helplessness and being useless for the pastoral work I came to do in this country. The whole situation made me lose my self-esteem at the time.

At that same time, people were complaining about my accent every day. Of course, I was not born or raised in this country and never learned the American accent, and being an old man, I felt that it would be hard to pick up the accent. I must confess that the mentality did not help my helpless situation. I am better now than then. Many people were also treating me as unfit to be a priest in their country and even unsuitable for the American citizenry and lifestyle. That honestly increased my situation of irritability as well as caused a loss of self-esteem and feeling of helplessness. I felt like one who had no cultural identity because the culture I know does not work in this country, and I had almost no knowledge of US culture. A combination of my lack of the host culture and my communication problem due to my accent and other communication skills for United States made it difficult for me to fully integrate myself into the society. It was a pitiful and stressful situation.

Adjusting to the food and weather was also a big problem, but the administrative aspect of my pastoral work is the one I wish I had known before coming to the States. I also wish that I knew about the different ethnic groups in the United States and their microcultures. I am taking care of two parishes, a Caucasian and an African American parish. There is a different way to work with each. One needs to know about those microcultures within the large US culture before coming to work in the United States in order to have an appropriate mindset for the kind of adaptation that is required in the United States.

What strategies are helpful to you to effectively adjust from Nigerian culture to US culture?

After many days of hard thoughts and prayers, I came up with two options: to go back or to be patient and humbly start learning the new culture. I chose the latter because I believe in my ability to adjust in any given situation. So, I decided to be mentally and socially active in learning the culture. I shared my problems with some of my parishioners and other Nigerians who have lived in the country for a long time. All were willing to assist me to adjust and asked me to feel free to call them for questions and advice. I was asking them many questions about the US lifestyle, values, pastoral expectations, and inappropriate actions to avoid. I gathered many helpful information from them.

I also read many books and magazines about the US history, culture, and church. I learned a lot from the internet and television too. I enrolled myself in an accent-reduction program. I learned so much from the various tools, such that after about nine months, I could not believe the change in my complex situation. I started seeing my initial mistakes and misinterpretations of the American people. I started understanding some of the US symbols and their meanings, which helped me to start having meaningful social interactions with both my parishioners and other people. I appreciated the time I was asked not to participate but watch and learn. Many Americans started to show me a feeling of belonging to their country. My self-esteem started to come back. Without losing my former culture, I may now proudly say that I also have a cultural identity in the United States.

I had problems with food and the cold weather, but meeting and interacting with other Nigerians helped me to know what to do. Some advised me to buy African raw food from the African stores and cook for myself, and some advised me to go to the Asian food buffets. I cooked only once and stopped because the American priest I lived with was not comfortable with the smell of the food. I am now a regular customer to the Chinese buffet. With the help of the advice of the Africans whom I talk to often, I started dressing better for the cold weather.

COULD YOU PLEASE BRIEFLY DESCRIBE THE IMPORTANT KNOWLEDGE OF US CULTURE THAT A NIGERIAN PRIEST COMING TO MISSION IN THE UNITED STATES SHOULD HAVE PRIOR TO DEPARTURE TO THE UNITED STATES?

A new priest to this country should have an open mind and seriously observe and learn before getting fully involved in the apostolate. He should not be afraid to ask questions. He should not be judgmental on how the people do things. He should rather try to be like them even though there is no time he will ever completely be like them. Humility to learn, openness to adaptation to the culture, and the mental tenacity toward adjustment are very important.

It is very easy to think that there isn't much pastoral work here, but one discovers that it is not true as soon as one knows the culture and is able to interact with the people effectively and develop interpersonal relationships with the parishioners. There is a lot to do, only that American people do not often ask because they do not want to get into somebody's space. Deep in their heart, they know the priest is supposed to care for them spiritually, and so they expect the priest to be the one to ask his parishioners how he could help.

For instance, I started having Mass for the sick people once a month after I asked about the need and had a positive answer to do it. Many people are now attending the Mass, more than I ever imagined. I started visiting the homebound every other week, and it now takes me a whole day to finish my visits because it is a need they wanted but never asked for it. Asking my parishioners how I could help them made them know that I am really there for them, and because of that, they have fully accepted me as a community member and relate with me better than they did when I arrived newly. They have taken me as one of them, despite my coming from a different culture, and got me more involved in some other pastoral and social things. An incoming priest needs to know that parishioners expect him to ask them about their problems and how he could help.

He should also be prepared to know that apart from being involved in the spiritual growth of the people, involvement in the people's social life is equally part of his pastoral work, for example, attending their children's graduation and ball games. There is lots of work. Just ask. I would not have known about this until a family who became my really good friends told me why parishioners loved a certain pastor who was in their parish at a time. These people know that they pay your salary, and they expect you to work for it, even though nobody will tell you.

Finally, given my experiences, I strongly suggest that no Nigerian priest should be sent to the United States without a cross-cultural preparation about the country. The US values, social life, symbols and meanings, and expectations from a priest must be made known to the incoming priest before he leaves for United States. He needs to know that the sexual scandal by some priests is still hurting some people and should learn to be careful while still serving everybody, old or young, male or female. Predeparture training while at home is very important. Without the prior preparation, it will be like throwing a kid into a pool to swim. The incoming priest needs the preparation as a stepping-stone in order to know what to expect and to understand what he would need to learn upon arrival. Without the predeparture cross-cultural training, he might arrive to the States in winter and think the snows are white grasses or get frustrated by some cultural things that might irritate him to the extent of going back to Nigeria, as some have done.

I would recommend that the Nigerians who have worked in the States and are now back at home should be asked to be involved in training or preparing the incoming priests because their personal experiences will be good instruments for teaching the priests. In addition to whatever they may be taught, they should learn more with the use of internet, books, and magazines. They need to watch American television channels and listen to the Voice of American (VOA) radio to get acquainted with the American accent. All these will help the priests to reduce unnecessary cross-cultural struggles, culture shocks, and early mistakes. The home preparation will help him to get acquainted with US culture and the US people upon arrival. Certain things that are normal at home are abnormal here. The priests should not shy away from letting any gifted person in his parish to use their gifts to serve in any of the parish committees, whether the person is a woman, youth, gay, or lesbian, as long as the Catholic teachings about the sacraments are respected.

PARTICIPANT D

4.1.5. WHAT IS YOUR GENERAL PASTORAL BACKGROUND, AND WHAT WAS YOUR KNOWLEDGE OF US CULTURE BEFORE MISSIONING IN THE UNITED STATES?

I was ordained in July 2004 and worked in Nigeria for six years before I came to the United States. My work is straightforward. I am doing exactly what I did in Nigeria. I was a high school teacher in Nigeria before I went to the seminary and became a priest. After my ordination, I was assigned to teach in a Catholic high school. Six years ago, I was asked to come and continue the same kind of work here in the United States.

Presently, I teach in a Catholic high school here in the States. My job is comprised of teaching, being a students' chaplain, and helping the pastor of my parish with youth apostolate and other pastoral duties in the parish, especially when the pastor is not available. I majored in counseling, and so apart from teaching, I do have counseling sessions with some of the students. I teach about four classes a day and spend the rest of my hours in counseling the students or helping out in the parish.

I was never in the States before I came to mission in the country. My initial knowledge came from those who have lived and worked in the States. I asked them many questions about the country and the teaching profession in the United States. The people I talked to were very helpful for my initial preparation. They told me the differences between the US and the Nigerian culture and teaching environment. Surprisingly, each of them emphasized that as a teacher in the States, I will be stepping into a delicate environment, and since I came, I have observed that delicate environment both in the school and the parish.

WHAT ARE THE CROSS-CULTURAL STRUGGLES OR CHALLENGES YOU HAVE EXPERIENCED IN THE UNITED STATES, ESPECIALLY PASTORAL STRUGGLES OR CHALLENGES?

Being the only African and foreigner in the faculty was not easy for me because of my accent and cultural values. My first year in the school was not easy for me. I felt lonely because of the individualistic life in this country. Interacting with the other staff members, students, and parents of the students were difficult because they looked down on me and have not known me well enough to have an open conversation with me. My accent did not help me to communicate effectively either. The whole situation made me develop a deep feeling of being alienated and a sense that unless a foreigner knows the various ways that Americans do things and the values they embrace and gets assimilated into their lifestyle, he will never get a feeling of belonging in the country. He would continue to feel lonely, and life will be full of complexities.

Naturally, human beings need a sense of belonging and want to relate well with people around them. Coming from a culture that is different from the American culture makes it very difficult to have interpersonal communications and relationships with the people around me. There were misinterpretations of what I do by many of them and of what they do by myself. I think many of them did not appreciate me because of some of my personal cultural values that I could not give up. I was a loner struggling to be a part of the society but did not know how to be a part of the society. It was a situation of discontinuity from the culture I know and struggling with how to continue with the new culture I live in.

Everything looked complicated to me. My entire situation irritated me because I was having cultural identity crises. Even though I was in the midst of many people, I always felt lonely. I was always aware that I was different in my thoughts and actions but did not know how to engage myself in the community, parish, and school. I was also treated differently in almost everything, probably because I was acting differently. Psychologically, my lonely situation was not healthy at all. The entire situation took away my self-esteem and nearly caused me a nervous breakdown. I was so irritated that I felt like going back to my home country.

Before I came, I thought there was one US culture. I did not know that there was a dominant culture and I would belong to a minority culture that would affect the way I would be treated. I was not happy with the different treatment of certain people because of their zip code, region, wealth, or race. It was very annoying. Seeing it happen in a Catholic school and a parish irritated me very much. I was very shocked to see racial discrimination both in the school and church. I did not know that the United States is such a divided society in terms of wealth, ethnicity, and race.

I struggled with understanding the level of wealth under the control of many of the students. For instance, in the school, many of the students drive to school with very expensive, intimidating cars. I am talking about expensive Mercedes and BMW cars as well as different kinds of expensive sports cars. Throughout my first year in the school, I was always wondering how the students would be motivated to work toward a great future if they are already exposed to that kind of luxury.

Being a priest, especially a foreign priest in the United States, is very stressful because of the outstanding bitterness of the laity toward the Catholic clergy due to the sexual scandal by some of the priests a couple years ago. I think the scandal has made many priests to be overly careful to the extent of keeping a great distance away from the youth and children in order to avoid being misunderstood. Being in a school environment, I was expected to be like most of the priests in the way I relate with the youths and children. I had to be extra careful and professional. It was a new situation and a different school culture for me and adapting to it involved mental complexities because I was not used to running away from the children and youth. I was used to being close to them without the paranoia of being labeled a pedophile. Of course, I was concerned with being misunderstood but not to the extent of being paranoid or running away from the younger folks. They also need evangelization.

Apart from the American school culture, I found the lifestyle of the Americans to be more formal and professional than in Nigeria. There is a more strategic planning and execution of actions as planned. Work ethics is a serious thing in the United States, and there are policies and procedures for almost every situation. Knowledge of the actual policies and procedures for various social situations challenged me.

This includes dress codes for various occasions. When I first arrived, there were situations where I was overdressed in certain occasions and situations where I dressed informally instead of dressing formally. For instance, I attended a funeral ceremony of a teacher, and I was the only male teacher not wearing suit. From my cultural point of view, I could not see the combination of sadness or mourning and best dressing.

Generally, the priestly culture in the United States involves extra carefulness. I think some of the priests prefer to tell parishioners what they would like to hear in order to be loved and socially accepted by parishioners than focusing on the actual apostolic message. This is my personal opinion, and I may be wrong. They value and share moral and spiritual teachings with their parishioners while making sure that none of the teachings costs them the love and social relationship with the parishioners. Nevertheless, the priestly culture of striving to have good social relationships with parishioners is admirable.

There are symbolic ways to greet people and relate with individuals that are different from the Nigerian symbolic ways of doing the same thing. When I first arrived, I misunderstood some of the ways to symbolically say hello. The American way of saying hello with the hand would mean "come" in the Nigerian interpretation. Sometimes the waving of hands as hello looks like expression of anger in the Nigerian culture. In Nigeria, we wave the hand strongly all the time to indicate hello. Any other way of moving the hand no longer signifies hello. The first time somebody greeted me with a hand signal after Mass, I thought he had asked me to come close and listen to him.

I also struggled with food and weather, especially the cold weather. I missed the Nigerian food, but I am not a big eater, and moreover, I like eating nuts. There are better nuts here in the States than in Nigeria. So, my problem with food is nothing compared with my issue with the cold weather. Moreover, I love potatoes, corn, rice, chicken, and beans, and there are many of them in this country, even though I prefer the way they are prepared in Nigeria to the way they are prepared here. I miss my favorite meat, goat, but it is nothing when compared with other serious issues like developing the American accent and social life as well as knowing all the things a priest needs to know about the US moral values. I must indicate that some of the American values are confusing to me. For instance, I still do not understand the legalization or registration of certain hate groups as legal associations.

WHAT STRATEGIES ARE BEING HELPFUL TO YOU TO EFFECTIVELY ADJUST FROM NIGERIAN CULTURE TO US CULTURE?

Honestly, adapting to a totally different culture is not easy, and adapting to US culture was a big struggle for me. After some kind of cross-cultural anxiety, I had to reflect and talk to myself and remembered the few discussions I had at home with a couple guys who had lived in the States before. I remembered the few tips they gave me about US culture. I wish I had more opportunities to listen to them and had taken everything they said seriously. However, their advice motivated me to face my cross-cultural situation and figured out a way to assimilate myself into the society and become a part of it. They advised me to start by being a participant observer. So, I decided to be one for many months. I became more interested in silent learning than practical involvement in certain things to avoid mistakes.

As a teacher who is constantly involved with students and staff (academic and domestic), I thought I needed to know the US Constitution because most of the time the behaviors of the students and staff are not devoid of the constitution. From reading the constitution, I started reading other books that would help me to understand the US culture and lifestyle. The books also helped me to understand the reality of the problem of race and helped me to figure out who I am as a black man in a country where people like me must be careful even if I have to be politically correct for the sake of acceptance and peace in my environment, as long as I do not betray certain moral values that hinge on equality of every human being. I engaged myself in a combination of diplomacy, moral truth, and avoidance of antagonistic environment, especially in my place of work.

So, with the help of reading many books and magazines, conducting observations, and asking questions, I picked up many of the US cultural values, some US symbols and their meanings, as well as certain phrases and their actual meanings. I realized that even though certain symbols and phrases are familiar to me, they have different meanings in the United States.

I think the greatest key toward my adjustment is the patience and humility to learn the culture like a child who is learning how to talk and the willingness to embrace the new lifestyle. We live in a new world of globalization where the key to success depends on the ability to embrace diversity. So, I had no option but to be open to embrace cultural diversity and learn the lifestyle of my new home.

I must say that I am lucky to be in the midst of educated people, fellow teachers, who are aware of the difficulty in learning a new culture. They always helped me with providing answers to my questions and appreciate my struggles to learn and be a part of the society. Actually, some of their attitudes toward me motivated me to keep learning the new culture.

Could you please briefly describe the important knowledge of US culture that a Nigerian priest coming

TO MISSION IN THE UNITED STATES SHOULD HAVE PRIOR TO DEPARTURE TO THE UNITED STATES?

Going back to the various ways I overcame my own cultural problems I would like to recommend the following for other priests coming from Nigeria to mission in the United States:

1. Try as much as you can to know about the US culture and lifestyle before entering the airplane to the United States. It could be done through reading, asking questions to those who have lived in the United States, or attending a workshop about US history, culture, and general lifestyle.
2. On arrival, see yourself as someone who knows little or nothing about the culture and be open to assimilate all the important aspects of the culture.
3. Think positively and try to do what is right. Always remember why you are in this country. Be tenacious in grasping the US values that would help you to be a part of the society and the ecclesial culture in order to be productive in the country.
4. Overlook some negative attitudes of a few people because there are many good Americans.
5. Put away any stereotypes in the mind about how the church must be and know that every culture has a way of doing things. A Nigerian can fit into the US society and do great things. Hold on to the belief that many Americans value God and the knowledge that there are many good US motivations.
6. While still in Nigeria, remember that normally when two cultures meet, there is always a shock, but the cultural challenges should not make you quit learning about how to be a member of the host country.
7. Even though you know and speak English, what you know is the King's English spoken with a Nigerian accent. You should therefore be open to learn how Americans speak their English.
8. The same thing applies to cultural symbols. Every culture has symbols and meanings that go with the symbols. A particular symbol might have a positive meaning in Nigeria but a negative

connotation in the United States. Thus, a lesson on symbols and the importance of paying attention to the meanings of symbols in another culture should be in the curriculum for preparing Nigerian priests assigned to work in the United States.

9. Remember that work ethics are highly respected in the United States. If one works hard, he would always get some support. Know the importance of being creative and being more of a collaborative worker, not one that imposes.

10. Know the negative effects of the past sexual scandal on the priests in the United States and how to handle the negativity and still be a devoted priest.

11. Before you leave Nigeria, be aware of the fact that there are certain behaviors about the host country, which you must acquire, and there are certain prior knowledge of your native culture, which you must put aside in order to succeed in the host culture. Have the mindset that what you know is not always the best, thus the importance of openness and flexibility. Finally, given the necessity of prior idea of the host culture before one departs his home country, a Nigerian priest coming to the United States needs to learn the US society and culture via internet, books, journals, and television channels that might help him to understand the various aspects of US culture.

PARTICIPANT E

4.1.6. WHAT IS YOUR GENERAL PASTORAL BACKGROUND, AND WHAT WAS YOUR KNOWLEDGE OF US CULTURE BEFORE MISSIONING IN THE UNITED STATES?

I was ordained twenty-five years ago in Nigeria and worked both as a parish priest and a lecturer in a senior seminary. I came to the United States ten years ago. I worked as an associate pastor for four years. Presently, I am a resident pastor and a full-time chaplain in a hospital.

I never lived in the United States before coming to work here. The only culture I knew and experienced prior to coming to the United

States was my native culture. I was born in it, had all my education in it, and worked as a priest in it. My very slight knowledge of US culture came from talking with friends from my hometown who reside in the United States and come home for vacation occasionally. I was always having an informal discussion with them for fun, and I never bothered to ask them about US culture because I never thought I would be in the United States one day.

Looking at the way they talked and dressed, I could notice a difference between them and our usual cultural way of dressing and speaking English, but I did not see a very big cultural difference because they had always wanted to be seen as homeboys and not as foreigners in their homeland. I know I admired their boldness and confidence when they talked, as well as their fluent way of speaking English, but I did not see a big difference in culture because they always tried to be fully involved in our traditional way of doing things at home.

What are the cross-cultural struggles or challenges you have experienced in the United States, especially pastoral struggles or challenges?

I was culturally ill-prepared before coming to the United States. It did not take me time to observe how the difference in culture was affecting every aspect of my life and work. The great use of the internet in almost everything was my first shock and embarrassment. I never used a computer before, and for the first time, I saw myself in an office where it is hard to function without the knowledge of computer technology.

I was also shocked by how elderly people are called by their first names by younger ones, even kids, without putting a prefix to show a respect to an elderly person. Back home, you must put a kind of prefix to show that you recognize that the individual is older than you are. It is a mark of respect for the elders. It is still taking me time to adjust to that.

I have been hearing the phrase "ladies first," but it sank deeply into my head when I came to this country. Women have more rights here when it comes to respecting people and woe to any man who disrespects or abuses any woman. The chairperson of the parish council in my parish is a woman and rules with an iron hand. It is not bad to have a woman as the chairperson even though it is my first experience. However, she and the other women in the council do not easily give up their ideas and suggestions, and often the men do not challenge them as they would challenge their fellow men.

I was surprised by the involvement of open gays and lesbians in my parish. I believe that they are children of God and deserve respect, but I struggled with their involvement in the positions of role models, and whoever questions it gets into trouble right away. There are gays and lesbians in Nigeria, but it is not open. The gays and lesbians tightly hide their sexual orientation. Those of them who are open are not usually allowed to be in the position of role models because it is morally unacceptable. There is no national or state law against them, but it is not culturally embraced, and people usually stay away from them to avoid being associated with them. So, my prior knowledge of gays and lesbians is that any association with them is morally unacceptable. Being in the States and working and relating closely with gays and lesbians were a big challenge for me when I first arrived. I was surprised to see some people tell me openly that they are gays or lesbians. Some are in different committees in the parish. If somebody had told me about their great involvement in the church when I was in Nigeria, I would have doubted it.

Everything in this country, including pastoral work, is solidly planned, and everybody follows the plan accordingly. Given that everybody knows what to do and knows that they are expected to get things done as planned, Americans are always busy, fast, and on time for every activity. Back home, life is more informal, laid back, and without the kind of serious work ethics I see in the States. Adjusting to strictly following the plans of the day as fast, as the culture expected, gave me a little problem initially. The fast pace of activities and strict timing of the activities was stressful. A particular time is allocated to every activity in our church, and everybody expects the activity to start and end as planned. For instance, in the church, many will be offended if Mass is started earlier or later than the agreed time, and many will be offended if Mass does not end at the expected time or earlier so that people will not be late to their next planned activity. It does not mean that an error of few minutes is not often ignored, but deep in peoples' minds, there are expectations, which are supposed to be respected. I used Mass as an example, but generally speaking, timing is a big deal in the United States. My parishioners do not expect the homily to be more than ten munities. After twelve minutes of homily, many people will begin to look at their wristwatches.

Earlier, I mentioned the use of an office and computer. Priests have offices in Nigeria and use them, but the priestly work in the United States keeps a priest more in the office than outside because he is always on his computer to track events, plan, and coordinate, making sure that the activities of the church are nicely organized and tallies with the parishioners' private activities for a maximum participation of the parishioners in the church activities. The priest is expected to be a collaborative and supportive leader who not only coordinates the parish activities but also gets involved in the individual activities of the parishioners, like attending graduation ceremonies of some students from the parish and going to their ball games and other social events. So, he is often in the office to organize parish events as well as marking where he could be involved in some families' spiritual and social events. At home, I never gave priority to family events of the parishioners, like attending graduations or ball games, unless a family invited me, which happened once a while. I never considered family social events as part of my pastoral duty. Here in the States, it is a pastoral duty.

In Nigeria, the priest is less collaborative in his leadership than here in the States. He gently tells people what to do, and often they do it without complaining. There are parish councils, but in most parishes, the councils are there to execute the wish of the priest except in situations where there is a lack of trust in the priest's ideas. The priest tells them his plans and then consults them regarding the plans, except for when he wants the council to do the planning.

Here in the States, the pastor and I, along with the rest of the parish staff, have meetings every Wednesday to plan the weekly activities in the parish, and everybody is welcomed to be a contributor in the plans. There is a real teamwork among us, and the pastor considers everybody's ideas at the meeting. It does not mean that he must carry out everybody's plans, but he listens and also lays down his own plans for critique, and all of us will collaboratively come up with a solid plan for the week and are on the same page for almost all the activities. In Nigeria there is nothing like staff meetings because everybody follows the plan mapped out by the pastor.

I did not work in a city parish in Nigeria, but I am aware that in some wealthy parishes in the cities, the priest gives annual financial reports, which is rarely challenged because of two factors: trust and the belief that the priest is in charge unless there is a serious reason to question the report. Here in my parish, the priest, his staff, and the financial council are expected to give a clean account of the yearly incomes and expenses at the end of every fiscal year. He gets into trouble if there is a problem in the reconciliation of incomes and expenses. So, the priest has to be at the computer every time to make sure the bookkeeper's records are as good as expected and questions the bookkeeper if there are discrepancies. This does not mean that the priests here are always in the office and do not go out for other pastoral works outside the church. Actually, the parish secretary is more engaged in the office work than the priest is, but most of the time, what the secretary does are the things already planned by the priest or the entire parish staff. So, adjusting to the US pastoral culture was challenging to me initially.

Basically, the same strategic plan we have in the parish is applicable in the hospital where I work, except minor differences because of certain rules in the hospital. Generally, both in the parish and hospital, the staff, and the rest of the people expect collaborative leadership, good execution of the plans, and accountability. Being a person who never engaged myself in a strict, formal way of doing things, adapting to this entire kind of leadership and responsibility took me some time.

Effective communication and interpersonal relationships were not easy for me at the beginning. Many people could not understand my accent and vice versa. My English is British-oriented and spoken with my tribal accent. It was hard to communicate effectively with many people when I first arrived, especially with those who never experienced any other accent except the American one. Without the effective communication, I found it hard to establish a good interpersonal relationship with many parishioners and some people at the hospital. It was really embarrassing when several people would talk with me for a very short time and go because we could not understand ourselves very well. Effective communication also includes certain general signs and symbols of expression. I could not understand many of those. The communication situation was really embarrassing, but it is better now.

I did not know that there are strong mini cultures within the general US culture, and sometimes the people of the mini cultures expect their pastor to relate with them in a way that is more meaningful to them. I am referring to mini cultures like Caucasian, African American, Native American, Hispanic, Italian, Irish, urban, rural, and ghetto cultures. When listening to the television, I often hear people talk about the Southern, Northeastern, Western, or Midwest cultures, which refer to the regional cultures in the United States. As a black man, many African Americans accused me of having the lifestyle of a white man instead that of a black man. Some of them occasionally find it hard to relate with me appropriately because of my ignorance of their culture. Others could not understand why I, a black man, could not understand their culture. They expected me, their black brother, to know their black culture. I am sometimes asked to help out in a black parish and doing it with an absence of the knowledge of their culture was challenging. Some could not understand why I was not familiar with their culture and were not happy with me. It made several of them not embrace me, which was shocking to me because while still in Nigeria I thought that every African American would embrace me because I am a black man.

I struggled with other cultural things. I struggled with food differences and the high level of feminism in this culture. I was surprised by the formality in almost every situation. For instance, I did not know that I was making certain sick parishioners feel uncomfortable by visiting them without a prior knowledge that I was coming. I did not know that I had to call the parishioner before the visit.

I knew there was racism in the United States, but I did not know that it was not as bad as I heard about. I thought there might still be secret lynching, but I have not heard of any, even though the constant unjustified excessive use of guns on people of color more than on Caucasians might be classified by some people as a modern way of eliminating people of color. However, the issue of race is not as bad as I thought when I was in Nigeria, and it took me some time to quit being afraid of the Caucasians. I was not aware of how the law protects everybody, irrespective of his or her ethnicity, even though some people sometimes abuse it. I was not aware that majority of the Americans respect the constitution of equality under law, even though some white folks never accept equality with black people.

I was shocked by how some people dress to come to the church during summer, and I struggled with it because I saw it as a lack of respect for the holy place of worship and the liturgy. Some wear the kind of shorts or dresses that parents in Nigeria would not allow their children to wear outside the house. The freedom in America is great, but I thought that sometimes it is overexpressed.

I struggled to comprehend the good morals I saw in some people who openly acknowledge that they do not believe in God. Some volunteer in the city or even our church. We have a food pantry in the church to help or support the poor. Some of the supplies of the food we get come from people who claim to be atheists. They even come to the church pantry on the days we give out goods to the needy and help in the work of serving the needy. I am still shocked by that gesture because I wonder what motivates them since they do not believe in any supreme being.

I do not think my cultural experiences will be complete without mentioning how I struggle with cold weather up till today. I knew that the US weather could be cold, but I did not know about the freezing condition of the weather at certain times of the year, just like I also did not know that the summer could also be hotter than the hot condition at home [Nigeria]. The white color of the snow is very good but driving on it or the icy road is not fun at all. While in Nigeria, I knew the weather could be cold, but I did not know about the extreme aspect of the winter and the extreme hotness of the summer.

I encountered other small challenges, but the heartbreaking thing is not having a person to talk to or someone you can genuinely trust with your problems and receive nonfiltered advice. I believe that everybody does have one problem or another, but the problem gets into one's skin or even becomes a psychological problem when there is nobody to offer help or encouragement. I am naturally an introvert and does not easily go to people for help unless I know the individuals very well. So being in a foreign country and not knowing who to talk to complicates my cultural struggles. I saw myself in the midst of a different social life, moral values, English accent, symbolic meanings, and way of connecting with people and doing my job but had no knowledge of the effective way of doing what I came to do or the required competence to do the job. There was nobody to show me the way to do it or what to do in order to be a productive member of the society. I felt like an outcast. My daily life was a life of complexity. There was a kind of helplessness and irritability I would never wish on anybody. The misinterpretation of my accent as not knowing English language did not help my anxiety.

WHAT STRATEGIES ARE HELPFUL TO YOU TO EFFECTIVELY ADJUST FROM NIGERIAN CULTURE TO US CULTURE?

Sometimes a mistake could open the door for a good thing. I did something that was not morally bad but culturally unacceptable. My pastor intervened on my behalf, and after that, he sat down with me to talk and advise me. During the discussion, he noticed that I really needed help to understand the US church and society. He later gave me two books about US history, culture, and church. The books exposed me to the knowledge of the United States, the various ethnic groups and regions in the country and their distinct lifestyles, as well as the general US lifestyle such as moral values, social and political life, certain symbols and phrases and their meanings, expectations from people, racial and gender issues, the civil rights movements and the progress that followed, and the present social and political issues in the United States. I also read about the US church and issues with the international priests.

The books opened my eyes. It also motivated me to read more to learn more about my host country. I bought some more books. The more I read, the more I noticed both the stupidity of sending a person to a culture he does not know without appropriate information about the culture and the danger the person is exposed to. The knowledge I got after the numerous readings and other information from asking questions helped me to start seeing my naïveté and my stereotypes. Then I started putting my original thoughts aside and embracing the lifestyle of the Americans as well as the best way to mission in my host culture. It has not been very easy because it is like a non-swimmer who is struggling to swim very well in order to stay alive. With persistence, patience, and humility, I started breaking through the cultural brick wall every day.

Moreover, when you imagine how you would feel if somebody from another culture comes to your own culture and relates with you like a member of your own, it motivates. This thought motivates me every day, even though there are certain difficulties like racism and accent proficiency that I have to overcome. Nonetheless, I have started to see joy and personal fulfillment in my mission, especially when more and more Americans relate with me cordially because they could now understand me better due to the improvement in my social life and accent. They now see me as one whose way of doing things is no longer very different from theirs.

Could you please briefly describe the important knowledge of US culture that a Nigerian priest coming to mission in the United States should have prior to departure to the United States?

Whoever is coming to the United States to work must have at least a basic knowledge of where he is going: the geography and history of the country, the US social lifestyle, the different ethnic groups in the United States, the importance of work ethics in the country, the importance of respecting law and order, the actual weather conditions, the pastoral expectations from a priest, and the actual racial issues as it is and the different ways it is expressed by people as well as how it is controlled by the law. He should also be aware of the differences in food and the importance of being on time for events. Basic computer knowledge is very important. The priest must be prepared to respect the equality of everyone, no matter the differences in age, gender, or social status. He needs to be aware of respecting people's sexual inclinations, gay or straight, as well as people's religious or atheistic inclinations to avoid illegal attitudes toward anybody and to avoid a person's judgment due to their looks or manner of dressing. The person must learn how to be patient and humble and know how to be a collaborative leader that can work with all kinds of people, no matter their gender or ethnicity.

Arrangements must be made with people who have already lived in the United States to educate incoming priests. In addition to that, the individual must read a lot about the United States and watch a lot of news about the country, especially the channels that broadcast the news with an American accent. Channels like CNN and others could now be watched anywhere on the television or the internet, and I strongly suggest that any individual preparing to come to the United States should make out time to watch those channels and pay attention to how the Americans pronounce certain words. He should also acquaint himself with the US accent. If possible, the individual should be allowed to visit United States for at least two or three months to see if he would be a good candidate for the US mission.

Finally I would suggest that any priest assigned to work in the United States must know that upon arrival, he should first be more of a student of US culture to avoid the exercise of his own culture in the host culture and know that as long as he has an accent and is a black man, certain people, including some of his parishioners and fellow priests, will always look down on him. But that should not deter him from exercising his duty with love. Moreover, certain people will also show him love, no matter how he looks, speaks, or dresses, as long as they see authentic dedication in the exercise of his duty.

Upon arrival, arrangement needs to be made for the priest to have a support group. Among the members of the support group should be some Nigerians who have lived in the United States for a long time and went through some cross-cultural struggles.

PARTICIPANT F

4.1.7. WHAT IS YOUR GENERAL PASTORAL BACKGROUND, AND WHAT WAS YOUR KNOWLEDGE OF US CULTURE BEFORE MISSIONING IN THE UNITED STATES?

I was ordained in 1994 and worked in Nigeria for twelve years before coming to the United States. Since I came to the States, my day-to-day work includes teaching catechism, administering the sacraments of the church, and acting as charismatic renewal director and youth apostolate. I was culturally challenged in the various works because I had never been in the States prior to my assignment to the country.

WHAT ARE THE CROSS-CULTURAL STRUGGLES OR CHALLENGES YOU HAVE EXPERIENCED IN THE UNITED STATES, ESPECIALLY PASTORAL STRUGGLES OR CHALLENGES?

Nigeria is different from the United States in many ways. Being culturally unprepared prior to coming was a big mistake by those who sent me. I had a postarrival program when I arrived, which was very helpful, but the period of the program was too short for all the cross-cultural training that one might need in order to adjust very well in the United States. I wish I had an idea of where I was going, especially the culture of the Americans and other things they value because it would have been a stepping-stone for the program I had, which was very short and did not address many differences between the US and my home culture. It was more of a general orientation program for priests from different parts of the world. So even though I had the postarrival program, I still struggle to put away some of the things that have already molded my life in order to genuinely immerse myself into the American lifestyle.

In my parish in Nigerian, I was the leader who made all the decisions. It is not the same here in the United States. Here, you are still the leader, but everybody expects you to be a collaborative leader who must consider the ideas of everyone in the church no matter their age, gender, and sexual orientation and work with them without dismissing anybody's idea because of gender, age, or sexual inclination. It was difficult for me to work with the gays and lesbians. It was hard to give serious consideration to suggestions made by youths and children. I believed that their parents should rather make the suggestions on their behalf. I was indifferent to work with a group of some strong feminist nuns, whom I thought were more interested in looking at their suggestions with the eyes of feminism instead of joining everyone in genuinely analyzing and critiquing suggestions and choosing the best. If their suggestions were not chosen because of genuine reasons, they would always misinterpret the reasons and claim that their suggestions were not chosen because they were women. If I had known the strength of feminism in this country, I would have worked better with the nuns. My ignorance of the strong feminism in the United States, the feminist way of pushing ideas by some women, was giving me anxiety, and so working with some of them in the staff team was a big challenge.

I was aware that there is lack of vocation to the priesthood in the United States, but I did not know that the church itself is stronger than I thought. I also did not know that the culture of the US church is not as liberal as I thought. I did not know that the great values of the church are highly practiced in the States, like fighting corruption, social justice, pro-life, and other great values that Jesus fought for. Certain individuals in the US church might be distorting the teachings, but a huge majority of the Catholics and other Christian denominations are very resilient in the traditional teachings of the church. It took me time to disregard my initial stereotype thoughts of the US ecclesial culture and accept the reality on the ground. I wish I were educated about the actual facts before I left Nigeria for United States.

Adjustment to the US climate and food has never been easy for me. I still have problems with them. The winter is very cold for me. I hate to drive on the snow or ice. The summer is better, but the humidity is sometimes worse than we have at home. I thought that it is usually cold every time of the year. I did not know that it could be colder than I initially thought while I was at home in Nigeria, and I did not know that the summer could be very warm.

Upon arrival it was not difficult for me to recognize that I was a second-class priest in the mind of many because of my accent, ignorance of the US social values, African ethnicity, and skin color. Some of the parishioners talked to me disrespectfully as a priest with little theology simply because I am from Africa. A parishioner who later became a good friend told me at one of our dinners that when they heard I was coming they were sad because they thought the African priests usually had only a one-year program in theology and were therefore unfit to serve in the United States. That kind of stereotype hurts because despite the differences in culture, I strongly believe that my theological training is not different from the theological training of the national priests. The church's theology is the same everywhere in the world. Moreover, many of my professors in the seminary were trained in the United States, and some were American citizens by birth. Thus, I struggled—and still struggle—with the US culture of classism and the demeaning of certain people because of how one looks and their ethnicity, accent, and some other variables, which include the idea that "made in America is always the best," including human beings. It hurts more when I get the demeaning stereotype from my fellow clergy. This issue of demeaning my priestly qualification because of the American patriotic culture of "made in America is always the best" was very challenging to me. It was always antagonizing when my accent is misinterpreted as not knowing how to speak English. I will not disagree that my English accent, especially when I first arrived, could have been very hard for some people to understand because my English is British-oriented and spoken with a Nigerian accent, but there is a difference between accent and bad English grammar. The misinterpretation of my accent as lack of English knowledge irritated me very much. Nevertheless, given what I know now, those who made the comments about my accent may not be blamed because I really was not speaking what they could understand, and I also misunderstood and misinterpreted some of the things they said.

I used my own tribal moral standards at home to judge and make decisions in the parish, and they backfired on me. My misinterpretation of their cultural values and their misinterpretation of the things I was doing with goodwill created a huge barrier between us. I had a feeling of being disliked.

To avoid further mistakes and problems, I stopped many of the pastoral and social things I was doing. Consequently, I felt useless to my parish community and the US church. I needed very good advice from somebody who trusted me and whom I trusted, but there was none. My entire situation could be described as stopping everything I knew without enough materials or information to replace what I knew before. I was helpless and psychologically agitated every time. I lost my self-esteem and was wondering whether to stay or go back to my country.

WHAT STRATEGIES ARE HELPFUL TO YOU TO EFFECTIVELY ADJUST FROM NIGERIAN CULTURE TO US CULTURE?

I talked to my spiritual director and friend about my problems. He told me that I was not the first to be in my kind of situation and that he would do everything he could to help me. He talked to my pastor, who introduced me to an American family that lived in Nigeria for seventeen years. An agreement was reached for me to live with the family for three months. The family understood my cross-cultural struggles and helped me to understand the cultural differences between Nigeria and the United States. For the first time, I felt like I had friends who understood my cross-cultural problems and knew how to orient me to US culture properly because of their knowledge of both cultures. I was open to them, and they helped me in many ways: accent reduction, public relations, people's expectations from a priest, how to minister in the United States, the importance of respecting the equality of everyone no matter their sexual inclination, gender, age, and the various American values I did not know before. They opened my eyes to the knowledge of the country, culture, and pastoral expectations from parishioners. From my relationship with them and everything they told me, it became clear to me that I must master the various ways Americans perceive things and their ways of behavior if I want to be accepted in the society and be successful in my missionary assignment.

After I left the house, I started to attend almost every activity in the parish and certain activities in the city to enrich myself culturally through participant observation. I would always get back to the family with some questions about certain cultural lifestyles that were complex for me to comprehend. I was never afraid or shy to ask questions in order to learn. My commitment to attend activities and be a participant observer and then follow up my observations with some questions when necessary have helped me tremendously to visually see the various aspects of the culture and be practically involved in the US cultural ways of doing things. I learned different aspects of the culture like when to address somebody formally, when to put a prefix to somebody's name, symbolic ways of showing courtesy and respect, and the expectation of everyone to serve himself in certain dinner parties unlike in Nigeria where the men would sit down and the women will serve them the meal and come back to collect their plates and clean the table. I observed that a majority of the women would prefer to be addressed as "Ms. A (i.e., their first name)" to "Mrs. A (i.e., their last name)" under normal circumstances except in formal and professional situations.

In addition to the learning activities, I also became a good friend of the television because that is another powerful means of learning both the culture and US accent. Since I met that family, I was always asking them why certain things are done certain ways, and they were always happy to explain to me. I can remember having long conversations with them about the influence of feminism in the United States and cultural ways of doing certain things. The family gave me some books that helped me to know more about US culture and history as well as the various ethnic groups and regions in the United States and how they influence the social, political, and religious activities in the country.

Could you please briefly describe the important knowledge of US culture that a Nigerian priest coming to mission in the United States should have prior to departure to the United States?

I think it was one of the US presidents, Eisenhower, who said that people must know before they act. Predeparture orientation or training or preparation is necessary for any priest coming from Nigeria to minister in the United States in order to work well with the people and for them. At the core of every kind of leadership is good relationship with people, especially in the church where the leadership role of the priest is expected to be close to perfection. A Nigerian priest coming to minister in the United States must be taught the importance of collaborative leadership with women, men, gays, lesbians, adults, and children.

The US values, including symbolic values and the American English accent, need to be told to the incoming priest. Psychologically, the individual should start tuning himself to the knowledge of the US appreciation of their culture and expectation of an immigrant who values their US culture. Thus, books, internet, magazines, CDs, and DVDs for mastering the various aspects of US culture and accent should be made available to the individual to help him with the appropriate preparation for the US mission. I suggest that those who have lived in the United States and are now residing in Nigeria and experienced cross-cultural struggles while in the States to be the cross-cultural trainers of the incoming priests. The incoming priests should know that a Nigerian who never experienced the US accent knows the King's English and speaks it with his Nigerian accent, which is totally different from the American way of speaking English.

I would also like to suggest that prior to selecting and training an individual for the US mission, it would be necessary to find out if the person will be comfortable to work in the United States. I have no problem with people who are introverts, but I think that whoever comes here should be someone who will not be shy to mix up with people and ask questions in order to learn. Adjustment to a new culture is not easy, and so the person must also be humble to put his own culture aside and embrace US culture. He must be patient and speak less until he acquaints himself with the actual differences between the US societal and pastoral culture and the Nigerian culture.

Bearing the differences between the two cultures in mind, the priests coming to the States need every predeparture training that will help them as a base for the postarrival training because I believe in having both the predeparture and postarrival training. The preknowledge will help the priests to understand that doing things according to his personal culture will be a bad idea. It might be hard to know everything about the host culture while in the home country, but I think a methodological cross-cultural preparation that starts at home and continues upon arrival will be very beneficial to the priests' adjustment. A combination of the predeparture and postarrival training will be like learning how to walk, in preparation to learning how to run without stumbling. Thus, both predeparture and postarrival training are very necessary.

I would also suggest that the place a person grew up in Nigeria should be a tool for choosing both the kind of place he will be assigned to work upon arrival and the kind of training he should get. Some people love to live and work in rural areas and so love rural ministry, and others love to live in the city and love city ministry. So, knowledge of the kind of place a priest prefers to work should be considered during the training, and when he arrives in the United States, efforts should be made to put him to that kind of place. If the individual will work in a US city upon arrival, the lifestyle of the US city should be incorporated in the training, and if the individual has not experienced a typical city life, he should be assigned in a city parish in Nigeria first before he departs for United States. The same thing applies to those who prefer rural parishes.

It will be nice to educate the person about the negative and positive things he will encounter in the United States. For instance, if the individual will work in a predominantly white parish, he needs to know that he will never be fully accepted by everyone in the community simply because he is not fully white and others will still love him, no matter his ethnicity or race if he does his job very well. Also important is the necessity of preparing the priest psychologically so he would always remain himself and never feel inferior because of the challenges he might encounter.

PARTICIPANT G

4.1.8. WHAT IS YOUR GENERAL PASTORAL BACKGROUND, AND WHAT WAS YOUR KNOWLEDGE OF US CULTURE BEFORE MISSIONING IN THE UNITED STATES?

I was ordained a priest in 1990 and worked in Nigeria for twelve years before coming to the States. I worked as an assistant parish priest and later as a lecturer in the senior seminary. I have worked in the States for ten years. Here, I mission mainly to the youths, which includes working with the youths in my parish and campus ministry. I teach the undergraduate students at the university as well as the chaplain of the Black Students Association. I also go to the psychiatric institute in the city to mission to the patients in the institute.

I had little knowledge of US culture before coming to the States. I did not have any formal training for the cultural experiences I would encounter. However, I gained a little experience in a very short assignment of working with people of different cultures, including Americans, in a parish in Nigeria with many expatriates.

WHAT ARE THE CROSS-CULTURAL STRUGGLES OR CHALLENGES YOU HAVE EXPERIENCED IN THE UNITED STATES, ESPECIALLY PASTORAL STRUGGLES OR CHALLENGES?

My first cultural conflict was how things move and change quickly in the United States. There are continuous technological transformations, and people quickly move with the technological changes. Americans like to be proactive and enjoy renovations as well as fast movement of ideas. Coping with that was a big challenge to me. For instance, there is a continuous change of announcement at the students' notice board. The students enjoy it and look forward to it. They feel bored if the same announcement remains on the notice board for a long time. I wish I were prepared for that before I was assigned to teach in the college.

As a college professor where students of different social backgrounds, ethnicities, and religious inclinations study, I wish I had known how to relate with people of the various backgrounds in the United States. I wish I had known the history of the African Americans and Native Americans and the lifestyle of the Hispanic Americans. I thought there was only one American cultural background and anticipated to see only one US culture. I did not know that there are microcultures within the general US culture. I wish I had known how to relate with the students of the various microculture within the general US culture.

As a black man, I ignorantly had a horrible relationship with African Americans in particular because they expected me to know the black culture and relate with them on that level. Thus, they were calling me a white man in a black skin. Knowing what I know now, I think that their criticisms were correct. They were not expecting a different treatment because they are black. Rather they were expecting me to use certain words and examples that resonate with the experiences of black people and their culture when I attend the black students' meeting or during private meetings in my office with some black students.

Surprisingly many of the white professors on campus know the importance of the knowledge of the black culture and relate very well with the black students. I struggled to relate very well with the black students due to my lack of knowledge of the black culture. The knowledge of the black culture gives the black students a feeling that the professor knows their peculiar situations and cares for them. This kind of students' feelings about a professor generates automatic rapport between the professor and the students, which indirectly enhances interest in learning among the students. They need a professor to visit with in times of stress: academic, family, and social. The professor needs to know their black culture in order to understand their situation. So, at school, I struggled with the appropriate advice and relationship with the black students. Generally, the misunderstanding between the African American community on- and off-campus gave me anxiety. When I was in Nigeria, I thought that they would embrace me automatically because of my skin color, but my ignorance of the African American culture made it hard.

I did not know that there are poor people in the United States. The first time I saw some people begging on the streets, I was so surprised that I took some pictures of them, but I have destroyed them. I realized that every society shares certain things in common. You will always have the rich and poor in every society, or people of high and low class. It is just part of every society's way of life. It took me time to understand that there is a certain level of poverty in the United States that needs pastoral attention. I thought that everybody is financially good.

The individualistic life in the neighborhoods is something I could not understand. Everybody minds their own business. Many people are not even ready to wave hands or greet when you pass them. It was hard for me because it is uncommon in Nigeria, and I love interpersonal relationship with people, especially neighbors. Joking and laughing with neighbors are part of the Nigerian culture, and in such situations, nobody will call the police on you because of what you said. It is also uncommon to meet somebody you know without going close to the person and giving a fraternal greeting like a hug.

Feeding was another problem for me. I found it hard to eat the American foods. Some foods are familiar but cooked differently with various spices that are not very tasteful to me, and some food items are totally different from the kind of food I knew. So, I struggled with the differences in food. The food challenge was always harder when I had to eat things I never saw before and tastes totally different.

Climate was another problem. I knew about the climatic changes in the United States but not enough to prepare myself with what I saw. I did not know about the changing of the tires of the car for icy winter roads. Living in the United States during winter and driving whenever there is continuous snowing and ice on the ground was difficult. I wish I had an accurate knowledge about the winter climate and how to drive and dress during such a period.

I thought I would not have problems with my English given my level of education. I had all my academic education in English and wrote my thesis for a master's degree and dissertation for a doctoral degree in English language, and I defended them in English language. My English language is British-oriented. Prior to my coming to the States, I was very confident with my English. Unfortunately, I was challenged by the American accent and how to write some of their English words. Some of the words mean the same thing in the British English but are spelled differently. In fact, many words have the same meaning in both American and British English but are spelled differently. It was embarrassing to be constantly corrected in the classroom by my students until I started to use the computer to check the spellings of the words I would write in the classroom.

Being a black person in the United States automatically makes one a second-class resident or citizen. For me, it is a truth that is being denied by many. Both on- and off-campus, I never love the way I am treated by some people just because of my skin color. It still gives me anxiety.

As an educated man, I am aware that there are gays and lesbians everywhere. There are many journals about gays and lesbians. In Nigeria, there are gays and lesbians too, even though it is a taboo to acknowledge it in front of people. Nevertheless, I was overwhelmed by how it is not a big deal for people to openly tell anybody, even those they do not know, that they are gays or lesbians. More shocking is a recognition of weddings by gays and lesbians. It might not have been a big deal for me if I were in a non-Christian country, but the United States is popularly known as a Christian country. I know that pastorally the Catholic Church in the United States and everywhere is against same-sex marriage, but I was unaware that US culture had no problem with it.

The level of decency and formality, which is good, is an aspect of US culture that I admired, but I was also surprised by the high level of decency and formality. There is always a way of doing or saying certain things for the sake of decency. Each time I encountered those, they remind me of the difference between United States and some developing countries. There are informalities in behaviors at some places in the United States, but it is very cultural to be formal at the expected places for formality. The decency includes what to say in certain places simply because of the presence of children or women. Violation of that could lead to a lawsuit.

The lack of great respect for elders by younger ones was surprising to me when I came to the States newly. In Nigeria, it is culturally unacceptable to talk carelessly to somebody who is older than you unless the person acted inappropriately. It is unacceptable to call an older person by his first name as if they are an age-mate. If you do that, everybody around will look at you as a crazy person. In some villages and towns, the younger person would be expected to render an apology or even pay a fine. Here in the United States, everybody calls you by your first name no matter the age difference, except on campus where formality requires students to address a professor with their professional achievement, like Dr. James.

The great regards for women in the US, which I actually admire, is new to me, but the high level of feminism drives me crazy. Some students and professors would never address God as a "He." Working with some of the women is really hard because of their misinterpretation of a genuine disagreement as a disregard of their opinion because they are women. I do not like the way some women are culturally treated in Nigeria, but I struggle with the high level of feminism in the United States, including the US Church.

What strategies are being helpful to you to effectively adjust from Nigerian culture to US culture?

I had to be patient and humble and learn from fellow professors and students. In the classroom I told students that I learned the British English and encouraged them to feel free to correct me if I wrote a word with the British spelling of the word. About accent, I was always paying attention to how the professors and students speak or pronounce words and learn from them. I am not a shy person, so I do not find it hard to ask a professor or student to assist me with how to pronounce certain words. Many students even enjoyed the fact that their professor was learning from them, and they felt free to correct me without being asked. I never felt offended.

I like to relate well with people. Considering the phrase, "if you cannot beat them, join them," I had to ignore the unnecessary aspects of feminism and leave some of the women to discover their mistakes by themselves instead of arguing with them since they might misunderstand me as being chauvinistic.

About racism, it was easy for me to ignore it. When you read about the atrocities before and during the civil rights time, it becomes easy to accept my present situation as a black man. Moreover, looking back to the history of black people in this country, one sees a steady progress, even though the situation has not reached perfection.

I needed to know a thorough history of the African Americans in order to relate well with them both on campus and in the church. So, I visited a colleague who teaches multiculturalism and borrowed many books about the African American history and culture. I read the books and learned from them. I also borrowed some books from the library and read them. Somehow the books helped me to understand what influences some of the actions of the black students and the questions they often ask me. I came to understand them better. I was also carefully asking them questions on certain issues about African Americans that were complex to me. With the help of the private studies I did and the information I gathered from some of the students and professors, a better relationship started between the African Americans and I, both on- and off-campus.

I learned every other aspect of US culture, like different ways of interaction, social relationships, and places of formality and cultural activities that require formality, pastoral expectations in the parish and on campus through constant observation, readings, and certain television programs. Perhaps being on campus where there are many people and activities almost every day helped me in a big way. The more I mixed up with the students and staff in the college, the more I learned. I cannot escape from the weather problem, so I had to ask some people about the different ways to remain warm and added heating gadgets in my room and office. I prefer to eat at the buffet restaurants so I would have many choices of food. I am gradually getting used to the individualistic lifestyle. It is just a different lifestyle from what I knew, and there is nothing to do about it except get used to it and socialize with some Africans in town whenever the opportunity comes. Moreover, the more I know and become friendly with the staff and students, the more I have better interpersonal relationships.

COULD YOU PLEASE BRIEFLY DESCRIBE THE IMPORTANT KNOWLEDGE OF US CULTURE THAT A NIGERIAN PRIEST COMING

TO MISSION IN THE UNITED STATES SHOULD HAVE PRIOR TO DEPARTURE TO THE UNITED STATES?

Every priest coming to work in the United States must have some kind of orientation before boarding the plane to this country, period. We have many priests and other professionals who have lived in the States and are now residing in Nigeria. Incoming priests should get orientation or advice from those people to maximize faster knowledge of the American culture prior to and upon arrival. The knowledge should come from people who have worked in different church ministries and other kinds of jobs. The trainers of those intending to mission in the United States must be people who know about the various microcultures in the United States in order to give the incoming priests a wider perspective of US culture. The incoming priests must be taught the US symbolic behaviors and meanings in order to avoid a misinterpretation of certain symbolic behaviors that look like the ones they know but do not mean the same thing in the United States. The priests should be advised to be open-minded, patient, and humble and to observe first and learn from American people upon arrival before jumping into quick conclusions on how to do things. I recommend that the priests should not limit their inquiries on US pastoral life and cultural values. They should also learn social things like the US-valued sports, valued celebrations, and political life in the country. Hollywood does not represent United States. The US movies we watch in Nigeria do not represent the real United States. So being prepared by appropriate people is important.

The priests should be aware of the US pronunciation of English words. For instance, when I came, I used the word "fourth nightly" and was later corrected that in the States it is common to say "biweekly." The King's English is different to some extent. I struggled to understand the Americans when I arrived and vice versa. A person coming to the States should be aware of this so he will be open to learn the US colloquial way of speaking and not assume that he knows everything about the English language. Some of the US colloquial expressions may not be correct English grammar, but one needs to know them in order to communicate appropriately with both the educated and non-educated Americans. The importance of communication is based on understanding one another and not always on speaking standard grammar.

Pastorally, I strongly suggest that the priests should have a strong knowledge of the history of the church in the United States so they would know they are not coming to a dormant church even though they are not coming to a vibrant church like the church in Nigeria. They should have a basic knowledge of computer technology and engage themselves in learning certain things by themselves via the internet and other sources of acquiring the knowledge of the American culture and lifestyle, like reading and watching or listening to the American news.

I would also like to suggest that upon arrival, the newly arrived priest should have a postarrival orientation. I did not have it, but it is good to have both preknowledge and visual/practical knowledge of the culture through postarrival training. A seasoned pastor could do it by making the Nigerian priest an associate pastor of the seasoned pastor, or he could be sent to one of the institutions where new arrivals receive enculturation training.

Participant H

4.1.9. What is your general pastoral background, and what was your knowledge of US culture before missioning in the United States?

I was ordained in Nigeria in 1990. I worked in Nigeria for twelve years. I was an assistant parish priest, a vocation director, and a postgraduate student. I then taught in a major seminary for five years and came to the States. Here in the States, I am an associate pastor and an adjunct professor at a community college.

It was my first time to be in the United States. As an associate pastor, I assist the pastor in almost all his pastoral duties. I have a meeting with the pastor and parish secretary every week, and we plan for the next week's works. Apart from assisting the pastor in the general pastoral and administrative works of the parish, I am in charge of the various religious organizations and the youths of the parish.

WHAT ARE THE CROSS-CULTURAL STRUGGLES OR CHALLENGES YOU HAVE EXPERIENCED IN THE UNITED STATES, ESPECIALLY PASTORAL STRUGGLES OR CHALLENGES?

I came into the country with a particular mannerism, which is different from US culture, and changing it was never easy. Immediately I had a feeling of complexities and stress. My first and greatest challenge is communication. I was confident with my English, which includes the grammar and various poetic ways of communicating in English, but I still had a problem with communication when I arrived. The communication I refer to includes accent problems and understanding the US symbolic ways of communication and some effective skills of interpersonal discussion that could help one to make sense to the American people during discussions. I struggled with knowing the meanings of certain US symbols. There are certain symbolic ways of communication in the US that are used in Nigeria, but the meanings in the United States differ from their meanings in Nigeria. There are certain jokes and phrases you can use in Nigeria to make your conversations or discussions very effective, but they do not have the same effect in the United States. The differences in accent and styles of effective communication between the two countries left me with confusion. While in Nigeria, I was hugging people, and it meant acceptance and happiness. I did it once in the United States and observed that I cannot do it unless to a person I know very well, such as a good friend or family member. Pastorally, it is even more dangerous given the priests' sex scandal that rocked the US church a couple years ago. America is a place where a priest must be very careful.

I did not know the meaning and importance of stop signs when driving. I never saw one in Nigeria before I came to the States. I could not understand why somebody must stop whether a car is coming from the other side or not. Even though it is a great thing for the sake of safety and I have come to admire its importance it was a surprising experience. Adjusting to it took me a while despite the fact that I read it in the guide for the driver's license exam.

As a person from a country where eating meant going for food when you are really hungry, seeing people eat as a part of every socialization or gathering—meetings, games, movie theaters, and following church services—was a new experience. There is food in almost every gathering in the parish. It seems to be part of the parish culture in the United States. It was also a shocking experience to see people throw away unfinished food instead of reserving it for another time. I have friends who cannot eat what was cooked on the previous day even if the food is still good. The reason for this is beyond my understanding, and I struggle to internalize the habit.

With respect, I would like to add that I found the American foods unpalatable to me because they are different from the kinds of food I was eating at home. Certain foods like chicken and rice, though familiar to me, are prepared differently and do not taste the same. So, I really struggled with the American food. I also struggled with the culture of discussing while eating. Back home, we have a culture of keeping silent when eating because discussions happen before and after meal.

The climatic changes in the States were new to me, and it has not been very easy to adjust to them, especially the winter season. I read about the climatic changes in the Western world at high school, but the lessons did not mean anything to me until I came to this country. I did not know about snow or how to even drive on the snow or ice. Moving from a place where it is almost warm every day of the year to the US winter climate is quite a challenge.

Extended family relationship (like being practically involved in the joys and sorrows of the extended family members or the village) is an expected responsibility in Nigeria. I have not stayed in the States long enough to make a general statement about the kind of relationship existing between a person and their extended families, but given what I have seen and heard, there are lesser responsibilities for extended family members in the United States. Some do not even know the names of their extended family members. I have visited some people at the nursing homes who have no children or siblings and observed that they have a feeling of loneliness because they have nobody to relate with as a family member. In my culture, there is nothing like not having a practical acquaintance with some sort of relatives. In the absence of immediate relatives, other people somewhere else who shares the same family tree with the individual will relate with them like immediate relatives. Not doing it is regarded as an abomination in my society.

Every child in my culture is regarded as the child of the entire village. If a child misbehaves, an elderly person from that village can discipline the child without the parents' permission. The same responsibility of caring for the child also applies in times of a child's need. When a child is in need and the parents are not available, any other person from the village steps in and helps the child as he would to his own child. There is even more expectation from a priest to discipline the child, but not here in the United States.

I grew up with a particular knowledge of dress codes. Of course, there are dress codes in the United States, but the occasions for certain way of dressing are different when compared with Nigeria. For instance, in Nigeria, a student is expected to dress formally for classes and worship in the church. My first experience of what some students were wearing on my first day in the college for classes and also in the chapel gave me a shock because I thought that we learnt our dress codes from the Westerners. On the same token, there have been occasions (like funerals) where I dressed informally and everybody else dressed formally.

I also could not comprehend the idea of greeting everybody, both young and old, the same way without a kind of prefix for the elderly as a sign of respect for the elderly. It is a serious thing in Nigeria to greet an elder without a prefix that signifies respect or to call an elderly person by their first name without some kind of prefix. In my culture, you must put a prefix when calling or greeting those who are older than you as a sign of respect. There are established ways of greeting senior citizens, and it is highly unacceptable to greet them as if they are age-mates of the younger folks. Initially I struggled with the US style of greeting the elders or calling them by their first names, but I am used to it now.

I felt very lonely when I first arrived because here in the States, the invitation of a priest to a home for socialization does not come easily unless there is some kind of friendship. Back home, invitation of a priest by parishioners, even those who do not know the priest personally as a friend, is common. Individualistic life seems to be a part of the culture here. Neighbors can be neighbors for several years without knowing themselves or even their names.

I come from a culture where neighborhood goes with fraternal relationship. I do not think that it applies here in the United States. I struggle with loneliness, especially with not having more social interactions with my neighbors and parishioners.

Working with the women and children on equal status with men was initially difficult for me when I came to the United States. There are more regards for women and children in the States than in Nigeria, and their opinions are taken more seriously in the States than in Nigeria. I admire this respect for women and children, but it was new to me, and it took me time to make it a part of my life. Sometimes they are not even allowed to express their opinions in Nigeria. Given the feminism in the United States and the respect for children, it was a big transformation for me to blend into the society with regard to relations with women and children. The same situation applies to relating with gays and lesbians, even though I am still struggling with the idea of men marrying men and women marrying women. It is unheard of in Nigeria.

In the parish where I reside, it is nice to work collaboratively with the staff and other members of the church. I like it, and it brings more achievement and happiness. When I was in Nigeria, I was making almost all the decisions. Priesthood puts the priest on the pedestal of a person who everybody needs to listen to unless the priest has no credibility. I came to the States with that mentality. It was not easy initially, but I have come to appreciate it.

If you want to know my main problem, it is the disconnection between what I was used to and the new reality around me. The initial discontinuation from what you know without something to replace it irritates, and it did put me in a helpless and complex situation until I gradually began to know the new reality or the expected values and behaviors of my host culture.

WHAT STRATEGIES ARE HELPFUL TO YOU TO EFFECTIVELY ADJUST FROM NIGERIAN CULTURE TO US CULTURE, ESPECIALLY PASTORALLY?

The key for my adjustment comes from my great interest to work in the States and the knowledge that each people has a culture. Being successful in a foreign culture depends on the ability to be patient and humble to put one's own culture aside and learn the host culture. With these ideas in my mind, I had no problem to observe, learn, and even ask questions to get the appropriate knowledge of my host culture. Luckily, the friend who helped me get the teaching job gave me some helpful cultural information. Moreover, I was on the college campus most of the time and surrounded by staff and students who were willing to help me learn US culture. I was always interested to observe and learn from them, and I was never shy to ask them questions, even if the person were a freshman. I think I have the personality of getting along with people and relating with them easily. So, it did not take me a long time to have friends, especially on campus. I would learn from them and then carry the knowledge I got from the campus to the parish. I also asked my pastor, a good man and a friend, to feel free to correct me at any time, and he does till today.

I connected with other Nigerians and Africans in town, and their advice concerning feeding, like going to African restaurants and Asian buffet restaurants, helped me to maneuver my food problems. They also educated me about the weather conditions, along with how to dress better to remain warm during winter and how to relate with women and the younger ones. They gave me the social support that helped me to handle the individualistic life in the United States.

COULD YOU PLEASE BRIEFLY DESCRIBE THE IMPORTANT KNOWLEDGE OF US CULTURE THAT A NIGERIAN PRIEST COMING

TO MISSION IN THE UNITED STATES SHOULD HAVE PRIOR TO DEPARTURE TO THE UNITED STATES?

There is a reason why the Second Vatican Council introduced inculturation in the church. The *Ad Jentes*, which refers to missioning in another culture, challenges every missionary with the importance of learning and knowing the culture of the host nation of the missionary in order to communicate the gospel values in the culture that the host nation understands, just like Jesus did not communicate to humans with the language of heaven but with the language that human beings understood. He used the language and culture of the people to communicate to them and did miracles. Just like God did not communicate to us with the angelic language, we need to know the language and culture that the host nation is familiar with. Incoming priests should be aware of this.

I taught in a seminary in Nigeria, and we had no preparation program for the US mission. Rather there is a general program of preparing people for missioning in different places. If a priest were to be sent to United States, he needs to be specifically prepared for the work in the host culture. I do not think it will be a hard thing to do. We can use the modality of African hospitality to prepare the individual. It means an integration of host and guest. In Africa, the host welcomes the guest. When the guest is integrated, he begins to contribute in the family. For instance, in the African culture, after staying in a family for a while as a guest, you will be expected to contribute toward the well-being of the family. After eating in the family for a while, you will be expected to go to the farm with the family. At this moment, one is no longer a guest but somehow a member of the family. So, a person coming to work in the United States should be reminded of the African modality of hospitality because it works here. It has worked for me, and I believe it could work for others since it is already part of the African culture and also US culture because Americans expect one to contribute appropriately after staying in their country for a while. After staying and working in America for a while, you will be expected to be part of the society, communicate appropriately, and respect every aspect of the US moral value. Thus, the individual coming to the States should be informed to be a guest upon arrival and learn the American way of doing things. This means he has to be patient, humble, and open to learn US culture while bearing in mind that he is a potential host. Upon arrival, he must put his own culture aside and learn the new way of life. Unless he learns and understands, he cannot contribute meaningfully to the host culture. The African modality of hospitality includes the importance of being part of the new community after staying with the host community for a while, and so the incoming priest should be trained with the use of the African modality of hospitality.

The incoming priest should learn the US symbols in order to avoid the use of the same symbols at home with a belief that they mean the same thing in the United States. Symbolic expressions could have different meanings in several cultures. Without knowing the symbols, he might be communicating another meaning even though he is using the same symbol. I strongly believe that one needs to know the US symbols and meanings, or he might get into trouble upon arrival.

While in Nigeria, the priest coming to Nigeria should be taught the importance of the word "why" in learning. In a new culture, one needs to be asking why certain things are done in certain ways. One needs to know the "why" in order to know the "how." This means he should not be afraid or shy to ask questions in order to learn.

I personally think it might be nice to prepare a group of priests first before choosing the appropriate candidates for the US mission and not choosing some people before preparation. During the preparations, the trainers would know who is fit for the country. Trainers need to know if a person can adapt easily and be productive in the United States before the predeparture preparation. Ability to adapt is very important because of the complexities in cultures. I believe that those who will be quick to adapt to a particular culture will find it easier to adjust to the new culture and learn the language/accent quicker. If a person lacks the ability to adjust to the new culture, he could easily be frustrated and even suffer depression because of the fear of ascertaining what is and is not culturally acceptable. Cross-cultural adaptation and job performance always need somebody who will be open to learn the new culture. Not everybody has the personality to mix up easily with foreigners or be humble and patient enough to ask questions in order to learn or even find it easy to change from the known to an unknown culture.

To decrease the problems of food, weather, accent, different spellings of certain words, and other ignorance, the trainers of the incoming priests should educate them about the availability of food buffet so they will have access to many choices of food, teach them how to dress during winter, and help them with pronunciations and writings of certain words as well as the appreciation of collaborative leadership in the United States. America is very democratic. A knowledge of the US history will help them to know the difference between the administrative style in both the US society and the church and the Nigerian style, especially in the area of the rule of law so they will know that in the United States, nobody is above the law and the clerical shirt or being a clergy would not prevent one from landing in jail if he breaks the law. They should know about the high sensitivity of sexual abuse in the United States as well as how the Americans value the equality among everyone, irrespective of age, gender, or sexual inclination. Having preknowledge is always important to reduce surprises, and so I really support predeparture cross-cultural preparation.

Participant I

4.1.10. What is your general pastoral background, and what was your knowledge of US culture before missioning in the United States?

I had a good pastoral background before coming to the United States. I had a solid eight years of college education that prepared me to be a priest. Four of the eight years were spent in learning different aspects of Christian theology. After ordination in 2004, I worked as the bishop's master of ceremonies and the associate pastor of the Cathedral parish. I was sent to the United States in 2007 to work in a parish and further my education. I had no knowledge of the actual US culture before my arrival. I was never in the United States before I came over here. My only knowledge about US culture came from the stories that people shared at home. I never read any book about the culture or had a solid foundation about the knowledge of the culture.

When I arrived, I was assigned to a parish as a full-time associate pastor. With the assignment, my pastoral work came first before my studies. I even counseled some courses if they clashed with my pastoral work. I was the youth director and chaplain of the parish's men and women club, in addition to all other pastoral and sacramental ministries that are shared between the pastor and me.

WHAT ARE THE CROSS-CULTURAL STRUGGLES OR CHALLENGES YOU HAVE EXPERIENCED IN THE UNITED STATES, ESPECIALLY PASTORAL STRUGGLES OR CHALLENGES?

I think there are a couple of them. The immediate one is the act of welcome with smiling gestures and waves of hands when you meet people. In my culture, when you meet a person the first time, even if the person is a stranger, once you have extended those acts of gestures through smiling faces or waves of hand, it means you are open to accepting the person within your space, even though the person is a stranger. That's not what I found here. Like somebody later told me, it is not an act of welcome here. It is an act of courtesy. It is not an act of friendship or that you are invited into their own space.

I had an encounter where I approached someone who repeatedly offered a smiling gesture. I approached this person in friendship, extended a handshake, and wanted to engage in a conversation as somebody who has welcomed me into this individual's space, only to be greeted with this confronting question, "Yes! How may I help you? How can I help you?" It is almost like, "Do I know you? What are you doing here? Hey, I don't know you."

So, it posited to be a contradiction from my own culture of what a smiling face and wave of hands mean, as opposed to what I experienced here. That was very serious to me. I had to deal with this for a while. Who is precisely welcoming me into this society? Who is actually open to be my friend and stuff like that? It is the same thing both in the neighborhood, within the church, and other places. So that's really one of them.

Another has to do with the Americans' definite idea of a guest and a stranger. As I have told some of my American friends, in my culture, we do not have a word for a stranger. They were surprised. What we have is a word for a guest, or a visitor, and as a result, there is a disposition to welcome. But in this culture, you will be a stranger if the person has not met or seen you before or may or may not have an idea of where you are coming from. Once you are visiting, they regard you as a stranger. A guest has a place of honor in my culture, so they will not be given a non-welcoming attitude. My cultural people will make you feel at home. They will provide for you and be the ones to make you believe that we are peaceful and will relate with you peacefully. So, they do the job for you as a guest, as a visitor.

Coming over here, what I saw is that I am a stranger, and even the people whom I supposedly should be visiting regarded me as a stranger. As a result, I was given the behavior that I am not trusted. "I don't know you. I don't know what you are capable of." So, it was almost like I have to prove myself before I am treated with a spirit of a guest. I was the one to do all the work, to reach out to the locals. I was the one to prove to them that I am not harmful. I am the one to show them that I am friendly and want to feel at home. That was burdensome, and I had to deal with it here.

It took quite a while to figure out what I am supposed to do, how I am supposed to do it, and whether the American people will understand what I do. If not, I would lose the chance of feeling at home and things like that. These challenges were as big for me as far as intercultural challenges or realities are concerned.

Obviously the more I stay in this country, the more I respect what I saw, what is obtainable here, and what it meant to them. Of course, there are all these other symbols, like exchanging smiles. When friends have known and accepted themselves, the smiles are totally different from the grins you get from a person who is not a friend. One is genuine; the other is politeness. It took me time to understand that the same smile might have different meanings, like "good to see you" or just being polite to a stranger.

About accent and communication, it is frustrating because I came to this country with a strong belief that I have a good command of the English language. Coming from Nigeria, a British colony that adopted

English as the national language, my initial observation is a sense of no communication even though I was speaking English. There were feedbacks that I was not being understood. It is both ways frankly. There have been instances where I didn't understand them either, so there is a break in communication, and at that point, gestures and constant repetitions helped to bridge that gap of communication. It is not a one-way traffic. As much as they have difficulty in understanding me, I also had trouble in understanding them.

This might be less serious, but there was an issue of weather and food. In my country, we have two seasons. It is either dry season or rainy season, but here, we have four. And when you talk about the two different cultural weather situations, there are no comparisons as such. Certain times of the summer season might be like home, but the beauty of my home weather, that is, my part of Nigeria, is that there is no humidity. The hot weather in some of the weeks of the summer season here in the States is very unbearable. If I may be specific, I am referring to some of the summer weeks around the Washington area where I live. It is terrible. The humidity makes it more uncomfortable, and it triggers some allergies. And then during the winter, I encounter snow. I encountered snow for the first time in the United States. Winter season is usually very cold for me. I enjoy it when the snow is white. It is pretty and makes the environment look awesome, but when it becomes slippery and forms ice or there are blizzards, I don't enjoy that part. It was challenging. I know of somebody who returned to Nigeria because he couldn't bear the weather.

About food, I love my African cuisine, and I miss it. I had to retrain myself on how to eat some of the American foods. I can't even tell the names of some of the American cuisine. Some I struggle with because I want to strive to develop the taste, but if I say that it were not a struggle, it would be lying.

I was in awe with how advanced the extent of some of the developments that have been here in the United States, for example, the power supply. In my culture, you can sometimes stay for days, weeks, and even months in some areas without power. Coming to the United States, I can't think of any time there was a loss of power, except in extreme weather situations, and it is usually announced about how long the power outage will last. That, for me, was a situation of the beauty of this society, of this culture.

Things are organized. Everything is allotted its own time, for instance, appointments with doctors, office visitations, and even visiting people at their homes. You are expected to call and make appointments, which is different from my culture and village setting where you just show up.

The differences between the US and Nigerian culture affected my work. I didn't know how to develop friendship with others or how to relate with people in my missionary work as a priest in general. With people seeing me like a stranger at the initial time, you could sense the reluctance of people being willing to receive my ministry. Sometimes it made me ask myself if my staying here was worth it. You could feel it. I couldn't relate well with people at that time because they did not trust me. Inviting me to their homes, which is normal for a priest in a new parish at home, was a challenge.

In fact, there was a big cultural shock. It was so hard that many times I thought of going back to my home country. The shock at that time of assimilation was so imposing that I could not even describe it very well up till today, but all that is gone now. Knowing and understanding certain things I did not know initially have helped me to be relaxed, open and patient to learn, and doing whatever I could to be a part of this great culture without losing my home culture.

WHAT STRATEGIES ARE HELPFUL TO YOU TO EFFECTIVELY ADJUST FROM NIGERIAN CULTURE TO US CULTURE, ESPECIALLY PASTORALLY?

The first thing I think about is the way I was trained in my family from my childhood to adulthood. My upbringing is such that you are constantly reminded and expected to understand that you can still make your future amid many obstacles. You can always work hard to survive. My siblings and I grew up on a farm, and we did not farm with mechanized equipment. We planted our crops with local types of equipment, and a lot of manpower and human energy was needed to operate the various types of equipment. There was always the encouragement that you have all it takes within you to finish the farming, no matter how tedious or big the landmass is. So that family background prepared me psychologically, even socially, without knowing that I would end up in this country. That's where it started. So, coming here as an adult now and facing these challenges I have shared with you, there was an aspect of me that kept informing me that I can make it or that I can meet the challenges. In it is the foundation of all my strategies.

The next is that I told myself that I don't know this society and I need to learn. So, I was open to learning, and because of that openness, I was very willing to ask questions. I still ask questions till today, and I will continue to ask questions because there are many more things I do not understand. In fact, the openness to learning and asking questions without feeling ashamed about it has helped me a lot. Also, by being patient to learn, I was able to endure the challenges until today. I have grown a lot in the knowledge of this environment. I have grown in making a distinction between my culture and this American culture that I live in, and I could find a balance between these two cultures. I still miss my culture, and I believe it is the best. However, there are many great things I have learned about US culture. There are great values that I have seen and love about US culture, but definitely I miss my culture.

COULD YOU PLEASE BRIEFLY DESCRIBE THE IMPORTANT KNOWLEDGE OF US CULTURE THAT A NIGERIAN PRIEST COMING TO MISSION IN THE UNITED STATES SHOULD HAVE PRIOR TO DEPARTURE TO THE UNITED STATES?

This is an important question. It is important to communicate to new missionaries coming here. I think the first thing I would tell the person is that this is different from the culture you are coming from. Within that context of difference, he needs to begin to tell himself that many things that work or that have worked for him in Nigeria may not work for him over here in the United States. He must be open to put his home culture aside and learn his host culture if he wants to be fruitful and relevant in this culture. It might be very difficult, especially if he is an adult who is used to doing particular things in a certain way. He needs to know that there will be challenges about food, weather, accent, modification in language and communication, and use of words. Certain meanings of the words that would ordinarily work in my culture would not work here.

An example is the use of fatness to describe somebody. It is not a compliment in the United States, but in our culture, it is something that we can play with. You can tell it to anybody, and the person will not lose sleep about it. In this culture, it is not something that you can say to somebody. That could constitute verbal abuse. So, the use of expressions and all that, is what I will tell them. This is different. He must be open-minded and ready to face the challenges that an African or Nigerian finds here.

Participant J

4.1.11. What is your general pastoral background, and what was your knowledge of the US culture before missioning in the United States?

I was ordained in the year 2001 and worked in my home diocese as an associate pastor and pastor till I came to the United States. Even though the work of a priest is defined most of the time, the definition of the work is non-definition. Apart from administering the sacraments and pastoral counseling, I feel that the work is about being all good things to all men and women in terms of service. I was a priest in Nigeria for eight years before coming to the United States.

The only experience I had about the United States is from the movies. I also had a professor who studied in the United States and shared some of his experiences when he was in the States. I got the impression that he did not like the United States because of racism, but the country itself is good in terms of cleanliness and patriotism. US culture, as I understood from him, does not tolerate bribery and corruption as it is in Nigeria. My unpreparedness affected me. I had many assumptions when I came here. I thought things would be the same as it is in Nigeria, and there were so many culture shocks.

WHAT ARE THE CROSS-CULTURAL STRUGGLES OR CHALLENGES YOU HAVE EXPERIENCED IN THE UNITED STATES, ESPECIALLY PASTORAL STRUGGLES OR CHALLENGES?

Thank you for giving me this opportunity to share a couple of cross-cultural struggles and challenges I have experienced. In America, there is so much emphasis on individualism. Where I come from, there is more emphasis on the group doing things together or helping one another, community support, collectivism. In America, time is money, and so the expected help from friends and family members do not come as quickly as I saw in Nigeria. I see much difference there. Another is, in Nigeria, there is so much emphasis on the past and traditions, but in America, there is so much emphasis on the future and discoveries for a change.

Nigerians are known to be very verbal in the way they communicate. Americans can also be verbal in the way they communicate, but they tend to interact more with symbolic attitudes, expecting you to understand what they are talking about. Direct discussions, especially about sensitive issues, are rare in America, probably to avoid lawsuits. Do not misunderstand me. In my culture, there is a sense of sensitivity in discussing certain issues, but most of the time we talk directly so people would have a good understanding without misconceptions. Explanations are more common during discussions in Nigerian than in the United States.

Where I come from in Nigeria, we have so much respect for elders, but here in America, there is so much respect for competence. While Nigerians lean toward traditional chieftaincy titles for honor, in America, emphasis is on results or what you can achieve. That's the reason Americans honor those who are known for improving the community or inspiring a change for human development more than they honor those who have lived for many years. In my country, honor is usually given more to the elderly whether they contributed anything to the society or not. The honor is an entitlement simply because of the age of the person, and the young people are expected to take care of the elderly. Given the importance of merit in America, there is an emphasis on working hard to make achievement and competing with others to earn an honor.

In Nigeria, families are so much into saving family members' face. We rarely condemn the bad deeds of family members even when a family member says or does something terrible. We want to save the face of the family and the person, but here in America, people take courage in saying stuff. They don't care very much about protecting the person who does a terrible thing, even if they are a family member. The culture of condemning the bad irrespective of the individual often makes people (Americans) have a feeling of guilt that leads to internal self-control, and it is vital for the Americans.

I would like to say again that symbols have always been a part of communication. Here in the United States, I have experienced some symbols that are similar to those I saw in Nigeria but have different meanings here in the United States. If somebody asks, "How are you doing?" in the United States, they might be referring to politeness or greetings if you are not a friend or a relative, and the individual's question is not an interest in knowing your situation. In Nigeria, it connotes the actual inquiry of the situation of the person who is asked the question. Saying hi to somebody in the States with a particular way of waving your hand could mean "come in" Nigeria and so on.

About verbal communication, it was difficult for me to speak the same way Americans do, and I could not understand everything they said and vice versa. After a while, I understood that I needed to improve my intercultural way of communication for us to work together. I had to put my culture aside to embrace the American way, to communicate both verbally and symbolically. So far, I think there is a significant improvement.

In Nigeria, we did not have a word for strangers. We have words for guests or visitors because of the sense of communalism. When I came to the United States, I felt very lonely because I was a stranger to the community, and nobody would talk to me. In Nigeria, you can meet someone and start talking with them in a friendly way because you are not a stranger, even though the person would not embrace you immediately like a person they knew many years ago. They would see you as a guest they are yet to understand better. So, you will be accommodated as an unknown guest or visitor. People will not run away from you or not relate with you because they have never met you before. You are not a stranger. You are an unknown guest. Americans may say hi or greet an unknown person, but it is not really from their heart. They do it as a social expectation. It is more of acting out a social expectation, but deep inside them, you do not belong because you are a stranger, an unknown and unidentified person. They may laugh and show you friendly teeth, but if you try to be friendly, the smile will disappear.

Also, we address people more formally like Mr., Mrs., or Reverend Father, but here, often they call you by your first name. Given that in Nigeria the priest is always called Reverend Father, part of my first culture shock was when some of my neighbors and parishioners called me by my first name. I am used to it now.

Life is more formal in the United States. You have to keep appointments for everything. If you are visiting, you are expected to indicate your arrival time and the day you will leave, even if the person is your best friend or relative. My first experience about it is when I visited a friend. When I arrived, one of the very first questions to me was when I would be leaving. In my culture, people are happy to have a guest, and you do not start asking them when they will be going. You could even stop around and say hi to a person without a prior appointment. The formality of life here was part of my first struggle. After a while I got used to it.

Here too they separate morals and religion. In Nigeria, it is believed that religion and morality go together. The moral value comes from somewhere. We don't put things in a bracket. We look at things from a holistic point of view (morals and religion).

The social support we get in Nigeria comes from the family, community, and society in general. It is not the same here. Sometimes there is no one to give you support. You have to work hard for it. It is a very individualistic culture. For example, if I needed help at home, most of the time I don't even ask for it. It comes from family and relatives, social friends, and even social groups, but here in the States, you have to seek for the support. In essence, what I am saying is that Americans are very individualistic. Where I come from, we are family-oriented and very communal.

I was also not aware of the idea of feminism or no feminism. We don't talk about it in my culture, but here it is something that people espouse. I mean they work hard at it. Nonetheless, it is good. In my culture, women are not lifted like men, but women do not look at it as wrong. Women have a particular role to play, which does not encourage empowerment, and they play that specific role. It took me a while to get used to it. So, I had to find a way to work with women. Those are part of the struggles and challenges I found when I came to America, and there is much difference between the two cultures.

What strategies are helpful to you to effectively adjust from Nigerian culture to US culture, especially pastorally?

I struggle every day to be effective in the cross-cultural challenges, and I think I am improving. One of the things that helped me to improve is the constant awareness that I have come from a different culture to US culture. That is important because it makes me begin to find ways in which I am supposed to act and even improve so I will be able to relate with my parishioners, fellow priests, and bishops. I also realized that many of the people I am working with had not been exposed to different cultures. So, I have to work out ways to get along with them without complaining. I compliment them too, given their limitations about their knowledge of other cultures. Sometimes I reach out to my parishioners to help me with solutions of the cultural challenges I face. My openness to parishioners and others to learn from them, especially by asking them many questions, has been very beneficial. Allowing them to understand me has also been very important, but above all, I did not give up because I come from a culture where people do not give up. In my culture, I am expected to work hard and succeed.

It is always important for one to be humble and learn in my culture. So, for me to succeed, I have to empty myself to learn about US culture. I ask a lot of questions because one learns by asking questions. When you ask a question and you get an get answer, then you learn. That is how I grew up.

Patience has also been helpful to me. It helps to observe and not be in a hurry to act out. When you are patient and you observe, then invariably those little things will not escape you, but when you are in a hurry, nothing will affect you, and you will learn nothing.

The orientation I got when I arrived also helped me. When I came, I lived with pastors who were exposed to other cultures and had an experience of cross-cultural struggles. I also attended a program about cross-cultural adjustment.

I ask questions to Nigerians and people from other cultures, and their advice remains helpful in my transition. Above all, some of my parishioners were very supportive and appreciative of my gradual improvements. The compliment from the Americans, such as, "Wow! You are doing very much better!" is very encouraging. Americans appreciate people's efforts. My improvements also help me to work harder to improve more. If I make any improvement, I am like "Wow!" And then that gives me the strength to make another improvement. Those strategies have helped me in this journey.

COULD YOU PLEASE BRIEFLY DESCRIBE THE IMPORTANT KNOWLEDGE OF US CULTURE THAT A NIGERIAN PRIEST COMING TO MISSION IN THE UNITED STATES SHOULD HAVE PRIOR TO DEPARTURE TO THE UNITED STATES?

I will recommend humility and patience to learn the new culture. I will ask them to read about US culture. That's very important. I will advise them to talk to those who have been in America. Watch American television stations, if possible. These things will give them an idea of what the culture is all about and expose them to the culture. They should also attend seminars and workshops about different cultures, especially about US culture. They must be participant observers on arrival and then move on from there. Another thing too is the importance of making a distinction between the King's English and American English because we come from Nigeria, where there is British English. For example, when asked the question, "How are you doing?" the British English would recommend, "I am well." Americans would say, "I am good." So, knowing the distinction makes a lot of difference and helps in communicating with people. Certain things in the United States have names that are different in the British English, like boot of a car/trunk of a car. It's the same thing but different words! Or flat/apartment.

The priests need to know that there are ethnicities in the United States. When on duty, an acknowledgment of your client's culture brings trust, and it helps in the ministerial work. Even though the United States is united in many ways, each of the ethnic groups in the United States is unique in how they do their stuff. Generally, the incoming priests must be open to learn the host culture because what one knows is not always the best in another place. That helped me a lot. What I knew before coming to America was best in my culture, but my culture cannot replace the American culture here in the United States.

I will also advise them to never give up in times of frustrations because sometimes we tend to give up when the going becomes very tough. There was a time I felt that way, but then I realized that I am here for good. It is not about me. It is about God's ministry in the United States, and it made me not to give up.

Stereotypes are not good. Open-mindedness is the key to learning a new culture. With stereotypes, you become myopic and gain nothing. Putting any stereotype about the United States aside is very important if one wants to learn US culture. They need to be aware that when two cultures meet, there is always a tendency for a culture clash, and they must get ready for those moments and how to manipulate the moments and move on. At those moments, priority has to be given to US culture because it is the host culture and the priest is expected to minister to people in a way that will make sense to them.

They need to know that here in America, work ethic is essential. So, to survive as a priest in the US church, it is imperative for the priest to be time conscious. In Africa, people do not care about time, but here, time is very important. That's why people make appointments and expect you to be there at that time. In Africa, people do not care, and we call it "African time." By African time, I mean that in Africa we are considerate about time and understand ourselves when it comes to that. In America, when people give you an appointment, they expect you to be there for that appointment. If not, the next time they will not show up. So. time consciousness is critical in America. These are the few things a person coming to the United States needs to know. They are not expected to be perfect, but then they must strive to integrate themselves into the culture and be able to relate better with other people and influence the peoples' lives positively.

Participant K

4.1.12. What is your general pastoral background, and what was your knowledge of the US culture before missioning in the United States?

After my ordination, I worked in my diocese for only two years and was sent to another diocese in a different tribe within Nigeria. The tribe speaks a different language, but their culture is not completely different from my tribe's. I enjoyed working in the area and was there for ten years. I went back to my home diocese, and after three years, I was sent to the United States. And here I am. The priestly work in Nigeria is easier than here in the United States. I was doing everything expected from a priest, from administering the sacraments to being part of the people's problems and joys.

I knew nothing about US culture before I came to the States. Upon my arrival, I felt like somebody in a different world. I was confused most of the time. I had zero experience about US culture before my arrival even though I was excited when I was told that I would be going to the United States.

WHAT ARE THE CROSS-CULTURAL STRUGGLES OR CHALLENGES YOU HAVE EXPERIENCED IN THE UNITED STATES, ESPECIALLY PASTORAL STRUGGLES OR CHALLENGES?

In the Nigerian culture, we were taught to be respectful to the elders. We were encouraged to greet our elders, teachers, and community and civic leaders and do it with the use of a prefix. Upon arrival, it was a shock to me when I ran into a group of younger folks and they would look at me and walk away, call me by my first name, or say hi if they wanted to be polite. At first, I thought that the kids needed training about greeting the elders. It wasn't long I came to understand that it was just the culture, and kids even call some people who are about the ages of their parents and grandparents by their first names. I struggled with it, but later I became ok with it.

Another challenge is that in Nigeria couples tend to stay together in marriage longer and divorce is rare because it will bring shame to the families. Divorce is avoided at all costs in Nigeria. Here in the United States, it is nothing, and as a priest, I couldn't understand it. You might see a kid on a Sunday school this week, and he is not there the other week because he is with one of the other parents who live afar. It gave me a feeling that the family dynamics in the States seem to be loose. When I studied it more, I found that the issue of divorce and separation are normal and usual in the US culture. Since then I have learned not to ask why people say that they are brothers and sisters but do not have the same last name.

Now let me talk about people's reaction and misunderstanding of my English because it was a big issue for me when I first arrived. I had a good understanding and writing of English before I came to the United States. Now coming from a culture where nobody has trouble understanding my English, upon arrival to the United States, I was faced with a communication problem. What I thought was a perfect English, that is, the British English, was welcomed with, "Sorry, say it again" and "Sorry, I can't understand you," all followed by "You have an accent." The reality is that I speak differently compared with a typical American, but it never occurred to me that my pronunciations are different and hard to understand.

From talking about the accent, I might use this opportunity to dive into the American symbolic way of communication and their meanings. Some of the symbols are the same as we have in Nigeria but have different meanings. For example, there is the waving of hands. Here in the United States, sometimes they wave their hands as if they are saying "come," but they meant to say "hello" or "bye." That was confusing because in Nigeria that style of waving hands symbolizes "good to see you."

In Nigeria, the idea of eating out every time is looked at as a taboo. A responsible man eats at home. I was trained in the seminary to be a responsible man. So, I never ate in a restaurant until I came to the States. When I got used to it, ordering from the presented menu became another challenge. Most of the time I could not see foods that are familiar to me, and when I look at some, such as rice, the meals are prepared differently from how they are prepared in Nigeria. The spices used to cook them are not the same, and they taste differently. For instance, some rice is made with butter and sugar. Back home we prepare our rice with hot spices. Also, back home, chicken is usually tough, strong, and delicious, and it has a pleasant smell. Here, the chicken meats are as soft as bread, and I don't like it.

It surprised me when people here say that they have had their fill and quit eating and then turn around and start eating dessert. In Nigeria, if you are full after eating, you would not eat another thing, and moreover, we do not know about desserts after a meal.

Weather is another shock. In Nigeria, we have a hot or warm season as well as wet or dry seasons, but here in America, they have four seasons, and the winter gave me the biggest problem, especially when everything outside is frozen. I will never forget my first winter here. Trying to operate in the extreme cold was a challenge.

I find working with women a little troubling because in Nigeria women do not challenge the authorities of the men, but here in the United States, women do not care. They question what you say, they have their opinions, and they can express it very well. They know they have the right and always love to exercise it. I think women in the States are compelling. Feminism is extreme and a force to recognize.

WHAT STRATEGIES ARE HELPFUL TO YOU TO EFFECTIVELY ADJUST FROM NIGERIAN CULTURE TO US CULTURE, ESPECIALLY PASTORALLY?

At first, I had to forget about the prefix before my name and relate with the people just as they would associate with themselves. I humbled myself to learn what works here in the United States and forget the unnecessary honors that are given to priests in Nigeria. I began to learn how the Americans spoke and discovered that when I make short and simple sentences, they understand me better. Sometimes I feel like my English sounds like an informative way of speaking English, but it works. Keeping it short and simple leads to better communication.

I also understood the American individualistic lifestyle. They love their space. Whatever they planned to do for the day is very important to them and taking their time without prior information is not appreciated. I constantly remind myself that I am in a different culture and I am here to stay, so I must learn their ways and recognize when I am with a fellow Nigerian or American.

I had to acquaint myself to be less severe with my own opinions and not take things personally because I am in a different culture and passing through a transcultural experience. It needs putting aside what you know before and learning the new lifestyle. I think the understanding that America is a busy culture where people work hard and are always on the go helped me to understand the importance of eating out. I hardly cook at home anymore. The work ethics in the country have now made me start eating out more and have more time for other important things I need to do pastorally and socially.

About the menu, giving every kind of American dish a chance to see what I may like has helped me to get used to some of the American food. I now eat hot dogs and hamburgers, which I would never try when I initially came here. Nonetheless I always search for restaurants with foods that are similar to African cuisine and food buffets. I particularly like Asian food buffets, because there are a lot of options that taste African and I can sample the food and have a good meal. Once in a while, I drive to the city to eat at the African restaurant or make the time to buy the African spices and cook my food.

One of the major things that helped me is not being afraid to ask questions and reading about US culture because my people say *"onye ajuju adi efu uzo"* (one who asks for directions never misses his destination), and that is true. The more I ask questions, the more people help me to know what to do to adjust to US culture, and it has worked.

COULD YOU PLEASE BRIEFLY DESCRIBE THE IMPORTANT KNOWLEDGE OF US CULTURE THAT A NIGERIAN PRIEST COMING TO MISSION IN THE UNITED STATES SHOULD HAVE PRIOR TO DEPARTURE TO THE UNITED STATES?

I will seriously encourage incoming priests to learn about US culture, such as their way of life, watch American movies, and stuff like that. I would like them to get introduced to the American food while they are still in Nigeria. That will be helpful for them so they will not be shocked when they come here and do not find the African menus in the American restaurants. They should be told the truth because I think that sometimes some of the people coming to the United States do not know the reality of the situation in America. I would like the incoming priests to know that in America, they would be expected to do things by themselves. You know, in Nigeria, the priest is surrounded with all kinds of help—house help and everything—but here in America, those kinds of aids are not always available. Priests take care of their private duties, and they need to know how to do things by themselves.

I will also explain to them that Americans are principled and cannot be taken for granted in their beliefs and philosophies of life. I will tell them about the difference between the King's English and American English. It is not that the King's English is not ok, but in America, you speak the American English. It is about communication. Even if you speak the King's English and believe it is a refined English, if people do not understand you, it is useless.

I will advise them to watch the US TV stations and then practice how people speak and get familiarized with the US accent. They should know about the US weather because when it is cold, it could be freezing sometimes.

They should know the importance of freedom and its effects among Americans. They should know the great power of women in the United States. In Nigeria, men make all the decisions, but here in America, women have equal rights with men, and sometimes the women even have more rights than men.

The incoming priests must be humble to learn and courageous to ask questions to learn. They need to know that once one steps out of his culture to another, there would be a culture shock. They have to prepare for the culture shock, no two ways about it. The better they prepare themselves, the lesser the shock. My pastor helped me a lot with my problems with assimilation, and I would always remain grateful to him. So, the incoming priests must be ready to learn from the experienced pastors they are assisting and learn from them.

May I finish by saying that American parishioners also need to be oriented about globalization and intercultural relations to work better with the foreign priest.

Participant L

4.1.13. What is your general pastoral background, and what was your knowledge of US culture before missioning in the United States?

I was ordained in 1994. I worked as an assistant parish priest and parish priest in my diocese in Nigeria for twelve years and came to the United States. I have never been to any other country. The United States is the only country I have lived in apart from Nigeria. As an assistant parish priest in Nigeria, I was just doing whatever the parish priest asked me to do in the ministry. I learned how to manage a parish from him. I became a parish priest in 1998 and came to the States in 2006.

I was never aware that I would ever come to the United States and never cared very much about the US culture. So, I did not know much about the United States before I came to the country. I watched some US movies at home for fun. I wish I had watched them with more attention to learn the culture, even though, given what I know now, many of the movies do not really represent the real America.

What are the cross-cultural struggles or challenges you have experienced in the United States, especially pastoral struggles or challenges?

I moved from a place to another where I visually did not know anybody. They are two different worlds for me. Moving aware from family—my parents and my siblings—the friends I went to school with, my parishioners, and an environment where I was very comfortable to another climate was harsh. In Nigeria, I could drive to friends and familiar places. I could do things very conveniently because I knew the culture. Leaving those things behind and getting into an airplane and flying thousands of miles away to a place I had not been before and begin to adjust to a new way of lifestyle was never easy. What made it unique was not that I have not seen people before. I have seen people—blacks, white, short, tall, or blond. I have seen some of them physically and many in the movies but coming over here to live a different lifestyle was different. I came to where I ultimately did not know anybody. The culture was entirely foreign to me. Alighting from the airplane, I had people who came and picked me up and then started to show me things.

Everything they were telling me was like a dream. I came during the winter season. I had never experienced winter before. The closest cold weather I knew was *hamartan*, and it was usually probably about sixty-five or seventy degrees. Coming to the United States in wintertime, especially in February, was difficult. It was freezing. The weather was so cold that I was like, "Do people live here?" So, the struggle about the weather was severe.

My friends took me out to dinner at a restaurant, a Chinese buffet. They said it was all you can eat. I was shocked because I never had seen a restaurant where a person could eat as much as he or she could, and everyone still paid the same price regardless of the content or amount of food one eats.

When my friends left, I had nobody to talk to. I began to experience real loneliness. I started to ask myself, "What did I get myself into?" So, moving from where I had people around me all the time to where I didn't have anybody, except those people who came to get me at the airport, was an experience I would never forget. The same people who picked me up at the airport took me to the school, where I had admission for studies, and I found out that it was difficult for me to adjust in the class or even learn what they were saying in the classroom. I wouldn't say that English language was the problem because, in Nigeria, English is the official language, though a second language after the tribal languages, but nobody graduates from a college like I did without having a command of the English grammar. Instead the American version of English was the problem. The British colonized Nigeria, so our Nigerian English leans toward the British accent. Coming to the American classroom two days after my arrival to listen to a professor at the school and even the students who participated was quite intimidating, but the professors were accommodating with one-on-one discussions with students in their offices for assistance, and it helped me very much.

I was working and going to school. In the church environment, it was not that easy too. I had somebody helping me with the American accent, but it still was not very easy because he had his program. And after a few minutes with me, he would be on his own and vice versa. So, loneliness was a big issue, apart from the accent problem. The loneliness is caused more by the missing of my family members and the American individualistic style of life. Back home we interact more, and people do not come to you asking for anything or vice versa because everybody looks out for the other and offers help before it is requested. But here, people need their space. Space is very important to people here. They want that space, and it was a struggle for me. It is an individualistic society. They are on their own. What counts for them is the individual, but back home, the emphasis is on the entire group, for example, family, and that's how I was born and raised.

Back home, people do not call me by my first name. They say Father. They use a prefix, and likewise, we do not address the older adults by their first name. You either use their children's name to address them such as Jessica's or Emmanuel's dad, but here, people can call you by your first name, no matter the age difference. I was surprised when some kids called me by my first name, and I felt like, "Do they not know about the usual formal respect? Do they not know that I am much older than them?"

I also struggled with what I call relationship differential because in the US culture feminism and women's right have asserted themselves and some women feminists love to control men in positions of leadership. Coming from Nigeria, you will see it immediately. One has to adjust to it, or he may get into trouble within a short space of time. When I first arrived, someone asked me, "Do you have a problem with women?" I didn't know where that question was coming from. I said, "In what regard, please?"

She said, "In Africa, men do not treat women nicely, but here in America, women are treated very well, and they are recognized for who they are."

Someone asked me that question. I asked her to elaborate more, and she told me that here in America, men would wait on women, but in Africa, given what they have heard or seen in the movies, women are treated like slaves. She even said that men are like kings to women and it is not like that in the United States.

Well, I did not know her intention or motives, but I disagreed with her because it was not very right. We have shared roles back home. Each gender have their functions. We have a division of labor. Actually, in cases where a woman is maltreated or abused, some people would speak up for her, even from family members. So, I did not know what this particular woman was talking about. However, that's the way many of these feminists see it from here. I completely disagree with her statements. Probably the reason she asked me that question was to find how I would work and interact with women and if I have the kind of mentality she had in mind about Africa and African women. I used that opportunity to tell her that Africa is a continent and not a country and it would be dangerous to generalize. When they say Africa, they talk about it as if Africa is a village. Africa is not a village.

WHAT STRATEGIES ARE HELPFUL TO YOU TO EFFECTIVELY ADJUST FROM NIGERIAN CULTURE TO US CULTURE, ESPECIALLY PASTORALLY?

The first things that come to my mind are time and patience because when you get into an environment that is not your familiar environment, you would need time and patience to acclimatize in that environment. You have to give yourself time to study and observe, talk less, and see what the setting is all about and what you also are going to learn from it. When I found myself in this new environment and went through some struggles, it became evident to me that I must stoop low and be a learner if I want to be a part of the society. With time and patience, I gave myself enough opportunity to face my immediate challenges and learn. I needed to know how they do things and why they do it the way they do it. Culture is about the people and who they are within their environment. If you do not step aside to have a right judgment of the culture, to question yourself on why they do things the way they do it, you may not be able to know much about the culture. You would follow the current and move in whatever direction without a single knowledge. So, I stepped aside and became a learner. I gave myself time and patience to learn my new environment and how or why they do what they do.

Another thing that helped me is better relationship and interactions with the priest I lived with in the same rectory. I go to him when I have questions, and he would guide and tell me what to do, where to go, what to buy, how to use things, and how to even drive, irrespective of the book you study to get your driving license. The rush hours make people ignore the laws in the book, and you have to be careful if you are on the road about that time. I used to drive in Nigeria. However, when I came over here, adjusting to the driving rules and the road signs - everything was all new, and I had to learn.

Now asking questions is one key factor in helping me to adjust, and I do very well with asking questions because when you do so, you open up conversations, and people can help you. Asking questions opened the way for me to have a better understanding of my new environment, people, and space.

I read books and newspapers, and I listened to the news. I watched the television, especially the local channels. They were part of the ways I got some important information about the culture. I did not only depend on people, but I also depended on print and media for my source of information about the people and their culture.

I handle food and weather a lot better now, but I still struggle, especially with food. My body has not adjusted to the American cuisine. I am just managing because if I don't eat, I will be hungry and starve, and it is not healthy. I am beginning to try the American foods. Some of them are really good, and others, such as cold food, bloody steak, and salad, are difficult for me to eat. I don't like raw food. I can handle some of the warm and spicy American food because back home we eat a lot of spicy stuff. I am handling those much better.

Could you please briefly describe the important knowledge of US culture that a Nigerian priest coming to mission in the United States should have prior to departure to the United States?

First of all, it depends on what part of the United States an incoming priest will be going. If the person is going to a place that is usually very cold, I will tell the person to get good winter jackets. I will also tell the person that there are apparently different ways American people handle issues. There is a standard procedure for doing things in this country. For example, back home, if you are the parish priest, you have control over a lot of things, but when you come over here, they already have their structure about how they do things. It is what I will call "standard operating procedure." They have a structure.

In a church setting, they have business managers and employees, and each person has a job description of what they do under the pastor's supervision. So, I will tell the person, when you come over, you have to give yourself one year of listening, learning the culture, and studying your environment. All he has to do for the first year is to keep quiet and do what he is assigned to do. Let them show him how to do it.

It is like an orientation. You have to be patient for one year, no matter what and who you were in Nigeria before you took off. You are coming into a new environment, so you have to be patient. You have to give yourself time to study your new environment. You have to be a learner. Open your mind, ears, and eyes so you can adjust well in your new environment. I do not think that there is any single formula that you give to somebody, except a general prior knowledge of the culture as a stepping-stone. Upon arrival, his new community or region where he will work will determine other necessary things to learn. Each environment is different. Wherever you go, people do things differently, and I will advise that where you are going is different and they have their structure of doing things. For me, there is not one specific thing, but a time frame of learning before working is important, and I emphasize not less than one year.

If you are fortunate to find yourself under a good role model, mentor, supervisor, or priest who can teach you, learn from him. With that, the incoming priest will get himself grounded and gradually work himself into the system.

I will not advocate that a person carries a full mentality of the Nigerian culture he knows and begins to figure out the ones to change after arrival. No! He needs to come with an open heart and mind. He is coming to learn. There might be some good things from him that could help to make his new community great, but the people can only learn it if you first know their culture and respect it very well. It takes time. Keep your home mentality aside and learn first. People here do not like impositions of any type. Where there is a structure already, people don't like some other people to come over and impose things on them. They would like to see your interest in them first, and gradually they will see some good qualities you have brought with you or the gifts you are bringing, but it is something that will take time for you to bring out.

So, whether you are a monsignor back home or an archpriest, whatever it is, when coming over, you must be open and flexible. The flexibility of mind will help you to adjust to your new environments.

When I came here, I did not have postarrival orientation. I was fortunate to have a good priest who was a mentor to me, and frankly I really cherished the way he went about it because some of these programs you are talking about (postarrival, orientations, summits, or conferences) are more like them giving you information on what you have to do and probably not listening to you. They feel that this is something you should know, which is fine, but somebody who has been a priest in Nigeria for some years before coming over here is not a kid. He is an adult, and adults don't learn things very quickly because it is difficult for them to change. Adults do not change very easily.

The people who give those programs should make it a learning process for themselves as well and learn where these people are coming from, what they are bringing, what needs to be changed, and what might be useful. So, make it an adult dialogue and not one-sided or a one way of doing things.

Finally, what people here do not do very well is they are not patient with other people. What made America great are ideas from the different countries that come to the United States and settle here. Being what it is, the home of people from different nations and cultures, there must always be new things to learn and share. Americans need to be patient with the new priest to adapt and see if there might be a great thing he could add to the culture. That's the advice I have.

4.2.1. INTERPRETATION OF DATA

The following are the key phrases, words, or sentences in the interviews. The phrases, words, and sentences are coded into themes. The themes are written and described after identifying and coding the key phrases, words, and sentences from the participants. The themes are strictly numbered during the description. So, each theme represents a category of some similar ideas that emerged in the form of phrases, words, or sentences. The first aspect of the key phrases, words, and sentences from the participants were extracted from the second and third questions that referred to the participants' challenges or struggles and the important knowledge of US culture that a Nigerian priest coming to mission in the United States should have prior to departure to the United States. The second aspect of the key phrases, words, and sentences from the participants were extracted from the third question that referred to adjustment strategies. The coding of the key phrases, words, and sentences from the participants are presented as "Par," which stands for participant. Alphabets are used to represent the participants' names to ensure confidentiality.

4.2.2. KEY THEMES AND PHRASES THAT EMERGED AS THE PRIESTS' CHALLENGES

1) Absence of major similarities	1) A vacuum between the known culture and the new host culture was a difficult thing	1) Culture shock
2) Culture shock/loner		
3) Lack of knowledge of the cultural norms		
4) Change from my culture was hard		
5) Difficult to put my culture aside		
6) I felt like a kid learning to walk		
7) Unprepared		
8) Like one without cultural identity		
9) It's like throwing a kid into a pool to swim very well		
10) Didn't know how to connect with American people		
11) Didn't know how to relate with Americans		
12) Didn't know how to be part of the society		

1) Challenged by the US accent
2) Could not understand me and I could not understand them
3) Misinterpreting my accent as not knowing English
4) Cannot understand my English
5) Symbolic gestures
6) Nonverbal behaviors
7) Symbolic meanings
8) Ignorance of other communication skills
9) Effective communication
10) Communication problem

2) Communication is more than words. It could also be symbolic. Thus, a problem of accent and understanding of symbols

Communication: Accent and symbols

1) The time allocated for the training was not enough
2) Did not have the postarrival training
3) No clue about the United States from friends or other sources
4) Upset about not having a predeparture training and had problems with adjustment
5) My diocese did not have enough fund for longer training

3) A majority of the participants did not have the postarrival training. Those who had the training complained that the program was short and not deep enough for proper adjustment

3) Short or no postarrival orientation

5) The diocese needed the service of priests as soon as possible for assignments

6) If I had a predeparture training, the program would have helped me to grasp the postarrival training within the short time

7) Predeparture training could have helped as a stepping-stone to grasp the postarrival training within the short time

8) All the international priests were having the program together, and so there was no time for personal assistance

9) No time for one-on-one discussions to know individual problems and the person's better way of adjusting

10) I had no predeparture training

1) Cultural discontinuity and no replacement

2) Discontinuity from a known culture

3) Felt like an outcast

4) Lack of knowledge of their new culture subjected them to a feeling of cultural discontinuity without replacement

4) Discontinuity from a known culture without replacement

4) Not knowing what to
   do or not to do
5) Stress of how to
   be part of my new
   society
6) Like one who woke
   up and saw myself
   in the middle of an
   ocean
7) Using their cultural
   standard to judge me

1) Loss of self-esteem
2) A feeling of useless
3) Helplessness
4) Mistakes/fear

5) Inability to adjust
   immediately and
   be a part of the
   society caused
   helplessness and loss
   of self-esteem

5) Helplessness and loss
   of self-esteem

5) Ignorance/mistakes
6) Afraid and confused
7) Afraid of mistakes

1) Confusion
2) Angry
3) Irritating
4) Complex lifestyle
5) Complexities
6) Stress
7) Complexities/stress
8) Mental torture
9) Agitated
10) Irritability

6) Inability to master
   the norms; what
   to do and what
   not to do lead to
   constant fear of
   mistakes, confusions,
   frustrations, and
   stress

6) Complexities,
   confusions,
   frustration, and stress

1) Feeling unaccepted

2) Feeling unappreciated

3) Felt being disliked

4) Initial thought of being lynched

5) Didn't see many of the things I thought

6) Didn't know that discrimination is this high

7) Unaware that Catholicism is still strong and lively here

8) Unaware that the core values of the church are still respected here

9) Was thinking of a very liberal Catholicism

7) Personal stereotypes before being in the States made many of them to misjudge things and situations initially

7) Personal stereotypes

---

1) At home, women have their roles

3) High level of feminism

4) Feminism is strong

5) Strong power of women

6) Women are more powerful than men here in the Unites States

7) Could easily be in jail if not careful with women; very powerful

8) Overwhelmed by the extent of the power of women and the accommodation of feminism in US culture

8) Power of women and feminism

1) Unaware of the different ethnicities	9) No idea of the many other microcultures in the United States and did not know what to do when solely with a particular ethnic group	9) Ignorance of microethnicities within United States
2) Microcultures in the United States		
3) Thought that there is only one US culture		
4) Some Americans are sometimes guided by their microcultures		
5) Would have loved to know about the different ethnic cultures and how to relate with them		
6) Thought the African American culture would be close to mine		
1) US lifestyle is very structured	10) US culture has a more structured lifestyle, work ethics, and formality than the life they knew in Nigeria	10) Very formal life, use of time, and strong work ethics
2) Very formal life		
3) Very high level of formality and decency		
4) Expected ways of greetings		
5) Following plans strictly		
6) Life moves too fast for me		
7) Fast lifestyle		
8) Sensitive about use of time		

1) Racial discrimination
2) Irritated by treatment of minority groups, including me
3) Microaggression
4) Misinterpretation and misjudgment because of cultural difference
5) Poverty and classism in are used to define people
6) Legality of different racist groups

11) Higher level of racism, marginalization, and unequal treatment was surprising

11) Racism/ microaggression

1) Did not like how they put down my culture
2) Cultural superiority
3) For them, "made in America" is always the best, even human beings
4) Demeaning of my cultural values
5) Being underestimated
6) Seen as unfit for United States

12) Offended by the degradation of their native culture

12) Unhappy with the demeaning of their home culture

1) Excessive collaborative leadership
2) At home, the priest is in charge of everything
3) The priest makes almost all the decisions

13) Difficulty in sharing major decisions with the laity, especially women

13) Exercising leadership

4) The women in my parish staff could be difficult to work with

5) Parish council easily goes with the priest's idea in Nigeria

6) Lack of computer literacy

1) Technological transformation	14) Computer illiteracy was a big challenge because of lack of computer literacy and the frequent use of computer for the priestly work in the United States	14) Computer technology
2) Never used computer before I came		
3) Back home, the work is more pastoral like visiting and helping those in need		
4) Not knowing how to use computer		
5) Wished I knew how to use computer		

1) US individualistic life	15) Each person minds their own business and it is the norm to avoid encroaching on another's space	15) Individualistic society
2) No interpersonal relations with people		
4) Each person minds their own business		
5) It is a norm to avoid encroaching on another's apace, uninvited		
6) Lack of interpersonal relationships		
7) Lack of strong extended family system		

8) Doesn't need others to be part of their private business

9) Respect of others' freedom and privacy is an expectation

1) Cold climate

2) Sometimes I felt like I am wearing my entire wardrobe to be warm

3) I was raised and lived in a warm climate

4) I hate the winter season

5) Feeding problem

6) Food and climate problem

7) I love my African cuisine

8) I preferred the restaurants with a food buffet

9) Sometimes the drive is far to an African restaurant

10) We like hot, spicy food

11) Some similar food like rice but prepared in a different way and taste different

16) They came from a country where most of the cuisine and the climate is very different from their experiences

16) Climate and food problem

1) Nigerians have greater honor for the elderly; Americans have greater honor for achievements and inventions
2) Talking to elders like age-mates
3) Calling elders by their first names
4) Calling elders without a prefix that indicates respect
5) Americans have more regards for achievements
6) Greater respect for inventors

17) In Nigeria, respect for the elders has a deep cultural value. In the United States, elders are respected too, but more respect is attached to achievement and inventions

17) Respect for tradition versus respect for achievement

1) Bitterness of some people toward Catholic clergies (because of sexual scandals)
2) Lower regards for priests
3) Priests are respected more in Nigeria
4) Some people in the United States hate Catholic priests

18) The respect for priests in Nigeria is greater than it is in the United States, probably because of the people's reaction against some priests for sexual scandal

18) Bitterness against priests because of the past sexual scandal

1) Pastoral life includes being part of family events like graduation ceremonies

2) In Nigeria, participation in people's family events is not considered pastoral

3) Parishioners expect you to be present at their children's events like ball games

4) Being to family celebrations is pastoral

5) 1 didn't know that being in family celebrations was part of a pastoral work

19) The priest in the United States is expected to be part of the activities of his parishioners outside the church activities most of the time

19) Pastoral life includes being part of family events

4.2.3. KEY THEMES AND PHRASES THAT EMERGED AS SUCCESSFUL STRATEGIES

1) Reflection

2) Reflect about people's expectations from me

3) Thinking always to master the positive and negative aspects of the culture

4) Appreciation of my own culture implies their own appreciation of their own culture

1) Motivated by a reflection that just as they expected foreigners in Nigeria to adjust to the Nigerian culture, the same would apply to them here in the U.S.

1) Reflection

5) Americans would expect foreigners to be part of their host culture

6) How could I fit in?

7) I looked inward to find out where I have been imposing my own culture in a foreign land

8) Where have I have not been doing well in respecting the host culture?

1) Not afraid to ask questions	2) Tried to socialize with the Americans and others, and not afraid to ask questions	2) Socializing and asking questions
2) Solicitation of knowledge		
3) Socialization/asking questions		
4) Socialization		
5) Felt free to ask questions		
6) Impossible without socialization and asking questions		
7) I wasn't shy to ask questions		
8) I was socializing with the Americans and other people who have lived in the States for a long time		

9) Friends with other Africans in the States to ask questions and learn

1) Practicing how Americans speak their English
2) Listen to American accents via the social media
3) My British English spoken with my tribal accent is different from the US accent
4) Acknowledge the difference between the American and British accents
5) Working on accent reduction
6) Accent-reduction classes
7) I was speaking English with my tribe's accent and so had to tell myself the truth about it and started making efforts to change like mimicking
8) Accent reduction is a necessity for adaptation to the new culture

3) Observe and practice how Americans speak as well as their words for certain things

3) Communication: Accent reduction

9) Started to observe how Americans pronounce their words and mimic them
10) Learning US symbols
11) Knowledge of symbols
12) Learn the US words for certain things that are named differently in the King's English
13) Mastering American symbols and meanings
14) Learning US symbolic expressions
15) Verbal and nonverbal expressions
16) Listen to American accents via social media

1) Humble and open to accept personal inadequacies
2) Humility and openness helped me to learn the new cultural values
3) Openness to diversity
4) Humility
5) Humility and openness
6) Open-minded

4) Humility and openness to accept personal inadequacies and loosen up to embrace the new culture

4) Humility and openness

7) Open-minded,
   patient, and humble
8) Humble and
   open-minded
9) Willingness to
   embrace the culture
10) Accepting my
    inadequacies, I had
    to be a child and
    open to embrace

1) Developing a strong
   mindset
2) Strong mindset
   to eliminate my
   mistakes
3) Mindset to eliminate
   unacceptable
   attitudes
4) Mindset for
   adjustment
5) Mindset to quicken
   adaptation
6) Mindset and focused
7) Interest to serve leads
   to the mindset to
   learn

5) Developed a strong
   mindset towards
   reducing mistakes,
   learn, and adjust

5) Having a mindset

1) Basic computer
   knowledge
   instructions
2) Took computer
   classes
3) Computer technology
   class
4) Hired a tutor for
   computer literacy

6) Learned computer
   literacy in different
   ways: taking a class,
   private tutorial, use of
   instructors' manual

6) Computer technology

5) Bought a tutorial computer book and started learning and practicing

6) Computer instructor's manuals

1) Appreciation of collaborative leadership	7) Experiencing the results that emerge from collaborative leadership made them love it	7) Learning collaborative leadership
2) Practicing consultation leadership		
3) US administrative style is good		
4) More is achieved through a division of labor		
5) Regular meetings with other staff members are very helpful		
6) Contribution of ideas serves the parish better		
7) Seek the opinion of everyone who might have a better idea irrespective of their age, gender, or sexual orientation		
1) An experienced pastor knows more about the locals and the local environment and how to navigate within the area	8) Those of them who had the opportunity to assist some experienced priests learned more from them	8) Living with experienced priests

2) Living with an experienced priest

3) My pastor understands cross-cultural difficulties

4) He was willing to help me with cross-cultural adjustment

5) I was fortunate to have a good priest who was a mentor to me

6) I cherished the way he went about it because the program I attended is more like them giving you information

7) With his knowledge and experiences, he knows all it takes to help a foreign priest

1) Patience and courage

2) Humility, patience, and observation

3) Observe first before doing

4) Faith, patience, and courage

5) Patient and undeterred by negative labels on me

6) Courage to put my own culture aside

7) Patient to be a participant observer

9) Patient to be a participant observer and the courage to put home culture aside in order to accommodate the host culture

9) Patience and courage

8) Took me courage and patience

9) Patient and courage during my period of culture shock

10) Patient and courage for "personal cultural exorcism"

1) Mental toughness for the complexities

2) When the going gets tough, the tough gets going

3) Desperate to learn

4) Determination to learn

5) Hustling to know the language and culture

6) Decided to be resilient

7) Ignored useless criticisms

8) Ignored negative attitudes of some people

10) The belief that determination is the key to success made many of them to persevere and learn the new culture, amidst their challenges

10) Determination

1) Missiology class in the seminary at home

2) Missiology class about being conscious of cultural differences

4) Learned valuing the host culture in a missiology class

11) The very few who took a missiology class while in the seminary in Nigeria knew some basic things to do when in a foreign culture

11) Missiology class in the seminary

5) The [missiology] class helped me in some ways to manage my cultural struggles

6) Aware of a possibility of a cultural clash when two separate cultures meet [from the class]

7) Aware that I am not going to change the people's culture [from the class]

8) Aware that I had to find a way to blend [from the class]

9) The class was very instrumental in my adaptation to US culture

10) The class reminded me the importance of being mentally, physically, and socially resilient when challenged by cultural differences

1) Readings, especially the US history and geography

2) Getting knowledge of US culture by reading and watching the TV

3) Read about the US

4) Watch the television

5) Learn via other social media

12) Readings, watching televisions helped most of them to know the U.S. culture

12) Readings, watching television, and using disc devices for learning

6) Readings, observations, and television

7) I read a lot about United States

8) Use of book and other sources . . . such as CDs and DVDs about US culture and lifestyle helped me

1) I was happy to get emotional and psychological support

2) Open to certain people I trusted for emotional support

3) In times of stress and confusion, friends accorded me emotional support

4) I have a friend I go to for advice whenever I am stressed out because of the adjustment problems

5) Some of my parishioners were always available to give me support and advice

6) Emotional support from some Americans motivated

7) Appreciation of my hard work by some Americans

13) Got emotional support and advice from the people they trusted and befriended

13) Friendship and soliciting advice for emotional support

1) The winter was more than I expected, and I shared the problem with friends who's been here for a long time	14) Learned from their friends about checking the weather through the weather channels and cell phones, and how to dress according to the situation of the weather	14) Adjusting to the climatic problems
2) Bought winter dresses and additional heaters for my room, as friends advised		
3) Taught to dress for the cold weather by friends		
4) Advised on how to drive on the icy and snowy roads		
5) Had to learn about the US weather and how and it changes		
6) Read about the US climatic changes especially here in Chicago		
7) Checking the weather through the weather channels and cell phones before going out		
1) Cooking my food and going to the buffet	15) Cooking African food, and food buffets for the sake of appropriate choices	15) Food
2) Trying the American cuisine and eventually started liking some of them		
3) Buying African food items and spices from African stores and cooking them		

4) Food buffet restaurants where I could carefully choose a kind of food I would enjoy
5) Making a distant drive to an African restaurant, though not very often

1) Listening more and talking less were beneficial	16) Listening more and talking less were essential to learn the new culture and avoid the implementation of the home culture.	16) Listen more and talk less
2) Had to know what is and is not culturally appropriate to say		
3) Being a participant observer and conscious of the common norms		
4) Interested in learning than in talking about my feelings		
5) Took the position of a college freshman listening and learning		
6) Put my culture aside and listen to learn		
7) More interested in observing and learning		

1) Postarrival training helped with relationship about inclusion

2) The rule of law in the United States about the importance of equality and freedom of expression

3) The postarrival cross-cultural training helped me in many ways

4) The training was helpful in the areas of accent reduction

5) Studied the reactions of Americans about inclusion in US culture

6) The training helped to know what is expected from priests in the United States

7) It was a key to understand how to navigate in the society

8) The program helped me to understand that United States has her own cultural richness

9) It helped me to know how certain things work or function in the United States

17) Post-arrival training was a key to their understanding of how to navigate in the society, how things work in the United States, realize that U.S. has her own cultural richness, and work on accent reduction

17) Postarrival cross-cultural training

10) Very helpful but it would have made more impact if one had a predeparture training

1) Accept feminism as part of US culture

2) Advice by some experienced priests about inclusion

3) Careful with some strong women or I might be in trouble

4) Advice by some Africans who have lived in the United States for a long time about equality and freedom

5) Importance of freedom and its effects among Americans

6) Mastering the culture of the host nation

6) Without joining them, I will not be important

7) There are certain behaviors of the home country we must acquire

8) Respecting people's sexual inclinations and opinions

18) Knowledge of the U.S. laws helped them to know the importance of equality, inclusion and freedom of expression in the United States

18) Equality and freedom of expression

1) Knowing the improvement of today's racism from the past	19) The priests were cautious about handling the issues of race, and some of them preferred to use the word micro-aggression during the interview	19) Cautious approach to the problems of discriminations in the United States
2) Careful with the use of the word "race"		
3) Accept the truth about race in America		
4) Discussing race could be dangerous		
5) Race discussion is a delicate discussion		
6) Avoided the use of the word "race" for the sake of unity		
7) Race issue is a sensitive issue		
8) Priestly profession unites and advocates peace		
9) Encountered racial discriminations but careful in confronting it		
1) Put my stereotypes away	20) Acknowledging how their stereotypes did not match with the reality they experienced, they dismissed it and opened up to learn the real U.S. culture	20) Dismissal of stereotypes
2) Listening to some Americans who are very objective and really cared about my adjustment helped me to realize some of my stereotypes		
3) I noticed that I was not committed to learn because of my stereotypes		

4) Believing that some Africans who have been here for a long time and wants me to adjust could not deceive me

5) Certain truths are very clear and helped to put away stereotypes

1) Very time conscious

2) Try my best to avoid a sense of the African time as much as I can

3) Use of alarm clock

4) Hanging clocks on a wall inside the church and other activity centers

5) Timing homilies and speeches before delivering them in the public

21) With the use of alarm clocks, proper record of the time for parish events, and conscious of being on the same page with parishioners

21) Being time-conscious and following the commonly agreed plan

1) Know that the lifestyle in the United States is more individualistic

2) Came to understand that Americans love their space and appreciate prior information before visiting with them

3) Tried to get acquainted with the US work ethics and structural lifestyle

22) They learned from their mistakes that Americans love their space, and prior information, even for a pastoral service

22) Americans love their space and prior information

4) By talking with them, it is easily noticed that they do not like encroachment into their space

5) One of the first things I learned is that they are organized people and planned their day's activities

6) Even pastoral visits to sick persons for prayers and administration of sacraments requires prior information

1) Thinking positively
2) Seeking ways to be part of the society
3) Encouraged by the fact that the derogatory remarks do not represent the views of all Americans
4) Ignored the derogations
5) Ignored the demeaning experiences
6) Remained positive to learn the host culture and render the pastoral services that brought me to the United States

23) They ignored derogatory remarks, think positively and remain focused to learn the U.S. culture

23) Remaining focused and thinking positively

7) There are many Americans who appreciate diversity

8) Some Americans helped me to adjust to US culture

1) Sensitive about child abuse

2) The anger toward the clergy about the abuse is a natural thing

3) Awareness of the bitterness was helpful to understand the people's anger and work with them

4) Evaluation of the bitterness of the people led to sympathy for the victims

5) Listening to the angry individuals helped to learn the best ways to relate with the children and youth to avoid any kind of accusations

6) The bitterness toward priests because of the abuses was even an important tool to be very cautious

24) An awareness of the bitterness, and the sympathy for the victims of the abuse helped them to continue their work and learn the best ways to relate with the children and youth

24) Sympathy for the victims of abuse by the Catholic clergy

1) Americans are comfortable about the social relationship between the elderly and the young	25) They learned that there are certain laws that protect the senior citizens, which is a kind of respect for the elderly	25) Understanding the issue about the respect of the elderly
2) Couldn't but embrace the cultural lifestyle of the people		
3) Later understood that there is no disrespect of the elders but a great respect for inventors and achievers		
4) "Personal cultural exorcism"		
5) Learned that there are laws that protect senior citizens, a kind of respect for the elderly		
6) Learned that there are certain exemptions for the senior citizens as a kind of respect for them		

4.2.4. EXPLANATION OF THE KEY THEMES AND PHRASES

Six of the interviews took place at a national conference. I interviewed three other priests in their homes, and three others were interviewed by telephone. I stopped after reaching a significant saturation with the twelfth interviewee. Not all the individuals who were approached agreed to participate in the study. There were concerns about privacy and a hesitancy to talk about challenging experiences, as well as the fear of saying something that might somehow jeopardize their immigration status. I appreciate the courage and honesty of those who were willing to be interviewed. Before interviewing each priest, the priest signed a letter of consent to indicate his willingness to participate in the study and also to assure him the confidentiality discussed during the conversation about the interview. All the interviewees were supportive of the research and gave informative answers to the questions they were asked. All the interviews were conducted in the English language.

Generally, the findings from the coded interviews suggest the need for predeparture cross-cultural training of Nigerian priests assigned to work in the United States. These themes are reported mainly because of their frequency of appearance from the various participants or their unpopularity in other research works in the literature but emerged in the interviews. The themes are presented in two sections. The first section about struggles or challenges came from the interviewees' answers to the second and third questions: What are the cross-cultural struggles or challenges you have experienced in the United States, especially pastoral struggles or challenges? What strategies are being helpful to you to effectively adjust from the Nigerian culture to US culture, especially pastorally?

The second interview question directly addressed cross-cultural challenges experienced by the priests. The fourth question about knowledge relevant to priests coming to the United States addressed the same issues, though in a more indirect and perhaps less threatening way. The two questions helped to harness the participants' cross-cultural problems, especially when they arrived newly to the United States. The third question, "What strategies are helpful to you to effectively adjust from Nigerian culture to US culture?" is a direct question and supplied direct answers. The answers provided the strategies that the priests used to adjust to US culture. While the second and fourth question gave an idea of the problems to consider during the cross-cultural training, the knowledge of the strategies helped to supply some of the skills to pursue for predeparture cross-cultural training. Question one was not used so much to discover their challenges and strategies because it focused on the introduction of the participants.

It was interesting to observe the differences in opinion and choice of words between the priests in the urban parishes and those in the rural parishes. Two major points were outstanding. While the priests in the urban parishes believed more on the role of personality traits in adaptation than those in the rural parishes, the priests in the rural parishes said little or nothing about personality traits. The priests in the rural parishes were more outspoken in interpreting their situations from the point of view of being misunderstood because of racial discrimination, but the priests in the urban parishes were more careful in their choice of words and so preferred microaggression or something similar. Nevertheless, all of them have a commonality of many experiences of challenges and the strategies for adjustment. I did not specifically solicit for these expressions. They came out on their own during the discussion, and the shared similar experiences were reported and analyzed.

4.2.5. Explanation of the Key Themes That Emerged from the Priests' Challenges

From the two questions, "What are the cross-cultural struggles or challenges you have experienced in the United States, especially pastoral struggles or challenges"? and "What strategies are being helpful to you to effectively adjust from the Nigerian culture to US culture, especially pastorally"?, the researcher noted that all the participants would have loved to have a predeparture pastoral and psychological cross-cultural preparation. They believed that being unprepared prior to departure is a mistake. All the twelve participants commented that predeparture preparation is a necessity. A priest needs to have a mindset about his future environment in order to have easier adaptation upon arrival. Knowledge of the differences between his home and new culture will help him to develop a strong mindset to withstand the cross-cultural struggles. A prior knowledge of the new culture will help the individual to know whether to go or not, which is good for both his health and a successful pastoral performance in the foreign culture. The prior knowledge would also help the priests to know what to collect and what may not be necessary for his assignment in the United States. The prior knowledge helps one to be open-minded to learn the new culture and assimilate himself easier without spending too much time in dealing with culture shock because there will be lesser surprises, patience, and mental toughness for the complexities he might encounter.

One of the participants summarized it very well by saying that "lack of preparation prior to departure is like throwing a non-swimmer into an ocean and expecting him to swim very well. He will either sink or barely be on top of the water until he gets help". After careful examination of the keywords, phrases, and sentences, the coded themes are carefully explained as follows.

4.3.1. CULTURE SHOCK

Most of the participants mentioned an experience of culture shock. In other words, the total lack of knowledge of their sudden new culture subjected them to a feeling of disorientation and confusion. The new lifestyle that was unfamiliar to them made it hard for them to relate with the people they came to minister to. They thought the lifestyle of the Americans was too individualistic for them. The normal attitudes and behaviors of the Americans were so complex for them that they simply did not know how to approach the people or pastoral work they came for. It took them a couple years to pass this stage after getting help from some people, making personal efforts to adjust, or a combination of both.

4.3.2. COMMUNICATION: ACCENT AND SYMBOLS

Communication is central to the life and work of a priest, and all the interviewees described struggles with understanding and being understood. They described communication challenges in three areas. Speaking American English challenged them. Despite their language fluency, the priests were schooled in British rather than American English. Many indicated that they spoke the King's English with some vocabulary and usage entirely different from American English. This, combined with their Nigerian accent, was a real barrier to being understood. Likewise, they had difficulty understanding American English pronunciation and usage. One of the interviewees said,

"Americans have a different way of speaking and writing English unlike the British style that is taught in Nigeria, e.g., the use and writing of certain words, such as bonnet (the hood of a car), lift (elevator), flat (apartment), and boot (trunk of a car)."

Many described episodes of misinterpreted communication. They misinterpreted aspects of the US way of life that they did not understand, and some of the Americans also misunderstood some of the priests' lifestyles unknown to the Americans. One said, "Americans value their space, but I misinterpreted it as being unfriendly and unwelcoming to foreigners. They are polite and respectful to people, but I misinterpreted it as an invitation for friendship."

Apart from spoken language, there was also a challenge of a nonverbal aspect of communication. The priests had a problem of understanding certain symbolic expressions of the Americans. While a majority of them talked about accent and not being understood or understanding everything the Americans said, they also added that the issue of communication also included their inability to understand the American symbols (nonverbal communication) and their meanings. Even though some of the American symbols are used in Nigeria, they do not necessarily communicate the same meaning. The wide range of communication includes the rules governing personal space and meanings associated with same sex touching that created some misunderstandings. One interviewee particularly described the misunderstandings that arose from putting his arm around a male friend. Common and neutral action in Nigeria was interpreted in the United States as gay behavior. One of the interviewees who had a similar experience said, "I wish I had known about the gay issues before coming here."

4.3.3. SHORT OR NO POSTARRIVAL ORIENTATION

Some of the participants who had postarrival training complained that the time allocated for the training was not enough for them to learn the culture and be ready to assimilate themselves into the society for a very fruitful pastoral work. While some dioceses do not have enough funds for longer training, others needed the priests as soon as possible for assignments. These participants acknowledged that the postarrival training was helpful but believed that if they had predeparture training, it would have helped them to grasp the postarrival training within the short time allocated to it and be ready for missioning. A majority of the participants did not have the postarrival training. They are the ones who mostly missed the predeparture preparation and had more problems with the host culture initially, which affected them psychologically and their pastoral work, especially at their early stage of being in the country.

4.3.4. DISCONTINUITY FROM A KNOWN CULTURE WITHOUT REPLACEMENT

Upon arrival in the United States, it did not take many of the participants much time to recognize the difference in both the sociocultural and pastoral lifestyle in the United States and the sociocultural and pastoral lifestyle in Nigeria. The inability to immediately become part of the new culture gave them a feeling of a discontinuity from a known culture without a replacement. It was stressful to them because there was a vacuum between the known and new culture, which led to loneliness and irritability that affected their pastoral work.

4.3.5. HELPLESSNESS AND LOSS OF SELF-ESTEEM

Some of the participants talked about feelings of helplessness and loss of self-esteem. They arrived and did not know much about their new culture, and they did not know how to be part of the social and pastoral life in the host culture. Many cultural values were new and complex. They did not know how to obtain assistance and become useful to their parishioners and the entire society. Some of their American parishioners regarded them as unfit for the ministry in the United States. The complexity of their situation and the inappropriate comments from the parishioners generated a feeling of helplessness and loss of self-esteem.

4.3.6. COMPLEXITIES, CONFUSIONS, FRUSTRATIONS, AND STRESS

Many of the participants used complexity for different situations. However, the common thing in their statements is the difficulty or problem of knowing what is and is not permissible in the foreign land due to their lack of knowledge of the new culture. The complexities led to confusion, frustration, and stress among some of them. Ignorance of the new culture created a situation of being afraid of making mistakes, which also created stressful moments in the pastoral duties.

4.3.7. PERSONAL STEREOTYPES

Some participants acknowledged that they had stereotypes about United States prior to arrival. One person indicated how he was afraid of being lynched because he thought that lynching is still common in the United States. On the other hand, some were surprised to see different kinds of discrimination or microaggression. Another indicated that he thought he was coming to a dead church, but upon arrival he realized that the US church is still vibrant. Another expressed his stereotype of being in a very liberal church, only to realize that there is more committed Christians than he thought. Almost all of them had their stereotypes about gays and lesbians but realized later that they live in a free country where everybody deserves respect irrespective of their sexual inclination. The US church respects the fact that everyone is a child of God but still reveres the core values of the church and has no room for same-sex marriage. The personal stereotypes prior to understanding cultural realities led to some initial mistakes.

4.3.8. POWER OF WOMEN AND FEMINISM

The priests were not familiar with working with strong women or women with strong feminist concepts. Culturally, feminism has not taken a strong root in Nigeria. The participants were amazed by the overwhelming accommodation of feminism in their new culture.

Having some of them on the pastoral staff was a challenge they were not prepared for.

4.3.9. IGNORANCE OF MICROETHNICITIES WITHIN UNITED STATES

A majority of the participants thought that there was only one culture in the United States and had no idea that some groups in the United States like Hispanic Americans, Native Americans, Italian Americans, and African Americans are sometimes guided by their microcultures. While most of them indicated their wish to have known about the various ethnic groups and how to relate with them in certain situations, two participants expressed their difficulty in relating with African Americans because of their ignorance of the African American culture. This ignorance of the African American culture hurt their pastoral work with the African Americans because the African Americans expected them to know the African American culture since they are their fellow Blacks.

4.3.10. VERY FORMAL LIFE, USE OF TIME, AND STRONG WORK ETHICS

All the interviewees indicated in one way or the other that the United States is a much more structured society than Nigeria, which is a very flexible society. There are stipulated rules, and almost everybody follows the rules. They observed that the convention of following the rules accordingly innately leads to great work ethics and time-consciousness. The work ethics influences the use of time. Unlike Nigeria where the common adage "African Time" affects work ethics, Americans are more time-conscious, and many people try their best to generate the expected work output within the time for it. They noted that almost every activity, including church activities like Mass or adult formation classes, are supposed to be conducted within the allocated time, and everybody is busy to meet up with the expectations of the day at the right time. They saw American society as quite structured:

- "There is a sense of order and framework … from driving to behavior in the bank or restaurant."
- "There are policies and procedures in almost every place, especially in places of work."
- "Americans take commitments very seriously."
- "Respect for the law, respect of traffic signs, even stop signs when there is no other car."

Lack of this knowledge at the initial stage led some participants to the misunderstandings of great formality in US culture.

4.3.11. Racism/Microaggression

The level of ethnic and social divisions in the United States was surprising to many of the priests. They wondered why a highly developed country such as the United States has not advanced beyond the level of ethnic and social divisions they saw. One of them, a high school counselor, expressed,

> The United States is like a movie stage that has different scenes … Even in the same state, there is a different reality depending on your social class, the zip code you live in or your ethnicity … I didn't know that the United States was such a divided society.

The priests expressed different experiences they had with some Americans that gave them a sense of unequal treatment. However, while some of them bluntly used the words "racism" or "marginalization," some preferred not to go that far. They would not use such words because they wondered if the negative experiences were racism or misinterpretation and misjudgment because of cultural differences. Whatever the case, there was a feeling of being treated differently in a negative way as second-class human beings. There was also a disappointment about the legality of some groups that are popularly known as discriminatory groups, for example, the Ku Klux Klan. Not knowing how to identify a true racist and how to work with them led to some internal tensions.

4.3.12. UNHAPPY ABOUT THE DEMEANING OF THEIR HOME CULTURE

The participants believed in the teaching of cultural anthropologists such as Brown (2008) about "cultural relativism," which teaches that cultures cannot be objectively ranked with the presumption that one culture is better or greater than the other. Many of the participants expressed that they felt offended each time their native culture was put down or demeaned as inferior. They wanted to learn the American culture because they are in America and needed to master the American culture in order to offer a good pastoral job. Their intention for mastering the American culture does not come from the idea of leaning toward a superior culture. So, they were offended each time their native culture was degraded.

4.3.13. EXERCISING LEADERSHIP

All the interviewees struggled with exercising leadership in US culture, especially handling the empowerment of the American women and working with gays and lesbians in the parish staff. One of them expressed, "in Nigeria, the priest has sole authority. He controls everything and tells people what to do. Parishioners obey him unless he engages himself in a big scandal." They were accustomed to a commanding leadership style, which is not well received in the United States. The same interviewee indicated that he later learned, "They were accustomed to a commanding leadership style. Authority must balance with a good relationship."

Regarding leadership and women, another stated, "In the United States, women have the right to express themselves as men, and men are expected to be gentle and careful in the way they talk or associate with women ... The bar is very high about how men are supposed to relate to women." Given the societal expectations of men toward women, these priests who were used to telling women what to do struggled with working collaboratively with the women on their parish staff. Nevertheless, all of them appreciated and understood the opportunity for women to express themselves and "to explore their potential and get to the apex of their career for the good of the society."

Regarding working with gays and lesbians, it was a new and difficult experience. Collaborating with them in making decisions about the parish was hard. Many admitted that there are gays and lesbians in Nigeria, but it is hidden from the public, and the Nigerian church forbids them to hold duties in the church. "So, it was a shock to see them in the US church as members of the church staff and various church committees."

It was hard to adapt to it, but the difficulty did not prevent them from seeing the beauty of collaborative leadership after internalizing the good things in working together and gathering ideas from all sorts of people within the work environment. Working with the strong feminist women was difficult, but they eventually appreciated the high level of collaborative leadership in the United States and its positive outcome. About gays and lesbians, they believed that everybody is a child of God and deserves respect and opportunities to serve God, but in all things the dogma of the church should be respected.

4.3.14. COMPUTER TECHNOLOGY

Surprisingly, they noted their lack of computer and technology literacy as a real hindrance to communication with Americans. Some of the priests expressed that it was hard to do their work appropriately with their little or no computer literacy. The use of computer for many things in the parishes, schools, and hospitals challenged them. They wished they had certain level of computer literacy before coming, and they wished they had known the magnitude of the use of computers in the US pastoral work. They cited the use of Facebook as a fast way to reach out to parishioners, especially for emergency announcements, or designing church programs and plans on the computer or contributing to tweets by parishioners as significant challenges. Such activities require an appropriate knowledge of technology. An interviewee who decided to take a class on computer technology said, "using technology in everything … is different from what we used to do in Nigeria. In Nigeria you are in a parish, you are in a school, or you go to the hospital to minister, and then you go back to your base." I need to add that the age of the interviewees made a difference in their views of computer literacy. Younger ones have lesser problems with computer literacy. It may not be surprising for the seminarians who are young and yet to be ordained to have a better computer literacy.

4.3.15. INDIVIDUALISTIC SOCIETY

During the interviews, the struggle from a lack of social support surfaced in different ways. They found America to be an individualistic society. Unlike the Nigerian culture, where the community, village, and extended family are part of the individual's life, the United States is a society where each person minds their own business. It is the norm to avoid encroaching on another's space and to respect people's freedom. One who remarked that he does have a feeling of exclusion said,

> Americans find it hard to associate with people they do not know. They regard such people as strangers. In my culture, there is no word for a stranger ... We rather have words for a guest or a visitor. He could be an unknown visitor but not a stranger.

The priests indicated that Americans are very good with cordiality, smiling faces, and shaking hands, but it is not always a sign of welcome for friendship. It is often a social virtue. In Nigeria, such gestures mean welcome and feel at home.

The priests expressed that the Nigerian culture encourages social support in which a person's issue is an issue for the rest of the villagers. Coming from that background, the priests found that the extended family system and family dynamics in the United States are not as strong as they are in Nigeria and affect social support. One of them who moved from one part of the United States to another region where there are many Nigerians and other Africans confidently said,

In Nigeria, we live more of a community-oriented life ... what I call communal life or life of togetherness but here [USA], I observed that you are an individual, you stand on your own and make your decision, and live your life … In my place, people often meet together, people interact, and people go out together, talk, and share experiences as a community. I know that Americans do it in their way, but not with the connecting force as we have in Nigeria.

In other words, the individualistic lifestyle in America affects social support. They also believed that one of the reasons they were not receiving social support is the American attitude of superiority. One of them asserted that Americans thought that "made in America is always the best, even human beings."

4.3.16. Climate and Food Problems

All the participants struggled with feeding because of the differences between the food they see in the United States and the ones they were familiar with until they discovered food buffets and the presence of African stores and restaurants. They also struggled with the cold weather. Some of them were aware of the differences in weather but not to the extent they experienced. Talking about harsh winter conditions, they wondered about the Americans' ability to have a normal life during winter. One of them said, "the coldest weather I knew is the harmattan, and it is usually about seventy degrees. Arriving here in February, I felt like a person in an icebox. I was like … Do people live here?" Coming from a continuously warm or hot temperate country, it was confusing for some of them to imagine how human beings navigate their daily duties in winter and how they (the priests) would carry on their regular duties in the cold winter.

4.3.17. Respect for Tradition versus Respect for Achievement

The priests come from a culture where age has a strong cultural value. They were surprised that older people are addressed by their first names by those who are younger than them without adding a prefix to indicate respect. They realized though that this was part of a larger issue. Nigerian culture has more emphasis on traditions, which includes respect for elders, while American culture has more respect for achievement, creativity, competence, and accomplishments. Americans are culturally more futuristic. One of the priests expressed it very well, "I see that ... in Nigeria, there is much emphasis on the past and also tradition. In America, there is so much emphasis on the future and change." So, the priests struggled with who deserves more respect, given what they were used to and their new understanding of what is admirable.

4.3.18. Bitterness against Priests because of the Past Sexual Scandal

Even though it is fairly long when the sexual scandal by some priests made big news all over the world, the participants were surprised to observe that many Americans do not know that certain disciplinary actions are being taken to restore the dignity of the priesthood. Unfortunately, the US priests are still negatively affected by the problem. The respect for priests is lower in the United States than in Nigeria. Given the issue of the distrust of the priests in the United States because of sexual abuse, the foreign priests are distrusted more, and it is hard to work in an environment where one is not trusted.

4.3.19. Pastoral Life Includes Being Part of Family Events

Pastoral life in US culture is different in some ways. Many of the participants expressed that one of the important pastoral ministries of a priest in the United States is to be part of some of the family events of parishioners. For instance, the priest is expected to be at the ball games of the children in his parish or at their graduation ceremonies. Initially the participants did not see it as part of a pastoral work because it is not considered as one in Nigeria.

4.4. Explanation of the Key Themes That Emerged from the Successful Strategies

Themes emerged from the fourth question, "What strategies are being helpful to you to effectively adjust from the Nigerian culture to US culture?" The suggestions given by the participants were also coded into themes. These emerged themes were very instrumental for the participants' ways of handling their cross-cultural problems and highlight the important knowledge that a Nigerian priest coming to mission in the United States should have in order to adapt to the host culture easier and serve the people without a severe dysfunctional cross-cultural stress. The themes are listed below along with short explanations.

4.4.1. Reflection

Through personal reflection, some of the interviewees came to understand that their appreciation of home culture also implies that the people of the host nation appreciate their culture and would expect foreigners to be part of their host culture. This kind of thought made the participants respect the host culture and became a part of it in order to fit in. In other words, they looked inward to find out where they have been imposing their home culture and where they have not been doing well with regard to respecting the host culture. Some of the priests suggested that cross-cultural training might need to consider an advice for some moments of reflection when one starts experiencing difficulties and stress after arrival to the host culture.

4.4.2. Socializing and Asking Questions

Some of the priests were flexible and open to making every social gathering a learning process. They believed that rigidity could damage relationships, and so they were open and flexible to ask questions and learn. Almost all the participants acquainted themselves with their new home by socializing with the Americans and other people who have lived in the States for a long time and through friendship were able to loosen up and feel free to ask questions in order to learn the new culture. Some found ways to be good friends with other Africans who have lived in the United States for a long time and asked them questions about adaptation. All the priests indicated that the adjustments in the United States could have been impossible without socialization and asking questions. One said,

A new priest to this country should have an open mind and be flexible enough to observe and learn ... Naturally, I am not a shy person, and I was always asking questions. So, he [a new priest] should not be afraid to ask questions, and he should let them [Americans] know who he is and what he thinks, for them to help him. He should not be judgmental on how the people do things. He should rather try to be like them even though there is no time he will ultimately be like them.

They found the idea of not being shy to ask questions so useful that they strongly recommended it for other priests who might be coming from Nigeria to serve in the States if they have the opportunity to be assisted with training prior to departure.

4.4.3. COMMUNICATION: ACCENT REDUCTION

Accent problem was one of their biggest problems because missionary work has much to do with talking and understanding. Even though the participants knew English prior to their arrival, they spoke the British English with the Nigerian accent. Americans could not understand everything they said, and they could not understand everything the Americans said. While many of the participants were initially angry because of certain negativities about their accent, there was an overwhelming agreement that accent reduction is a necessity for adaptation to the new culture. So, they started to observe how Americans pronounce their words and mimic them and learn the US words for certain things that are named differently in the King's English. The priests also recommended a predeparture program for accent reduction prior to departure, if possible. One may be angry or feel insulted with regard to his English accent upon arrival, but after some time he would realize that the problem is not lack of English knowledge but lack of American accent.

4.4.4. HUMILITY AND OPENNESS

They were humble and open-minded to accept their inadequacies and unsubstantiated stereotypes in order to learn the new cultural values. Most believed that their success could have been impossible without the attitude of humility and openness. The two attitudes helped them to put their home culture aside and learn the host culture. One said, "like a chicken in a new home, I had to stand on one foot with open eyes to learn the accepted norms and unaccepted norms." Another said, "I assumed the position of a kid who is learning to walk again." Another also said, "I had to decide to be a grade one learner … and it helped."

Humility and openness helped the priests to relax, observe, and ask questions from whoever would help them. Humility and openness helped them avoid bitterness, ignore unhealthy criticisms, and have an open heart to embrace a positive attitude for the host culture and its people. Humility and openness helped them to transform from domineering leaders to collaborative leaders and become sensitive about imposing their own culture. They became less judgmental and more interested in what one of the interviewees called "personal exorcism," which he explained as "removing personal accretions to align oneself with the culture that welcomes him."

A couple of them even suggested the personality of openness as one of the traits to be considered before the choice of a priest for the US mission. They also believe that some people may not have that personality trait, but a predeparture cross-cultural training could help them with some strategies to loosen up and learn new ideas.

4.4.5. HAVING A MINDSET

All the interviewees expressed that they made many mistakes upon arrival, but the interest to serve in the country made them develop a strong mind set to eliminate the mistakes and blend into the society. The decision helped to eliminate early mistakes and quicken adaptation. It was not easy for them because they had to understand the differences between the Nigerian and US culture and think of various ways of stopping the attitudes that are not acceptable. They suggested that it would be very helpful for priests coming to the United States from Nigeria and other cultures to have a good knowledge of the US social and ecclesial cultures and develop the mindset for adjustment before departure.

4.4.6. COMPUTER TECHNOLOGY

The necessity of computer literacy for their work made them look for different ways of mastering the use of computer. Some took computer classes in schools. Others had private tutors, and a few decided to teach themselves with the use of instructors' manuals. Generally, all of them are now happy to know how to make use of computers for their works and other useful things. Some of them expressed that, in this modern time, computer literacy is a kind of a necessary language to know what is happening in the United States and beyond and a fast way of communication.

4.4.7. LEARNING COLLABORATIVE LEADERSHIP

Americans prefer division of labor to dictatorship. Collaborative leadership is highly appreciated and expected from leaders in the United States. The priests were used to exercising leadership alone in Nigeria. Even though they found it hard to share leadership initially, they later appreciated the beauty of sharing leadership or proper division of labor because they witnessed how contribution of ideas from different people and division of labor serve the parishes better. They even recommended the importance of collaborating with the parish staff, whether they are gays, lesbians, children, women, or men for priests assigned to work in the States as long as the dogma of the church and the diocesan rules are not compromised.

4.4.8. LIVING WITH AN EXPERIENCED PRIEST

Living with a priest who has also experienced other cultures, understands cultural differences, knows the cross-cultural struggles of international priests, and is willing to help a foreign priest was the most powerful aid to cross-cultural adjustment. Not all the interviewees had lived with an experienced priest who was aware of intercultural relations, but those who had the opportunity stated that it worked better for them than the postarrival training program.

One of them said,

I was fortunate to have a good priest who was a mentor to me. Frankly, I cherished the way he went about it because the program I attended is more like them giving you information on what you have to do, and probably not listening to you.

The priests expressed that the United States is a big nation; specific environments within it are different from the others and require suitable orientations for the environments. An experienced pastor knows more about the locals and the local environment and how to navigate within the area. With the knowledge of his intercultural experiences and the local situation, he has all it takes to help the new priest who will work within that local environment to assimilate very well into the environment. Those who had received mentoring seemed happier and felt more adjusted than the rest of the participants.

4.4.9. PATIENCE AND COURAGE

Moving from one's own culture to live and work in a foreign culture demands adjustment to the new cultural way of doing things in order to be successful. A majority of the interviewees for this study believed that it takes courage to put their native culture aside and be patient to learn the new culture. With patience and courage, they put their native culture aside, became participant observers, and did other things to learn the new culture. One of the participants expressed that it really took him a strong courage and patience to undertake what he called "personal cultural exorcism," that is, putting his culture aside for the space to accommodate the new culture.

Without patience and courage during the period of culture shock and abuses by some uninformed Americans, they could have packed their things and go back to their home country. They asserted that given the unfamiliarity of the American culture and lifestyle, patience and courage were helpful to them and will also be to the priests who will come from Nigeria to the United States in the future.

4.4.10. DETERMINATION

Most of the participants expressed that the determination to learn is one of the keys to their success. Their native culture encourages the tenacity to face and defeat difficulties if one wants to be successful. One of them said,

The first thing I think about is the way I was trained in my family from my childhood to adulthood. My upbringing is such that you are constantly reminded and expected to understand that you can still make your future amid many obstacles. You can always work hard to survive. My siblings and I grew up in a farm area, and we did not farm with mechanized equipment. We planted our crops with local types of equipment, and a lot of manpower and human energy was needed to operate the various types of equipment, and there was always that encouragement that you have all it takes within you to finish the farming, no matter how tedious or how big the land mass is. So, that family background prepared me psychologically, even socially, without knowing that I would end up in this country. So ... there was an aspect of me that kept informing me that I can make it, or that I can meet the challenges. In it is the foundation of all my strategies.

Having been raised that way, they had to be tenacious, despite many odds, in order to learn and become part of the host culture. Certain days may be more difficult because of homesickness and other environmental or cultural problems, but they kept reminding themselves the popular comment that, when the going gets tough, the tough gets going. That spirit of tenacity helped most of the interviewees to adjust to the new culture. Thus, tenacity needs to be encouraged when preparing some priests to mission in the United States.

4.4.11. MISSIOLOGY CLASS AT THE SEMINARY

Some of the interviewees had attended a missionary seminary. There is no cross-cultural training in the seminary curriculum, but there is a course on missiology. The course is about being conscious of cultural differences when ministering in a different culture and valuing the host culture to be successful in one's job. The missiology class helped two of the interviewees to manage their adjustment struggle. For example, they indicated their awareness of the possibility of a cultural clash when two separate cultures meet. They were also aware that a missionary is not expected to go and change the peoples' culture but rather accept and blend with the people. One of them concluded,

I must acknowledge that the Missiology class I took while in the seminary in Nigeria was very instrumental in my adaptation to US culture. The course is helpful … The class was on missioning in a different culture other than mine. The class reminded me of the importance of being mentally, physically, and socially resilient when challenged by cultural differences.

Even though the priests who took the course did not know much about America while in Nigeria and were never prepared for the US mission, the class helped them with adjustments amid their various challenges.

4.4.12. READING, WATCHING TELEVISION, AND USING DISC DEVICES

Many of the participants indicated that they improved their knowledge about the American culture through readings and watching television. Interestingly, all indicated the importance of reading as one of the antecedents of their adaptation. They suggested that such readings should start when one is still in Nigeria so he would have known certain things about the United States prior to his arrival.

Apart from reading and watching television, they indicated that the use of other sources of learning, such as CDs and DVDs about US culture and lifestyle helped them and suggested that they could be used by a person intending to mission in the United States to learn the culture of the host nation while still at home.

4.4.13. Friendship and Soliciting Advice for Emotional Support

These strategies helped many of the participants to conquer their emotional or psychological problems with regard to adjusting to the new culture. They were open to certain people they trusted. In times of stress and confusion, these friends accorded them emotional support and gave them advice on what to do. Some of them, especially the egalitarian ones, had friends within their parishes who accorded them the valuable support and advice. As it were, the idea of having friends in the host culture and reaching out to the friends for advice and emotional support need to be incorporated in the predeparture cross-cultural preparation.

4.4.14. Adjusting to the Climatic Problems

All the participants had problems with the climate, especially the winter climate. They had problems with the cold weather and driving on the icy and snowy roads. Prior to coming to the United States, most of the participants had little or no accurate knowledge of the US climate and how it changes. Some of the participants who knew about the US climate from their geography class in the high school did not learn much about the US climate. Many of the participants learned from their friends about checking the weather through the weather channels and cell phones and how to dress according to the situation of the weather. They suggested that priests assigned to the United States should be given accurate knowledge of the US climate and how it changes and then taught how to dress and drive on the snow or icy road upon arrival.

4.4.15. Food

Feeding is another problem, which all the participants encountered in a country where there is abundance of food. It was problematic for them to enjoy the American foods because the foods are either prepared differently or foreign to them. While some of them learned to be buying African food items and spices from African stores and cooking for themselves, others preferred food buffet restaurants where they could carefully choose a kind of food they would enjoy. All of them suggested that the cross-cultural training of the incoming priests should include an awareness of the differences in food and spices and how to adapt in a situation where there are unfamiliar foods.

4.4.16. Listen More and Talk Less

Upon arrival and being aware that one is in a different culture, listening more and talking less were beneficial. They helped to know what is culturally appropriate to say and what is not. Thus, being a participant observer in the host culture was very essential and helpful to avoid dictating what might be strange in the host culture.

4.4.17. Postarrival Cross-Cultural Training

Many of the priests had postarrival cross-cultural training when they came to the United States. All of them who attended the training believed that the training was helpful in the areas of accent reduction and what should be expected from them as priests in the United States. It was a key to their understanding of how to navigate in the society and how things work in the United States. The program also helped them to realize that the United States has a cultural richness that needs to be remembered and used while working in the society.

However, even though the training was helpful, it was not entirely adequate. Some of them felt it was too short and did not address each individual's cross-cultural issues because all the international priests from different countries were taking the class together. Some expressed that they are adults who were used to doing certain things in a particular way, and therefore expected to be involved in their change process. One of them, who believed that he learned more from an experienced priest he is assisting in the parish, strongly asserted,

The training is more like them giving you information on what you have to do. It is fine but somebody who has been a priest in Nigeria for some years before coming over here is not a kid. He is an adult, and adults don't learn things very fast because it is difficult for them to change. Those people who give the program should make it a learning process for themselves about us to know where we are coming from and what we are bringing. So, make it an adult dialogue and not one-sided or one-way of doing things.

Overall, they found the training positive, but all agreed that it would have been more helpful if they had predeparture training as a stepping-stone to the postarrival training.

4.4.18. KNOWLEDGE OF EQUALITY AND FREEDOM OF EXPRESSION IN THE UNITED STATES

Knowledge of certain US laws helped them to understand the importance of equality and freedom of expression in the United States. The knowledge helped them to see the risk in depriving women and even feminists, gays, lesbians, and youth from being involved in activities because of who they are. The knowledge helped them to balance the responsible teachings of the church and the US rule of law.

They suggested that those who prepare the missionaries should have a program that inculcates the respect of women, even feminists, and everybody in the United States into the missionaries' minds. From the priests' experiences, they advocated that every priest on mission in the United States must know how to balance the church dogma with the US laws and freedom of expression that extends to everyone, irrespective of gender, age, or sexual inclination. The incoming missionaries should know that it is normal to have different kinds of people on the parish team as well as respecting everyone while keeping the dogmatic teachings of the church.

4.4.19. Cautious Approach to the Problems of Discriminations in the United States

The participants approached the problems of microaggression, racism, and other ethnicity problems without violence. Through observation, reading, and asking questions, they knew the issue of ethnic divisions and discriminations in the United States and how discussing them could sometimes be delicate. Given that their profession is supposed to unite everybody and advocate peace, they were diplomatic in addressing the issues as sensitive. When affected, they console themselves with the teachings of the scripture. When others are affected, they preach peace and nonviolence. When appropriate, they help the perpetrators to examine their conscience.

4.4.20. Dismissal of Stereotypes

The interviewees acknowledged that holding on to personal stereotypes blocked their opportunities to learn the host culture. Some of the participants were able to learn the new culture when they dismissed their stereotypes and opened up to learn new ideas. Acknowledging how stereotypes made them have a false knowledge of their real experience, they advised that predeparture preparation could help to remove the stereotypes if unbiased people who know US culture very well deliver cross-cultural training to priests coming to serve in the United States. Some of the participants suggested that those who lived in the United States for a long time and now residing in Nigeria might be the best people to deliver the predeparture training.

4.4.21. Being Time Conscious and Following the Commonly Agreed Plan

For the Americans, time is precious. They like to be in a place at the appropriate time and leave at the appropriate time. Many of the participants had problems with timing their events. Even though some of them expressed that Americans are very structured or have a fast lifestyle, they also expressed that it is because the Americans have particular time for each event and are often strict with the timing of events in order not to be late for the next event. Events and their times are often commonly agreed on, and everybody wants to be on the same page with others.

Thus, the priests started to make use of alarm clocks and keep proper records of the time for every event to avoid being late. Some indicated how they hung clocks in their churches and activity centers so as to monitor their events and finish on time. They also expressed how they write their homilies or speeches and check the number of minutes it might take to deliver it before the actual deliverance. All the interviewees recommended that a foreign priest coming to the United States from Nigeria or other African countries must start to practice being time-conscious and understand that lateness or "African time" is not tolerated in the United States. Here in the United States, every activity is expected to start at the exact time for it and end at the expected time of its stoppage.

4.4.22. Observing that Americans Love Their Space and Prior Information

The lifestyle in the United States is more individualistic than in Nigeria, and they appreciate prior knowledge, if possible. They do not like people to encroach on their time and space without prior information because it might mess up their plans for the day. Making a home visit for the sick requires prior information, or the priest might be politely be dismissed even though he is going for a good pastoral work. "Americans have plans for their day," said one of the interviewees. The interviewees indicated that Americans appreciate having an agreed time with whoever they are dealing with so there would be general consent for every activity that involves more than one person, including a consent for the time of the pastoral works that are rendered to them, to avoid thwarting their day's plans.

4.4.23. Remaining Focused and Thinking Positively

Some of the interviewees expressed the Americans' belief that "made in the USA" is always the best, including human beings, and how the Americans constantly devaluated their home culture. Some of the Americans even described the priests as uneducated, uncivilized, and unfit for the US mission because of their lack of American accent. However, these priests believed that those Americans do not represent the perceptions of every American. So, they remain focused in their efforts to get acculturated and be a part of the society. They ignored the derogations and the demeaning experiences and remained positive to learn the host culture and render the pastoral services they came to offer in the United States. Moreover, there are also many Americans who appreciate diversity and were helping them to adjust to US culture without much stress.

4.4.24. Sympathy for the Victims of Abuse by the Catholic Clergy

The interviewees believed that as long as the sexual molestation of children by some priests remains in people's minds, the bitterness toward the clergy by some people will not disappear easily. Given the freedom of expression in this country, the bitterness would often be expressed by some people, especially those who were hurt most. An awareness of the bitterness and the sympathy for the victims of the abuse helped them to continue their work and learn the best ways to relate with the children and youth to avoid any kind of accusations. Some expressed that the bitterness toward priests because of the abuses was even an important tool to be cautious and avoid any action that might lead to accusations.

5.2.25. UNDERSTANDING THE ISSUE ABOUT THE RESPECT OF THE ELDERLY

One of the cultural surprises expressed by the participants is how the younger people relate with the elderly as if they are age-mates. It is one of the cultural differences, and the host nation is comfortable with it. The surprise stems from the priests' home cultural values. Putting the home cultural values by the side in order to embrace the new culture took care of the issue. They also learned that Americans respect their senior citizens in different ways and even have laws that protect the senior citizens, even though a great respect are mainly given to great achievers and inventors.

CHAPTER 5

Discussion

THIS STUDY INVESTIGATED THE CROSS-CULTURAL CHALLENGES AND
other relevant experiences of the Nigerian priests working in the United
States. The outcome of the research indicates that the cross-cultural
experiences of these priests are consistent with those of expatriates in
other professions, yet the roles and responsibilities of a priest greatly
influence the nuances of the priests' experiences and the importance that
these challenges be overcome. Understanding and being understood is
central to the life and work of the priests as expressed by one who said,

I need a sense of belonging and want to relate well with people
around me. Coming from a culture, which is different from the American
culture makes it very difficult to have interpersonal communications and
relationships with the people around me. There are misinterpretations
of what I do by many of them and misinterpretations of what they do
by myself ... It was a situation of discontinuity from the culture I know
and struggling with how to continue with the new culture I live in.
Everything looked complicated.

The priests' statements indicate the importance of predeparture
training about US culture before coming to minister in the United States.
Many of the priests saw the need and even suggested a combination of
a predeparture cross-cultural training at home with the postarrival
training they get in the United States for a better adjustment during
the interviews. One strongly asserted, "no Nigerian priest should be
sent to the United States without a cross-cultural preparation about the
country." The suggestion of the priests is consistent with the widespread

use of both trainings by other intercultural groups and businesses (Wurtz 2014; Godiwalla 2012; Elmadssia and Hosni 2012; Sperry 2012; Nicole 2011; Vogeh, Van Vuuruen, and Millard 2008).

LIMITATIONS OF THE STUDY/RECOMMENDATIONS

It is the aim of this research study to provide an analysis of the cross-cultural difficulties of the Nigerian priests who mission in the United States in order to enhance a better predeparture cross-cultural training of future priests intending to mission in the United States. During the study, some difficulties in adapting to US culture due to cross-cultural challenges and various ways of adaptation emerged. While the study contributes to an understanding of the cross-cultural challenges and strategies of adjustment in the United States by the Nigerian Catholic priests, the study is not without limitations.

The researcher is a Nigerian priest serving in the United States, and as a human being, it cannot be taken for granted that he is immune from the human nature of bias. Nevertheless, every methodological safeguard was taken to avoid author's bias. I also suggest that an outside group researcher might replicate the study for the sake of the accuracy and quality of the study to make sure that it is free from "collective self-esteem contingency and intergroup bias" (Amiot and Hornsey 2010, 84).

The sampling of twelve priests is relatively a small number for the representation of all the Nigerian priests in the United States and may not adequately represent the experiences of all the Nigerian priests in the entire United States. Even though the experienced phenomena do not differ very much from the literature but instead provide further reasons for predeparture cross-cultural training, the truth remains that the experiences of twelve participants may not adequately represent the experiences of all the Nigerian priests in the various geographical regions or in the entire United States. This limits the generalization of the result of the study.

As much as I feel confident that the results of the study are encouraging, future studies are needed to investigate the results since no other major study has been done on the predeparture cross-cultural training of Nigerian priests coming to mission in the United States.

Other research designs and methods of collecting data could be used for the same investigation to find out if the same result will emerge. For instance, a quantitative research method with more samples or a case study research approach could be used to replicate the study to find out if the same findings will emerge.

Furthermore, the emerged result from the study automatically led to certain reasons for predeparture cross-cultural training for missioning in the United States. However, like every other research, this study leaves room for other prospective researchers to press on and investigate related areas that may not have been completely covered in this work. I will like this study to be an open-ended investigation. The participants for the study have worked in the United States for ten years or more. Some scholars, such as Chew (2004), believed that expatriates who lived in a foreign country for a long time often forget their actual adjustment problems after cultural adjustment. So, I would suggest that another research be done on this topic with participants who have not stayed very long in the United States to find out if the same result might emerge.

Now that specific categories of challenges have been established, survey research could gather data from a larger number of Nigerian priests. The experiences of other international priests whose culture is very different from the American culture could also be studied to find out the characteristics of their cross-cultural challenges and adjustments.

Further study could also be done on the Nigerian priests who have finished their missionary works in the United States and are retired to know if a similar result will come out with regard to the cross-cultural difficulties and better ways to adjust in the United States. The study might either consolidate this particular study or bring new findings that could enhance a more sophisticated pastoral and psychological cross-cultural predeparture training of the Nigerian priests on mission in the United States.

British grammar and a Nigerian accent proved to be a problem for the priests. The Nigerian priests in the United States are highly educated and know the English grammar very well, but there is still a problem of communication, that is, understanding and being understood. The interviewed priests found it hard to understand the host people; the host people found it hard to understand the priests because of the problem of accent. Given that the English grammar of the Nigerian priests is British-oriented and spoken with the Nigerian accent, which seems to be a problem, a study could be done on the best way to facilitate accent reduction.

Since this problem needs to be addressed in the predeparture training, how will it be done? There might be a research to find out the appropriate way of teaching and acquiring the American accent during the predeparture training in order to reduce the initial anxiety of the priests who dislike the misinterpretation of their accent as a lack of English knowledge. The acquisition of the accent will improve communication and better relations between the priests and their parishioners upon arrival.

Given that many of the priests indicated that some personality traits enhanced their adjustment, such as flexibility and openness, humility and patience, friendship and soliciting for advice, and dismissal of personal stereotypes, these attitudes should be examined as indicators for Nigerian priests' adaptability in the United States. The assertions may or may not be true. We need to know more about the influence of personality traits, especially extrovert personality traits in cross-cultural adjustment. Since the majority of the priests in the urban missions expressed the importance of personality in adaptation than those in the rural missions, a study needs to be done to find out why those in the urban parishes seem to think more about the importance of personality trait in adaptation than those in the rural parishes. There could be a study that measures the actual relationship between the personality of openness and cross-cultural adjustment given the numerous positive remarks about the personality of openness as a tool for easier adjustment. We need to know if this personality trait could be a major determinant for choosing and preparing missionaries for United States.

While some of the participants seem to think that it might be better to give many priests a cross-cultural preparation prior to choosing the suitable candidates for the mission, others indicated that appropriate training could help any priest to work on his weaknesses and he will be good for the mission. Research needs to be done to figure out the best methodology for choosing priests to mission in the United States.

CHAPTER 6

Implications

DESPITE THE LIMITATIONS OF THE STUDY, THE MAIN CONTRIBUTION OF this study is in demonstrating that the positive effects of predeparture cross-cultural training of Nigerian priests coming to mission in the United States could eliminate their maladjustments to US culture upon arrival. Therefore, this study adds to the understanding that predeparture cross-cultural training effects a better adjustment of foreigners in US culture and supports the need of predeparture cross-cultural training programs that would enhance cultural competence among Nigerian priests assigned to mission in the United States.

From the participants for the study, we learned that a prior knowledge of certain cross-cultural skills and knowledge of the culture of the host country is a *sine qua non*. If it is delivered with clarity, it can improve the priests' intercultural and interpersonal skills for adjustment and success in the host culture. All the research participants favored predeparture cross-cultural training with a belief that the critical questions and discussions that might arise during the preparation will provide the incoming priests with some important information. The incoming priests would know the useful framework to manage the cultural differences and transition. They would have a prior solid understanding of the cultural values of the foreign culture to avoid the application of preconceived notions that worked at home but does not in the host culture or the notions that stem from stereotypes.

The predeparture training of the Nigerian priests will help the priests to know how to cope with the cross-cultural struggles they will encounter in their new environment. This aligns with Arthur's (2001) recommendation that predeparture preparation is necessary because it is an anti-stress inoculation that helps people who might struggle with the intercultural conditions in a foreign land and prepares one for the strategy to manage their stress in the foreign culture.

The study justifies the perspectives of well-acknowledged psychological theories and the studies of cross-cultural scholars because it is evident from the research participants that predeparture cross-cultural training helps to avoid unnecessary complexities and unanticipated situations that might affect the priest's cultural adjustment and his health. Given that cross-cultural adjustment can be challenging, the theories of cross-cultural psychologists serve as a motivation that can reinforce efforts of the Nigerian priests on mission to the United States to learn and have a better adjustment upon arrival to the United States. The theories can energize the learning of the host culture prior to departure.

Some studies have advocated the importance of cultural competence on our increasing globalizing world, which is great. This study has also added the importance of preparing for the cultural assimilation (Arthur 2001) of other cultures. The fast globalizing world evokes knowledge of other cultures in order to have intercultural awareness and more personal feelings of other cultures. It helps to prepare for the best management situation when in another culture among many other options.

The priest going to mission in the United States will obviously need a specific expert view of US culture and the most appropriate behavior in the United States in order to be a good missionary in the United States. This means that those who might be involved in designing the programs for the priests would consider both the awareness and sensitivity in cross-cultural differences and the programs that enhance the knowledge of the target culture in order to appropriately adjust to the required behaviors of the host culture. According to Arthur, the idea of learning a targeted culture enforces a certain feel for the culture, the likelihood of fruitful collaboration, and the avoidance of offending the sensibilities of the host nationals.

Due to personality differences (introverts and extroverts) and their effect on learning a new culture, predeparture preparation could help the cross-cultural trainers to assist the priests with the essential cross-cultural skills that suit the personality of each priest to adjust to the new culture. If the priest is an introvert who has problems with relationship building, it will be observed during the predeparture preparation, and the priest will be helped to develop confidence and the ability for a collaborative teamwork as well as the opportunity to develop the required skill prior to his departure. The same kind of help will be accorded those who have intercultural communication skills. They will also be given the chance to develop the skills before their departure, as suggested by Kealey, Protheroe, Macdonald, and Vulpe (2005).

Given that the Nigerian culture is very different from US culture, this study will help the Nigerian priests hoping to work in the United States to know more about US culture, the differences between their home and US culture, and the key for adjusting to US culture. It will help them to understand the US cultural contexts. It will help to prepare the priests for a vital and effective ministry in the US church and expose them to enjoy the U.S social life.

According to Cremagic and Smith (2011), lack of cross-cultural preparation of an expatriate prior to departure to a foreign country negatively affects the success of the expatriate. On the other hand, cross-cultural preparation before departure to a foreign land does educate a person of a particular culture to get involved efficiently with people of other cultures and become accustomed quickly with the new environment (Hassan and Diallo 2013).

This systematic assessment of how some Nigerian priests who are ministering in the United States struggled to get adjusted to US culture and its future use as an informative tool to prepare the forthcoming priests will help the incoming priests to gain self-esteem and self-confidence, lessen some of the stress normally encountered by new priests in an unfamiliar culture, and quicken adjustment and better performance. It will also benefit the Catholic Church in the United States because fast and effective adjustment according to Evans (2012) is critical to job performance and profitability. The predeparture preparation will help the incoming priests to be critically conscious of the culture of the American people they will serve and facilitate integration and job performance. The USCCB (2010) has exhibited an interest in having suitable international priests for the US Catholic Church. This study will give them a new knowledge of the struggles and challenges of the Nigerian priests and how to assist the priests to perform better in their dioceses.

The study will benefit the Nigerian Catholic bishops who send their priests to work in the United States. Borrowing the ideas of Hassan and Diallo (2013) and Ramalu, Rose, Uli, and Kumar (2010), a predeparture training saves the sender of the expatriates the shame of failure or low performance by their expatriates. Just as in the business world where multinational corporations do not enjoy having a bad reputation because of the low performance of the expatriates (Hassan and Diallo 2013), the Nigerian bishops would not wish to suffer the bad reputation of sending non-performing priests to work in a foreign land.

Moreover, whenever a priest is repatriated because of maladjustments and low performance, there is a loss of the financial cost of sending him overseas to work. The predeparture training will reduce both the number of priests who are sent home and the cost involved in sending them to work in the United States. So, this study will help the Nigerian bishops to acknowledge the importance of predeparture cross-cultural training.

Given that research is a continuous process, other researchers in this field of study will benefit from this study. Other researchers could compare this study with their own and make some critical analyses and suggest further strategic planning. They could also discover other opportunities that may benefit both the Nigerian priests and other international priests to adjust better and work better in nonfamiliar cultures. A critical analysis of the study by other researchers could also help to highlight other essential issues on the predeparture training of professional expatriates and cross-cultural adjustment that may have been neglected in the study.

GENERAL SUMMARY

THE SITUATION OF PRIESTLY SHORTAGE IN THE UNITED STATES HAS created a phenomenon where relatively few priests are scrambling to meet the needs of well-established Catholic communities and a growing Catholic population generated by (1) the continuous immigrant population in the country (Welch 2009), (2) retirement and death of older priests (Gray 2015), and (3) lack of interest among many young American men in becoming priests (Mann 2012). These factors leave the average age of priests in the United States at sixty-three (Sheehy 2014).

While US Catholicism continues to witness the decline in the number of priests, it also sees a continuous growth in the number of Catholic members (CARA 2014). The inadequate supply of priests due to the decline in ordinations and the aging of the priests started to lead to closure or consolidation of parishes. In response to this problem, US Catholic bishops started to recruit priests from overseas, especially from the Southern Hemisphere, and Nigeria is one of the biggest suppliers of those priests (Owen 2014).

Even though a great number of these international priests are doing a great job, differences in culture between Nigerian priests and the US laity sometimes create cultural tensions in the US Catholic parishes and institutions being managed by the Nigerian priests (Allen 2010; Owan 2014).

This phenomenological study specifically examined the cross-cultural challenges or struggles - misunderstandings, cultural conflicts, and other challenges that Nigerian priests working in United States have encountered during their intercultural adjustments in the United States and the effects on their priests' job performance. By analyzing the interviews of twelve priests who have worked in different regions of the United States, this research uncovered the challenges encountered by the priests and the strategies they adopted to adjust to US culture. The cross-cultural experiences of the priests served as a tool for recommending a strategic predeparture cross-cultural training of Nigerian priests intending to work in the United States. The aim is totally geared toward achieving a better and understandable ways of carrying out successful missionary work in a US culture, which is different from the Nigerian culture.

Conclusion

This study has given a rich literature review of the history of the shortage of priests in the United States and how the problem led to the recruitment of priests from Nigeria and other countries that have a different culture from the United States. Responsive pastoral work in the United States requires knowledge of US culture. The absence of that knowledge among the Nigerian priests who are serving in the United States presents a challenge both to the Nigerian priests and to many of the people they serve because of the cultural differences.

I heard directly from the Nigerian priests who experienced hurtful cross-cultural challenges and their adaptation processes. The twelve participants for the study saw their entry adjustment periods as challenges. Their helplessness forced them to discover the positive and productive ways for adjustment in the different culture. Research studies have demonstrated that this kind of situation of cross-cultural struggles leading to the discovery of adjustment patterns is not abnormal in intercultural settings (Kim 2005). According to Kim, the development of intercultural transformation has the possibility of including the "dynamic of stress, adaptation, and growth" (394).

Though difficult and challenging, when the adjustment is acquired, the person gains a special privilege to feel, think, and act beyond the enclosure of a single culture. He becomes a proud member of a bigger culture without losing his primary or original culture.

I used phenomenological qualitative research to investigate the cross-cultural challenges and their strategies of adjustment to find out if there could be a need for a predeparture cross-cultural training of the Nigerian priests who leave their home culture to mission in US culture. A consistent pattern of cross-cultural challenges among the Nigerian priests was clearly evident. The priests' employment of a variety of strategies to understand and adjust to the American culture was also evident. From the priests' challenges and their employed strategies to tackle the challenges, I have recommended a predeparture cross-cultural training that considers both the challenges and strategies of adjustment. I also suggested a particular training program. This training program does not underscore the goodness of other training programs that might also be of great importance, even though I recommended it after a careful examination of some other programs.

CHAPTER 7

Suggested Training Program

PREDEPARTURE TRAINING IN MULTINATIONAL COMPANIES AND institutions has led to the use of some successful learning models or theories to design predeparture cross-cultural training programs to reduce cross-cultural challenges and facilitate intercultural competence in a foreign culture (Ashby 2012; Steve, Hendrick, and Morris 2007; Caligiuri, Phillips, Lazarova, Tarique, and Bürgi 2001). Since the participants in this study requested a predeparture cross-cultural training, which has also been favored by the researchers in other cross-cultural businesses and institutions for their expatriates, I developed a predeparture training program to assist the priests' adjustment and job performance. I preferred and used Kolb's experiential learning theory (ELT), which Yamazaki and Kayes (2004) once used for a different group of expatriates. I used ELT to develop a predeparture training program for the Nigerian priests to overcome their cultural challenges and increase their intercultural competence.

KOLB'S EXPERIENTIAL LEARNING THEORY (ELT)

Kolb's theory of experiential learning provides a structure that is useful in the cross-cultural training of expatriates (Yamazaki and Kayes 2004). In ELT, training and learning begins with a cognitive process in which an individual confronts abstract concepts in a way that suits the individual learner. There are four stages of learning in the theory; learning begins with concrete experience, followed by a reflective observation, which produces the abstract conceptualization that is then used for active experimentation (Kolb 1984). The concrete experience refers to the direct experience of the content to be learned. Abstract conceptualization refers to knowing the content and forming a theory from what is observed. The reflective observation refers to the individual's thoughtful review of the observed experience for proper understanding, and active experimentation refers to the individual's application of the perceived experience to the individual's surrounding world for an appropriate knowledge of the abstract (Chiong 2011). The four stages are integrated and supportive of one another such that sufficient learning only occurs when a learner can master and be capable of using all the four steps of knowledge. One of the great things about ELT is its nonrigidity in the preferred way of learning. It accommodates each's preferred method of learning. Kolb (1984) described the theory as "a process whereby knowledge is created through the transformation of experience" (38), and the center of learning is the subjective experience of the learner. Every individual has the opportunity to learn, no matter their preferred style of learning.

Embedded in ELT is what Boyatzis and Kolb (1995) later called the skill of developmental learning. It is a higher level of learning that refers to mastering skills from extensive learning processes and experiences that help the individual to respond to the changing circumstances (Yamazaki and Kayes 2004). Through it, an individual learns to respond to variations in role and situation, which is crucial for cross-cultural learning. Acquaintances with the four stages of learning, the skill of developmental learning, and the accommodation of individuals' learning style have the potential for effective cross-cultural training (Yamazaki and Kayes 2004).

"ELT embodies a comprehensive set of skills, including valuing, thinking, deciding, and acting, necessary for a variety of activities related to cross-cultural learning" (Yamazaki and Kayes 2004, 365). Its consideration of individual's different ways of learning "place the expatriate, or similar learner, at the center of the cross-cultural learning process" (Yamazaki and Kayes 2004, 365). Everything about ELT provides a framework for interaction between the home and the host cultures and the strategies that will be necessary for the expatriates in the face of particular cross-cultural situations (Boyatzis and Kolb 1995). ELT has been tested and found useful for cross-cultural training and learning (Yamazaki and Kayes 2004) and is therefore an appropriate model for assisting the Nigerian priests who are challenged by US culture.

APPLICATION OF ELT TO THE CROSS-CULTURAL TRAINING OF NIGERIAN PRIESTS

In the ELT model, the concrete experience for the Nigerian priests would be the unknown cultural challenges that the priests will face when they arrive in the United States. The experiences will be made known to them. The priests will then apply their various styles of learning to analyze the challenges for an appropriate knowledge of the cultural problems. Understand the challenges require information gathering, sense-making, and information analysis (Yamazaki and Kayes 2004). A precise definition or theory of the abstract (the challenges) by the learning priests indicates a good comprehension of the challenges. The priests would gather insight into the cultural concept and intercultural difficulties with the help of learning and knowing the specific stressful situations in their home culture. This particular activity inculcates cultural sensitivity, intercultural respect, and ability to deal with cultural ambiguities (Information Science Reference 2014). Its conceptualization contributes to accepting the cultural norms of another culture. Kolb (1984) described it as "a holistic process of adaptation to the world" (31). Finally, the learning priests would engage in active experimentation by using their acquired concepts from the problematic aspects of their home culture to interact with the unknown host culture. The involvement of returned expatriates from the host culture can be beneficial at this stage of interacting with unknown host culture by playing the host culture role for the cross-cultural interaction (Polon 2017; Yamazaki and Kayes 2004). External service providers who know the host culture may also be hired for this activity of acting as Americans (Polon 2017). This transactional meeting of the known and unknown has the capability of generating the skill of developmental learning (Yamazaki and Kayes 2004), which the priests need for their ministry in the United States. The interaction of the acquired skills from the home culture with the required cross-cultural competencies for the host culture will generate the expected cross-cultural congruence that should produce the effective cross-cultural adaptation. It is achievable if the learner sets his goal and applies all the required initiatives (Yamazaki and Kayes 2004). See figure 2 for the application of ELT to the specific cultural knowledge and cross-cultural challenges to be addressed in the predeparture training.

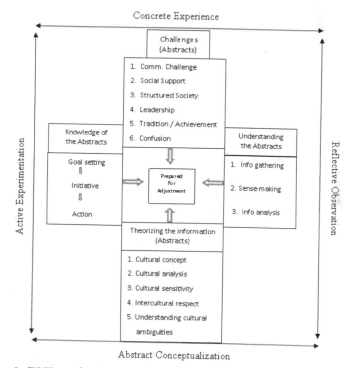

Figure 2: ELT applied to predeparture training for Nigerian priests.

Authors such as Wurtz (2014) have expressed a concern that predeparture training may be less effective if there is not enough time for the assimilation of the appropriate behavior. They therefore advocated for in-country cross-cultural training because of their belief that the pressing issues confronting the expatriate while in the host country would force him to learn and retain what was learned. In answer to the concern, Selmer (2001) who initially expressed that predeparture cross-cultural training is useful for constructing adequate expectations and reducing the anxiety of the unknown later suggested a fusion of both types of cross-cultural training. He called it sequential cross-cultural training because it "progresses in steps starting at pre-departure and continuing to the post-arrival phase" (Selmer 2006, 47), thereby leaving no gap to forget what was learned previously. A combination of ELT with the post-arrival training that the priests get in the United States fits into the sequential purpose of cross-cultural training. The mix of the two pieces of training is what most of the participants of this study requested. They believe that predeparture training would enhance the post-arrival training for better adjustment.

FORMAT FOR THE TRAINING

There is no curriculum in the Nigerian seminaries specifically for missioning in the United States. Instead there are missiology classes in very few seminaries, and the classes cover general clues about behavior in a different culture. Not being sure of the best format for the training, I consulted some Nigerian seminary staff for a better format for the training. After conferring with the faculties of some of the seminaries with a missiology class in their curriculum, we determined that the cross-cultural training for the US mission would fit better into a workshop format rather than a regular seminary class. In light of the demands placed on seminary students, the nature of the training, and the content to be covered, I have proposed twenty-four hours of instruction and activities over three days.

DAY 1: AN INTRODUCTION TO CULTURE

"In many cases, the success or failure in management is caused by the way leaders understand the cultural environment" (Vasile and Nicolescu 2016, 35). It is therefore necessary for the priests to understand the cultural variations within Nigeria as the first step in knowing differences in culture as well as the specific cultural situations faced by Nigerian priests in the United States. The day's exercise will help the priests to know the actual meaning of cultural variations and differences between Nigerian and US culture in order to have an appropriate mindset to learn US culture.

LEARNER OUTCOMES

1. Define culture and describe some of the ways in which cultures vary.
2. Analyze cultural variations within Nigeria.
3. Describe some specific situations that Nigerian priests have faced in the United States.
4. Compare Nigerian and US culture in terms of Hofstede's cultural dimensions.

SAMPLE TEACHING/LEARNING ACTIVITIES

1. Lecture/presentation on the definition of culture and ways in which cultures vary.
2. Group discussion of cultural variations within Nigeria (e.g. regional and urban versus rural). Lecture/presentation on Hofstede's cultural dimensions.
3. Discussion of prior cross-cultural experiences of members of the group (e.g., what they experienced and how they felt about it).
4. Review a series of written scenarios of situations encountered by Nigerian priests in the United States that involved cross-cultural misunderstandings or challenges (based on data from the study).
5. Group discussion (e.g., comparing Nigerian and US culture in terms of Hofstede's cultural dimensions).

DAY 2: LIVING AND MINISTERING IN AMERICA

There is a big cultural distance between Nigeria and the United States (Allan 2010). Some of the interviewees felt like kids learning to walk again. They made every social gathering a learning opportunity. Pursuant to their recommendation, priests assigned to the United States need a prior knowledge of the characteristics of US culture and its challenges and must prepare to encounter them. This day's exercise will help to encourage immersion into the society and satisfaction with living and working in the United States.

LEARNER OUTCOMES

1. Describe cross-cultural challenges experiences by Nigerian priests in the United States.
2. Describe the characteristics of modern American culture, including regional, ethnic, and socioeconomic variations.
3. Describe ways in which daily life in the United States differs from daily life in Nigeria, including practical matters such as transportation, communication, and shopping.
4. Analyze the cross-cultural challenges described in number 1 in light of the characteristics of US culture.
5. Anticipate other cross-cultural challenges that might arise.

SAMPLE TEACHING/LEARNING ACTIVITIES

1. Presentation/lecture of the cross-cultural challenges experienced by Nigerian priests as documented in the study. (Include quotes from the transcriptions of interviews.)
2. Presentation/lecture on the characteristics of US culture.
3. Presentation/lecture on daily life and meeting practical needs in the United States.
4. Group discussion of the cross-cultural challenges described in number 1 in light of the characteristics of American culture.
5. Group discussion of other areas of potential cultural conflict in life and ministry.

DAY 3: SKILLS AND STRATEGIES FOR CULTURAL UNDERSTANDING AND ADJUSTMENT

When two different cultures meet, there will be a culture clash and a culture shock by those who are foreign to the culture. This study has indicated some strategies of minimizing the culture shock and adapting to the host culture. The priests assigned to the United States need to be equipped with those necessary adaptation strategies to lessen both stress and resistance to adapt to the US sociocultural life.

LEARNER OUTCOMES

1. Describe specific strategies used by Nigerian priests to help with cultural understanding and adjustment.
2. Describe typical stages of culture shock and how it can be minimized.
3. Demonstrate an understanding of culturally appropriate interpersonal communication and ministry.

Sample Teaching/Learning Strategies

1. Presentation/lecture on strategies used by Nigerian priests to address the cross-cultural challenges (data from the research).
2. Group discussion on putting these strategies into practice.

Presentation/Lecture of the Nature of Culture Shock and How It Can Be Minimized

1. Role-play/simulation of typical situations encountered in life and ministry that require cultural sensitivity and understanding.
2. Interaction with Americans or others with direct experience with American culture.

Rehearsals

The objective of this ELT training program is to help the priests understand how to facilitate their adjustment to the United States. Wurtz's (2014) concern that predeparture training may be less effective if there is not enough time for the assimilation of the appropriate behavior before departure is considered in this suggested training program with the rigor of the training and some rehearsals. The three-day training will be an intensive training, followed by two rehearsals before departure. The first rehearsal will be done two weeks after the training; the second rehearsal will be done three weeks after the first rehearsal. Repeated rehearsals have been shown to have substantial effects on retention and confidence (Black and Mendenhall 1990). The choice of the intervals between the time of the training and the first rehearsal and between the first rehearsal and the second rehearsal are influenced by Caligiuri et al. (2001), who believed that the gaps between the training and the rehearsals have the capacity to facilitate mental rehearsals and retention of the learned behavior. During the intervals, the learned behaviors are likely to be employed beyond the training sessions inside the mind of the recipients of the training (Wurtz 2014).

REFERENCES

Ahanotu, L. U. 2019. "Navigating between Cultures: Cross-Cultural Challenges of Nigerian Catholic Priests Working in the United States." *SAGE Journals* 48 (1): 315–335. https://doi.org/10.1177/0091829619858597.

Addleman, R. A., R. C. Nava, T. Cevallos, C. J. Brazo, and K. Dixon. 2014. "Preparing Teacher Candidates to Serve Students from Diverse Backgrounds: Triggering Transformative Learning through Short-Term Cultural Immersion." *International Journal of Intercultural Relations* 43: 189–200. https://doi.org/10.1016/j.ijintrel.2014.08.005.

Albu, G. 2015. "Intercultural Education, a Key Issue in the Innovation of the Initial Training of the Future Teacher in Primary and Pre-rimary Education: Case Study." *Journal Plus Education* 12 (2): 151–157. http://eds.a.ebscohost.com.oralroberts.idm.oclc.org/eds/pdfviewer/pdfviewer?vid =7&sid=68fdbe1f- c8d8-4cb8-9235-36253e816dd9%40sessionmgr4007.

Allen, J. L. 2010. "Foreign Priests and the Risk of Plunder." *The National Catholic Reporter*, February, 2010. http://ncronline.org/blogs/all-things- catholic/foreign- priests-and-risk-plunder.

Aneas, M. A., and M. P. Sandin. 2009. "Intercultural and Cross-Cultural Communication Research: Some Reflections about Culture and Qualitative Methods." *Forum: Qualitative Social Research* 10 (1): 51–70. http://www.qualitative-research.net/index.php/fqs/article/view/1251/2738.

Amiot, C. E., and M. J. Hornsey. 2010. "Collective Self-Esteem Contingency and Its Role in Predicting Intergroup Bias." *Self and Identity* 9: 62–86. https://doi.org/10.1080/15298860802605895.

Arthur, N. 2001. "Using Critical Incidents to Investigate Cross-Cultural Transitions." *International Journal of Intercultural Relations* 25 (1): 41–53 https://doi.org/10.1016/S0147-1767(00)00041-9.

Ashby, W. 2012. "Employing Constructivist Models of Culture Teaching for Enhanced Efficacy in Pre-Departure, Cross-Cultural Training." *Applied Language Learning* 22 (1–2): 1–20. https://eric.ed.gov/?q=source%3a%22Applied+Language+Learning%22&pg=2&id=EJ1000094.

Bakel, M. V., M. Gerritsen, and J. P. V. Oudenhoven. 2011. "Impact of a Local Host on the Success of an International Assignment." *Thunderbird International Business Review* 53 (3): 391–402. https://doi.org/10.1002/tie.20416.

Bank, M., and S. Rothmann. 2006. "Correlates of Expatriates Cross-Cultural Adjustment." *Management Dynamics* 15 (4): 29–39. https://www.questia.com/library/journal/1P3-1273049031/correlates-of-expatriates-cross-cultural-adjustment.

Beck, N. 1992. *Shifting Gears*. Toronto: Harper Collins.

Becker, M. A., and D. Bhugra. 2005. "Migration, Cultural Bereavement and Cultural Identity." *World Psychiatry* 4 (1): 18–24.

Berg, I. K., and S. Miller. 1992. *Working with the Problem Drinker: A Solution Focused Approach*. New York: Norton

Berg, I. K. 2016. *"About Solution-Focused Brief Therapy."* SFBTA: Solution-Focused Brief Therapy Association. Retrieved from http://www.sfbta.org/about_sfbt.html

Biggerstaff, D., and A. R. Thompson. 2008. "Interpretative Phenomenological Analysis (IPA): A Qualitative Methodology of Choice in Healthcare Research." *Qualitative Research in Psychology* 5 (3): 214–224. https://doi.org/10.1080/14780880802314304.

Black, J. S., and M. Mendenhall. 1990. "Cross-Cultural Training Effectiveness: A Review and a Theoretical Framework for Future Research." *Academy of Management Review* 15 (1): 113–136. http://eds.a.ebscohost.com.ezproxy.oru.edu/eds/pdfviewer/pdfviewer?vid=1&sid=85eb8c8e-d170-4b5d-9233-90b90895539f%40sessionmgr4008&hid=4111.

Blum, L. 2004. "Stereotypes and Stereotyping: A Moral Analysis." *Philosophical Papers* 33 (3): 251–289.

Bogan, J. 2011. "Foreign Priests Help in U.S. Shortage." *The Post and Courier,* June 19, 2011. http://www.postandcourier.com/article/20110619/ARCHIVES/306199927.

Boyatzis, R. E., and D. A. Kolb. 1995. "From Learning Styles to Learning Skills: The Executive Skills Profile." *Journal of Managerial Psychology* 10 (5): 3–17. https://doi.org/10.1108/02683949510085938.

Braxton, E. 2008. "Cross Cultural Ministry: One Church in Two Different Worlds." Keynote address at the 2008 African Conference of Catholic Clergy and Religious in the United States. The National Black Catholic Congress. https://www.diobelle.org/bishop-emeritus/biography

Breitenstein, D. 2014. "As Number of U.S. Catholics Rise, Some Parishes Lack Suitable Leaders." *The News-Press* January 14, 2014. https://davebreitenstein.files.wordpress.com/ … /call-to-the-priesthood.pdf.

Brown, M. F. 2008. "Current Anthropology." *The University of Chicago Press* 49 (3): 363–383. https://doi.org/10.1086/529261.

Caligiuri, P., J. Phillips, M. Lazarova, I. Tarique, and P. Burgi. 2001. "The Theory of Met Expectation Applied to Expatriate Adjustment: The Role of Cross-Cultural Training." *Journal of Human Resource Management* 12 (3): 357–372. https://doi.org/10.1080/09585190010026185.

Caligiuri, P., and I. Tarique. 2012. "Dynamic Cross-Cultural Competencies and Global Leadership Effectiveness." *Journal of World Business* 47 (4): 612–622. https://doi.org/10.1016/j.jwb.2012.01.014.

Caligiuri, P., and R. Tung. 1999. "Comparing the Success of Male and Female Expatriates from a US-Based Multinational Company." *The International Journal of Human Resources Management,* no. 5, 763–781. http://eds.b.ebscohost.com.ezproxy.oru.edu/eds/pdfviewer/pdfviewer?vid=1&sid=7fb3d97a-1500-46a2-9c0c-2dae29641188%40sessionmgr120&hid=108.

Cave, A. 2009. "Foreign Priests, Enculturation Programs Proliferate." *The National Catholic Reporter, July 30* https://www.google.com/search?q=Cave%2C+A.+%282009%29.+Foreign+priests%2C+enculturation+programs+proliferate%

2C+The+national+Catholic+reporter%3A+Kansas+City%2C+ MO+&ie=utf-8&oe=utf-8.

Chan, Z. C. Y., Y. Fung, and W. Chie. 2013. "Bracketing in Phenomenology: Only Undertaken in the Data Collection and Analysis Process?" *The Qualitative Report* 18 (59): 1–9. http://nsuworks.nova.edu/tqr/vol18/ iss30/1.

Cerimagic, S. 2012. "Cross-Cultural Characteristics and Training of Australian Project Managers Working in the United Arab Emirates." Doctoral diss., Bond University, Queensland, Australia. http://epublications.bond.edu.au/cgi/viewcontent.cgi?article= 1111&context=theses.

Cerimagic, S., and J. Smith. 2011. "Cross-Cultural Training: The Importance of Investigating in People." *COBRA: RICS Construction and Property Conference* 667–675. http://works.bepress.com/jim_ smith/27.

Cernera. A. 2005. *Lay Leaders in Catholic Higher Education.* Fairfield, CT: Sacred Heart University Press.

Chew, J. 2004. "Managing MNC Expatriates through Crises: A Challenge for International Human Resource Management." *Research and Practice in Human Resource Management* 12 (2): 1–30. https:// rphrm.curtin.edu.au/2004/issue2/expats.html.

Chiong, S. 2011. Kolb's Learning Styles Model and Experiential Learning Theory.
From **ETEC**510.
http://etec.ctlt.ubc.ca/510wiki/Kolb%27s_Learning_Styles_Model_ and_Experiential_Learning_Theory.

Chien, T., N. Gary, and G. N. McLean. 2011. "Intercultural Training for US Business Expatriates in Taiwan." *Journal of European Industrial Training* 35 (9): 858–873. https://doi.org/10.1108/03090591111185556.

Constantine, M. G., G. M. Anderson, L. A. Berkel, L. D. Caldwell, and S. O. Utsey. 2005. "Examining the Cultural Adjustment Experiences of African International College Students: A Qualitative Analysis." *Journal of Counseling Psychology* 52 (1): 57–66. https://doi. org/10.1037/0022-0167.52.1.57.

Creswell, J. W. 2007. *Qualitative Inquiry and Research Design.* 2nd ed. Thousand Oaks, CA.: SAGE Publications

Cunningham, L. 2005. "Spirituality and Lay Leaders in Academe." In *Lay Leaders in Catholic Higher Education*, edited by A. Cernera, 79–89. Fairfield, CT: Sacred Heart University Press.

Davis, D. W., and B. D. Silver. 2003. "Stereotype Threat and Race of Interviewer Effects in a Survey on Political Knowledge." *American Journal of Political Science* 47: 33–46. https://doi.org/10.1111/1540-5907.00003.

Deck, A. F. 2012. "Intercultural Competencies: The Opportunities and Challenges of the Present Reality." *Seminary Journal* 18 (2): 48–52. http://www.sjvcenter.org/assets/uploads/pages/Seminary_Journal_Fall_2012.pdf.

De Shazer, S. 1988. *Clues: Investigating Solutions in Brief Therapy*. New York: W.W. Norton.

De Souza, R. J. 2012. "Nigerian Catholicism at Forefront of Universal Church." *The Catholic Register, May 29, 2012* http://www.catholicregister.org/columns/item/14590-nigerian-catholicism-at-forefront-of-universal-church.

Drummond, P. J., E. McLafferty, and C. Hendry. 2011. "Interpretative Phenomenological Analysis: A Discussion and Critique." *Nurse Research* 18 (3): 20–24. https://doi.org/10.7748/nr2011.04.18.3.20.c8459.

Ellis, C. M., and J. Carlson. 2009. *Cross-Cultural Awareness and Social Justice in Counseling*. New York: Rutledge Taylor and Francis Group.

Elmadssia, T. H., and M. Hosni. 2012. "Impact of Intercultural Training on the Development of Intercultural Competences. *European Journal of Business and Social Sciences* 1 (2): 35–47. http://www.ejbss.com/Data/Sites/1/mydata/ejbss-12-1110-impactofinterculturaltraining.pdf.

Eoyang, E. C. 2005. *Two-Way Mirrors: Cross-Cultural Studies in Glocalization*. Lanham, MD: Lexington Books.

Evans, E. H. 2012. "Expatriate Success: Cultural Intelligence and Personality as Predictors for Cross-Cultural Adjustments." Master's thesis, University of Tennessee, Chattanooga. http://scholar.utc.edu/theses/19/.

Farh, C. I. C., K. M. Bartol, D. L. Shapiro, and J. Shin. 2010. "Networking Abroad: A Process Model of How Expatriates Form Support Ties to Facilitate Adjustment." *Academy of Management Review* 35 (3): 434–454. http://eds.a.ebscohost.com.ezproxy.oru.edu/eds/pdfviewer/pdfviewer?sid=b9e414b0-b64a-4b56-905f-fa58f6a04032%40sessionmgr4006&vid=2&hid=4111.

FAQ—The Center for Applied Research in the Apostolate. 2015. "Frequently Requested Church Statistics." http://cara.georgetown.edu/frequently-requested-church-statistics/.

Finlay, L. 2009. "Debating Phenomenological Research Methods." *Phenomenology & Practice* 3 (1): 6–25. https://journals.library.ualberta.ca/pandpr/index.php/pandpr/article/view/19818/15336.

Firmin, M. W., H. J. Holmes, L. Ruth, R. L. Firmin, and K. L. Merical. 2013. "Personal and Cultural Adjustments Involved with an Oxford Study Abroad Experience." *Procedia - Social and Behavioral Sciences* 89: 555–558. https://doi.org/10.1016/j.sbspro.2013.08.893.

Freeman, M. 2011. "Validity in Dialogic Encounters with Hermeneutic Truths." *Qualitative Inquiry*, no. 17, 543–551. https://doi.org.ezproxy.oru.edu/10.1177/1077800411409887

Gao, F., C. Tilse, J. Wilson, A. Tuckett, and P. Newcobe. 2015. "Perceptions and Employment Intentions among Aged Care Nurses and Nursing Assistants from Diverse Cultural Backgrounds: A Qualitative Interview Study." *Journal of Aging Studies* 35: 111–122. https://doi.org/10.1016/j.jaging.2015.08.006.

Gautier, M., M. Gray, P. Perl, and M. Cidade. 2014. *Bridging the Gap: International Priests Ministering in the United States*. Washington, DC: Center for Applied Research in the Apostolate.

Gautier, M. L., P. M. Perl, and J. Fichter. 2012. *Same Call, Different Men: The Evolution of the Priesthood since Vatican II*. Collegeville, MN: Liturgical Press.

Gill, P., K. Stewart, E. Treasure, and B. Chadwick. 2008. "Methods of Data Collection in Qualitative Research: Interviews and Focus Groups." *British Dental Journal* 204: 291–295. https://doi.org/10.1038/bdj.2008.192.

Giorgi, A. 2011. "IPA and Science: A Response to Jonathan Smith." *Journal of Phenomenological Psychology*, no. 42, 195–216. https://doi.org/10.1163/156916211X599762.

Godiwalla, Y. H. 2012. "Training and Development of International U.S. Executive." *Journal of Modern Accounting and Auditing* 8 (1): 32–39. http://www.davidpublishing.com/davidpublishing/Upfile/3/14/2012/2012031469377585.pdf.

Goodstein, L. 2008. "Divine Recruits: Serving U.S. Parishes, Fathers without Borders." *The New York Times,* December 28, 2008. http://www.nytimes.com/2008/12/28/us/28priest.html?pagewanted=all&_=0.

Gray, M. G. 2015. "The U.S. Catholic Family: Demographics." Center for Applied Research in the Apostolate (CARA) and Holy Cross Family Ministries: 1–13. http://cara.georgetown.edu/staff/webpages/Catholic%20Families%20Demographics.pdf.

Gray, M. G., M. L. Gautier, and M. A. Cidade. 2015. "The Changing Face of U.S. Catholic Parishes." Center for Applied Research in the Apostolate (CARA) and Holy Cross Family Ministries. http://cara.georgetown.edu/caraservices/parishes%20phase%20one.pdf.

Grunlan, S. A., and M. K. Mayers. 2015. *"Enculturation and Acculturation."* In *Cultural Anthropology, edited by* S. A. Grunlan and M. K. Mayers, 2nd ed. Grand Rapids, A Christian Perspective, 69–87. Minneapolis: Zonderan Publishing.

Hafitah, A., M. Tahir, and M. Ismail. 2007. "Alternatives: Cross-Cultural Challenges and Adjustments of Expatriates: A Case Study in Malaysia." *Turkish Journal of International Relations* 6 (3–4). http://alternatives.yalova.edu.tr/article/view/5000159622/5000144033.

Hamilton, T. G. 2014. "Do Country-of-Origin Characteristics Help Explain Variation in Health among Black Immigrants in the United States?" *Social Science Quarterly* 95 (3): 817–834. https://doi.org/10.1111/ssqu.12063.

Hanson, F. A. 2006. *Meaning in Culture: Anthropology and Ethnography.* Abingdon, UK: Routledge.

Haslberger, A. 2005. "Facets and Dimensions of Cross-Cultural Adaptation: Refining the Tools." *Personnel Review* 34 (1): 85–108. https://doi.org/10.1108/00483480510571897.

Hassan, Z., and M. Diallo. 2013. "Cross-Cultural Adjustments and Expatriate Job Performance: A Study on Malaysia." *International*

Journal of Accounting and Business Management (IJABM) 1 (1): 8–23.

Hershkowitz, M., and C. Tenenbaum. 2008. "The Critical Shortage of Military Chaplains: One Possible Solution." *State Defense Force Journal* 4 (1).

Hendershott, A. 2009. *Status Envy: The Politics of Catholic Higher Education.* New Brunswick, NJ: Transaction Publishers.

Henning, R., and S. Mahfood. 2009. "Opening the Reception Process: Distance Learning and the International Priest." *Seminary Journal* 15 (3): 62–68. http://www.sjvcenter.org/assets/uploads/pages/Seminary_Journal_Fall_2012.pdf.

Hoge, D. R., and A. Okure. 2006. *International Priests in America: Challenges and Opportunities.* Collegeville, MN: Liturgical Press.

Hugo, A. K. 1997. "African Immigrants in the United States: The Challenge for Research and Practice." *Social Work* 42 (2): 154–165. https://doi.org/10.1093/sw/42.2.154.

Hofstede, G. 1993. "Cultural Constraints in Management Theories." *Academy of Management Executive* 7 (1): 81–94.

———. 2009. "A Kuhnian Revolution in Cross-Cultural Research Hofstede on Hofstede. Geert Hofstede Is Interviewed by Delia Chiaro, *Cultus,* no. 2, 21–32.

Holmes, P. A. 2014. *A Pastor's Toolbox: Management Skills for Parish Leadership.* Collegeville, MN: Liturgical Press.

Hopfenspenrger, J. 2019. "Catholics Turn to Foreign Priests to Ease Clergy Shortage." *Star Tribune,* October 12, 2019.

Howell, B. M., and J. W. Paris. 2010. *Introducing Cultural Anthropology: A Christian Perspective.* Ada, MI: Baker Academic.

Hullinger, H., and R. Nolan. 1997. "Antecedents of Intercultural Adjustment of American Expatriates in the People's Republic of China." *New Prairie Press,* http://newprairiepress.org/cgi/viewcontent.cgi?article=1952&context=aerc.

Information Science Reference. 2014. *Cross-Cultural Interaction: Concepts, Methodologies, Tools and Applications.* Hershey, PA: IGI Global.

Ishlyama, F. 1989. "Understanding Foreign Adolescents' Difficulties in Cross-Cultural Adjustment: A Self-Validation Model." *Canadian Journal of School Psychology* 5: 41–56.

http://journals.sagepub.com/doi/abs/10.1177/082957358900500105.

Iveson, C. 2002. "Solution-Focused Brief Therapy: Advances in Psychiatric Treatment." *BJPsych Advances* 8 (2): 149–156. https://doi.org/10.1192/apt.8.2.149.

Irving, J. A. 2009. "Intercultural Competence in Leadership Education for Educating Global Leaders." *Journal of International Business and Educational Leadership* 1 (1): 3–13. http://people.bethel.edu/~irvjus/PDF/JBEL_2010_Intercultural_Competence-in-Leadership-Education.pdf.

Irving, J. A. 2008. Exploring Intercultural Competence in Leadership Education. *Journal of Intercultural Business and Cultural Studies,* (3)1–14. http://www.aabri.com/manuscripts/09392.pdf.

Javidan, M., G. D. Stahl, F. Brodbeck, and C. P. M. Wilderom. 2005. "Cross-Border Transfer of Knowledge: Cultural Lessons from Project GLOBE." *Academy of Management Executive* 19 (2): 59–76. http://eds.a.ebscohost.com.ezproxy.oru.edu/eds/pdfviewer/pdfviewer?vid=1&sid=27286940-66a5-4104-9af5-5d2b6fe3283b%40sessionmgr4009&hid=4111.

Jia, H., and F. J. R. Van De Vijver. 2012. "Online Readings in Psychology and Culture." *Intercultural Association for Cross-cultural Psychology* 2 (2): 1–19. https://doi.org/10.9707/2307-0919.1111.

Joshua-Gojer, A. E. 2012. "Cross-Cultural Training and Success versus Failure of Expatriates." *Learning and Performance Quarterly* 1 (2): 47–62.

http://lpq.sageperformance.com/journal/article/view/24/pdf.

Kealey, D. J., and D. R. Protheoroe. 1996. "The Effectiveness of Cross-Cultural Training for Expatriates: An Assessment of the Literature on the Issue." *International Journal of Intercultural Relations* 20 (2): 141–165. https://doi.org/10.1016/0147-1767(96)00001-6.

Kealey, D.J., D. R. Protheroe, D. Macdonald, and T. Vulpe. 2005. "Re-examining the Role of Training in Contributing to International Project Success: A Literature Review and an Outline of a New Model

Training Program." *International Journal of Intercultural Relations* 29: 289–316. https://doi.org/10.1016/j.ijintrel.2005.05.011.

Klenke, K. 2008. *Qualitative Research in the Study of Leadership.* Bingley, United Kingdom Emerald.

Kim, Y. Y. 2005. "Adapting to a New Culture: An Integrative Communication Theory." In *Theorizing About Intercultural Communication,* edited by W. B. Gudykunst, 375–400. Thousand Oaks, CA: SAGE Publications.

Ko, H. and M. Yang. 2011. "The Effects of Cross-Cultural Training on Expatriate Assignments." *Intercultural Communication Studies* 20 (1):158–174.

Kolb, D. A. 1984. *Experiential Learning: Experience as the Source of Learning and Development.* Englewood Cliffs, NJ: Prentice Hall.

Kolb, D. A., D. Wolfe, et al. 1981. "Professional Education and Career Development: A Cross

Sectional Study of Adaptive Competencies in Experiential Learning." From ERIC ED209493: Professional education and career development: Across sectional study of adaptive competencies in experiential learning. Lifelong learning and adult development project. Final Report. https://eric.ed.gov/?id=ED209493.

Langdridge, D. 2007. *Phenomenological Psychology: Theory, Research and Method.* Harlow: Pearson Education.

Lee, G., and M. J. Westwood. 1996. "Cross-Cultural Issues Faced by Immigrant Professionals." *Journal of Employment Counseling* 33 (1): 29–42. http://eds.a.ebscohost.com.oralroberts.idm.oclc.org/eds/pdfviewer/pdfviewer?vid=2&sid=0462f5b5-2cbd-420b-9695-395abaaf1c27%40sessionmgr4010.

Lefevere, P. 2006. "Study Looks at Foreign-born Priests Serving in U.S." *The National Catholic Reporter, February 24,* http://findarticles.com/p/articles/mi_m1141/is_17_42/ai_n16107683.

Liu, M., and J. L. Huang. 2015. "Cross-Cultural Adjustment to the United States: The Role of

Contextualized Extraversion Change." *Frontiers in Psychology* 6: 1–15. https://doi.org/ 10.3389/fpsyg.2015.01650.

Lunenburg, F. C. 2011. "Expectancy Theory of Motivation: Motivating by Altering Expectations." *International Journal of Management, Business, and Administration* 15 (1). https://pdfs.semanticscholar.org/6ce0/a17c0c51aadd099b9425a6e149f092befa95.pdf.

Mainemelis, C., R. E. Boyatzis, and D. A. Kolb. 2002. "Learning Styles and Adaptive Flexibility: Testing Experiential Learning Theory. *Management Learning* 33 (1): 5–33. http://journals.sagepub.com/doi/abs/10.1177/1350507602331001.

Malda, M., F. J. R. Van de Vijver, and M. Q. Temane. 2011. "Rugby versus Soccer in South Africa: Content Familiarity Contributes to Cross-Cultural Differences in Cognitive Test Scores." *Intelligence* 38: 582–595. https://doi.org/10.1016/j.intell.2010.07.004.

Mann, B. 2012. "Church Officials Say Priest Shortage Will Worsen." *New York Regional News*, March 8, 2012. http://www.northcountrypublicradio.org/news/story/19453/20120308/church-officials-say-priest-shortage-will-worsen.

Marriam, S. 2009. *Qualitative Research: A Guide to Design and Implantation*. San Francisco: Jossey-Bass.

Matheson, K. 2008. "Priest Shortage Could Alter College Identities." Associated Press, http://amarillo.com/stories/101808/fai_11516137.shtml.

McMohon, J. M. 2008. "Clergy Update: Consider Yourself One of the Family." *National Association of Pastoral Musicians* 12 (2): 1–4. https://npm.org/wp-content/uploads/2017/07/PM%20Vol%2031-2.pdf.

Memiah Limited. 2016. *Counseling Directory: Connecting You with Professional Support*. Camberly, UK: Therapy Directory.

Meyer, K. E. 2013. "What Is, and to What Purpose Do We Study International Business." *Academy of International Business Insight* 13 (1): 10–13. http://www.klausmeyer.co.uk/publications/2013_Meyer_what_is_why_study_international_business.pdf.

Morgan, H. J. 2015. *Clinical Psychotherapy: A History of Theory and Practice from Sigmund Freud to Aaron Beck*. Mishawaka, IN: GTF Books.

Morgan, H. J. 2015 *Clinical Pastoral Psychotherapy: A Practitioner's Handbook for Ministry Professionals*. Mishawaka, IN: Graduate Theological Foundation.

Morgan, J. 2005. *Naturally Good: A Behavioral History of Moral Development from Charles Darwin to E. O. Wilson*. South Bend, IN: Cloverdale Books.

Morey, M. M., and J. J. Piderit. 2006. *Catholic Higher Education: A Culture in Crisis*. New York: Oxford University Press.

Naithani, P., and A. N. Jha. 2010. "Challenged Faced by Expatriate Workers in Gulf Cooperation Council Countries." *International Journal of Business Management* 5 (1): 98–103. https://doi.org/10.5539/ijbm.v5n1p98.

Nicole, F. 2011. "Pre- and Post-Migration Attitudes among Ghanaian International Students Living in the United States: A Study of Acculturation and Psychological Well-Being." Doctoral dissertation, Virginia Commonwealth University, Richmond, Virginia. http://scholarscompass.vcu.edu/etd/2551.

Nolan, E. M., and M. J. Morley. 2014. "A Test of the Relationship between Person Environment Fit and Cross-Cultural Adjustment among Self-Initiated Expatriates." *The International Journal of Human Resource Management* 25 (11): 1631–1649. https://doi.org/10.1080/09585192.2013.845240.

O'Donnell, P., E. McAuliffe, and D. Diarmuid O'Donovan. 2014. "Unchallenged Good Intentions: A Qualitative Study of the Experiences of Medical Students on International Health Electives to Developing Countries." *Human Resources for Health* 12 (49). https://doi.org/10.1186/1478-4491-12-49.

O'Dwyer, L. M., and J. A. Bernauer. 2013. *Qualitative Research for the Quantitative Researchers*. Los Angeles: SAGE Publications.

Onwuegbuzie, A. J. 2007. "Sampling Designs in Qualitative Research: Making the Sampling Process More Public." *The Qualitative Report* 12 (2): 238–254.

Okpara, J. O., and J. D. Kabongo. 2011. "Cross-Cultural Training and Expatriate Adjustment: A Study of Western Expatriates in Nigeria." *Journal of World Business* 46: 22–30. https://doi.org/10.1016/j.jwb.2010.05.014.

Ortiz, F. A., and G. J. McGlone. 2012. "Model for Intercultural Competencies in Formation and Ministry: Awareness, Knowledge, Skills and Sensitivity." *Seminary Journal* 2. http://www.sjvcenter. org/assets/uploads/pages/Seminary_Journal_Fall_2012.pdf.

Osman-Gani, A. M., and T. Rockstuhl. 2009. "Cross-Cultural Training, Expatriate Self-Efficacy, and Adjustments to Overseas Assignments: An Empirical Investigation of Managers in Asia." *International Journal of Intercultural Relations* 33 (4): 277–290. https://doi. org/10.1016/j.ijintrel.2009.02.003.

Owan, V. A. 2014. "An Analysis of the Concept of Cultural Competence in a Cross-Cultural Priestly Context: Implications for Priestly Formation in the Twenty-First Century for Service Abroad." Doctoral dissertation, Kent State University. https://etd.ohiolink. edu/ap/10?0::NO:10:P10_ACCESSION_NUM:kent1397824661.

Ozar, S. 2015. "Personality and Social Psychology Predictors of International Students' Psychological and Sociocultural Adjustment to the Context of Reception While Studying at Aarhus University, Denmark." *Scandinavian Journal of Psychology* 56: 717–725. https:// doi.org/10.1111/sjop.12258.

Palinkas, L. A., S. M. Horwitz, C. A. Green, J. P. Wisdom, N. Duan, and K. Hoagwood. 2013. "Purposeful Sampling for Qualitative Data Collection and Analysis in Mixed Method Implementation Research." Administration and Policy in Mental Health and Mental Health Services Research 42(5), 533–544.
https://doi.org/10.1007/s10488-013-0528-y.

Panthaplamthottiyil, J. *CMI: North American guide.* Brooklyn, New York: Carmelites of Mary Immaculate, 2006.

Peltokorpi, V. 2008. "Cross-Cultural Adjustment of Expatriates in Japan." *International Journal of Human Resource Management* 19: 1588–1606. https://doi.org/10.1080/09585190802294903.

Peltokorpi, F. J., and V. Froese. 2012. "The Impact of Expatriate Personality Traits on Cross-Cultural Adjustment: A Study with Expatriates in Japan." *International Business Review* 21 (4): 734–746. http://dx.doi.org/10.1016/j.ibusrev.2011.08.006

Petriccione, R. C. 2009. *A Descriptive Study of Lay Presidents of American Catholic Colleges and Universities.* Ann Arbor, MI: Pro Quest.

Pionzo, M. 2010. "International Priests Help Support Catholic Parishes in Connecticut and the U.S." *Hartford Courant*, October 13, 2010. file:///Volumes/USB20FD/International%20priests:%20Connecticut%20and%20the%20U.S.%20-%20Hartford%20Courant.html.

Polón, M. 2017. "Impact of Cross-Cultural Training on Expatriate Performance. European Business Administration." Bachelor thesis, Helsinki Metropolia University of Applied Sciences. https://www.theseus.fi/bitstream/handle/10024/129376/Polon_Menni.pdf?sequence=1.

Pop, A., D. David, D. Triff, and C. Florea. 2012. "Designing an Intensive Bespoke Course in Cross-Cultural Communication." *Procedia—Social and Behavioral Sciences* 46: 2347–2351. https://doi.org/10.1016/j.sbspro.2012.05.482.

Porter, L. W., and E. E. Lawler. 1968. *Managerial Attitudes and Performance*. Homewood, IL: Dorsey Press and Richard D. Irwin.

Pringle, J., J. Drummond, E. McLafferty, and C. Henry. 2011. "International Phenomenological Analysis: A Discussion and Critique. *Nurse Research* 18 (3): 20–24. http://journals.rcni.com/doi/abs/10.7748/nr2011.04.18.3.20.c8459.

Puri, A., M. Kaddoura, and C. Dominick. 2013. "Student Perception of Travel Service Learning Experience in Morocco." *Journal of Dental Hygiene* 87 (4): 235–243. http://jdh.adha.org/content/87/4/235.full.

Reese, T. 2013. "Pope Francis and Reforming the Vatican: The National Leadership Roundtable on Church Management." *National Catholic Reporter, March 19, 2013* rest-pope-francis-gang-eight.

Roberts, B. 2007. *Glocalization: How Followers of Jesus Engage a Flat World*. Grand Rapids, MI: Zondervan.

Ross, D. 2009. "Lincoln and the Ethics of Emancipation: Universalism, Nationalism Exceptionalism." *Journal of American History*, no. 96, 379–99. http://www.journalofamericanhistory.org/projects/lincoln/contents/ross.html.

Rothmann, S., and M. Van Der Bank. 2006. "Correlates of Expatriates' Cross-Cultural Adjustment." *Management Dynamics* 15 (4): 29–39. https://www.questia.com/library/journal/1P3-1273049031/correlates-of-expatriates-cross-cultural-adjustment.

Roy, S. H. 2013. "Educating Chinese, Japanese, and Korean International Students: Recommendations to American Professors." *Journal of International Students* 3 (1): 10–16. http://eds.b.ebscohost.com.oralroberts.idm.oclc.org/eds/ pdfviewer/pdviewer?vid=4&sid=1d4ff449-cf5c-4795-adba-7c6625d01bb%40sessionmgr104.

Sandage, Steven J., and P. J. Jankowski. 2013. "Spirituality, Social Justice, and Intercultural Competence: Mediator Effects for Differentiation of Self." *International Journal of Intercultural Relations* 37 (3): 366–374. https://doi:10.1016/j.ijintrel.2012.11.003.

Schenk, C. 2013. "International Priest Organizations, Lay Leaders Meet to Discuss Church Reform." *The National Catholic Reporter*, October 17, 2013. http://ncronline.org/news/theology/international-priest-organizations-lay-leaders-meet-discuss-church-reform.

Schwartz, S. H. 2013. "Rethinking the Concept and Measurement of Societal Culture in Light of Empirical Findings." *Journal of Cross-Cultural Psychology*, no. 45. https://doi.org/10.1177/0022022113490830.

Selmer, J. 2006. "Munificence of Parent Corporate Contexts and Expatriate Cross-Cultural Training in China." *Asia Pacific Business Review* 12 (1): 39–51. https://doi.org/10.1080/13602380500337002.

Sheehy, K. 2014. "More International Priests Help Serve Southwest's Growing Catholic Population." *FRONTERAS The Changing American Desk*, August 5, 2014. http://www.fronterasdesk.org/ content/9741/more-international-priests-help-serve-southwests-growing-catholic-population.

Shen, J., and B. Lang. 2009. "Peer-Reviewed Articles: Cross-Cultural Training and Its Impact on Expatriate Performance in Australian MNEs." *Human Resource Development International* 12 (4): 371–386. https://doi.org/10.1080/13678860903135763.

Shi, L., and L. Wang. 2014. "The Culture Shock and Cross-Cultural Adaptation of Chinese Expatriates in International Business Contexts." *International Business Research* 7(1) 23–33. https://doi.org/10.5539/ibr.v7n1p23.

Shinkman, P. D. 2013. "The Catholic Crunch: Inside the Shortage of Catholic Military Priests." *U.S. News & World Report*, October 30, 2013.

http://www.usnews.com/news/articles/2013/10/30/the-catholic-crunch-inside-the- shortage-of-catholic-military-priests.

Smith, J. A. 2011. "Evaluating the Contribution of Interpretative Phenomenological Analysis." *Health Psychology Review* 5 (1): 9–27. https://doi.org/10.1080/17437199.2010.510659.

Smith J. A., P. Flowers, and M. Larkin. 2009. *Interpretative Phenomenological Analysis: Theory, Method and Research.* London: SAGE Publications.

Smith, A. R., and G. N. Khawaja. 2011. "A Review of the Acculturation Experiences of International Students." *International Journal of Intercultural Relations* 35 (6): 699–713. https://doi.org/10.1016/j.ijintrel.2011.08.004.

Sperry, L. 2012. "How Cultural Competence Develops." *Seminary Journal* 18 (2): 48–52. http://www.sjvcenter.org/assets/uploads/pages/Seminary_Journal_Fall_2012.pdf.

Stock, J. T. 2008. "Are Humans Still Evolving?" *EMBOR Reports* 9 (15): 546–574. https://doi.org/10.1038/embor.2008.63.

Sugg, R. A. 2013. "Finding God's Promise in Lonely Places." *The Military Chaplain* (87)2 1-45 https://mca-usa.org/wp-content/uploads/2017/04/TMC_Summer_2013_Web.pdf

Tarique, I., and P. Caligiuri. 2009. "The Role of Cross-Cultural Absorptive Capacity in the Effectiveness of In-Country Cross-Cultural Training." *International Journal of Training and Development* 13 (3): 148–165. https://doi.org/10.1111/j.1468-2419.2009.00324.x.

Townsend, T. 2013. "Belleville Bishop Outlines Gradual Plan for Parish Merges." *St. Louis Post-Dispatch*, April 5, 2013. http://www.stltoday.com/lifestyles/faith-and-values/belleville-bishop-outlines-gradual-plan-for-parish-mergers/article_5e0c4196-64d7-5a6d-90d6-132a595b53c1.html.

United States Conference of Catholic Bishops. 2000. *Welcoming the Stranger among Us: Unity in Diversity.* http://www.usccb.org/issues-and-action/cultural-diversity/pastoral-care-of-migrants-refugees-and-travelers/resources/welcoming-the-stranger-among-us-unity-in-diversity.cfm.

USCCB, 2010a. *International Priests 2010—United States* ... http://www.usccb.org/issues-and-action/child-and-youth-protection/upload/2010-International-Priests.pdf.

USCCB, 2010b. *International Priests and the Charter for the Protection of Children and Young People: A Resource for Dioceses/Eparchies.* http://www.usccb.org/issues-and-action/child-and-youth-protection/upload/international-priests-charter-resource.pdf.

USCCB, 2010c. *Keeping Our Promise to Protect: International Priests and the Protection of Children and Youth People.* http://www.usccb.org/issues-and-action/child-and-youth-protection/upload/2010-International-Priests.pdf.

Vasile, A. C., and L. Nicolescu, L. 2016. "Hofstede's Cultural Dimensions and Management Incorporations." *Cross-Cultural Management Journal* 18 (1): 35–46.

Vogel, A. J., J. J. Van Vuuren, and S. S. Millard. (2008). "Preparation, Support and Training Requirements of South African Expatriates." *South African Journal of Business Management* 39 (3): 33–40. http://eds.a.ebscohost.com.ezproxy.oru.edu/eds/pdfviewer/pdfviewer?sid=ae61ab9a-93b9-4880-8e7964889d53dc55%40sessionmgr4009&vid=11&hid=4208.

Vroom, V. H. 1964. *Work and Motivation.* New York: John Wiley & Sons.

Walker, K. A. 2014. *Called to Serve Catholics in the Military: An Interview with Archbishop Timothy Brogolio and Those Who Serve with Him.* New Providence, NJ: National Register Publishing. http://www.officialcatholicdirectory.com/special-feature-article/catholics-in-the-military.html.

Waxin, M. F., and A. Panaccio. 2005. "Cross-Cultural Training to Facilitate Expatriate Adjustment: It Works!" *Personnel Review* 34 (1): 51–67. http://www.emeraldinsight.com/doi/pdfplus/10.1108/00483480510571879.

Welch, B. J. 2009. "Unlocked Possibilities: Albany Parishes Should Find Other Uses for Buildings after Churches Close." http://timesunion.com/AspStories/storyprint.asp? StoryID=759808.

Wertz, F. 2005. "Phenomenological Research Methods for Counseling Psychology." *Journal of Counseling Psychology* 52 (2): 167–177. https://doi.org/10.1037/0022-0167.52.2.167.

Wurtz, O. 2014. "An Empirical Investigation of the Effectiveness of Pre-Departure and in Country Cross-Cultural Training." *The Journal of Human Resource Management* 25 (14): 2088–2101. https://doi.org/10.1080/09585192.2013.870285.

Xin, H., S. Morrion, J. Dharod, M. Young, and M. Nsonwu. 2014. "Cross-Cultural Allies in Immigrant Community Practice: Roles or Foreign-Trained Former Montagnard Health Professionals." *Health, Culture, and Society* 6 (1): 2161–6590. https://doi.org/10.5195/hcs.2014.143.

Yamazaki, Y., and D. C. Kayes. 2004. "An Experiential Approach to Cross-Cultural Learning: A Review and Integration of Competencies for Successful Expatriate Adaptation." *Academy of Management Learning & Education* 3 (4): 362–379. http://eds.a.ebscohost.com.oralroberts.idm.oclc.org/eds/pdfviewer/pdfviewer?vid=1&sid=c80ebf0f-ee66-462b-b1e3-80c10277729a%40sessionmgr4009.

Zhang, J., and P. Goodson. 2011. "Predictors of International Students' Psychosocial Adjustment to Life in the United States: A Systematic Review." *International Journal of Intercultural Relations* 35: 139–162. https://doi.org/10.1016/j.ijintrel.2010.11.011.

Zhang, J., M. Heinz, and W. Erping. 2010. "Personality, Acculturation, and Psychological Adjustment of Chinese International Students in Germany." *Psychological Reports* 107 (2): 511–525. https://doi.org/10.2466/07.09.11.17.PR0.107.5.511-525.

ABOUT THE AUTHOR

THE AUTHOR, REV. DR. LEONARD U. AHANOTU, EARNED FIVE DEGREES: a Doctor of Philosophy (PhD) in pastoral psychology, a Doctor of Education (EdD) in education leadership, a Master of Education (MEd) in special education, a master of arts (MA) in theology, and Bachelor of arts (BA) in philosophy from different universities and institutions in the United States. He is a Catholic priest of the Diocese of Tulsa, Oklahoma, in the United States and a member of the International Honor Society in Education, known as Kappa Delta Pi (KDP).

Before settling in the Diocese of Tulsa, he was a missionary overseas, where he worked as a missionary priest, a college professor, and a department head at St. Benedict College, Wewak, Papua New Guinea. As a priest of the Diocese of Tulsa, he serves as a pastor and sometimes combines it with teaching as an adjunct professor.

Rev. Ahanotu was born in Nigeria, where he attended the Seminary of the Holy Ghost Fathers and Brothers and was ordained as a priest in July 1994. Ahanotu enjoys experiencing other cultures and has traveled to several countries in Europe, Africa, Asia, Australia, and the region of the South Pacific. In his two doctoral dissertations, he studied cultural diversity, intercultural relationships, our fast-globalizing world, and the various ways of being a better leader at one's home culture and as an expatriate in a foreign culture. He still studies and writes about these issues that interest him. SAGE Publishing published his last work, *Navigating between Cultures*, last year 2019.

Printed in the United States
By Bookmasters